MY
COUNTRY

VERSUS
ME

The First-Hand Account by
the Los Alamos Scientist Who Was Falsely
Accused of Being a Spy

By Wen Ho Lee

with Helen Zia

MY
COUNTRY

VERSUS
ME

New York

ISBN 0-7868-6803-1

First Edition
10 9 8 7 6 5 4 3 2 1

This book is for all Americans,

especially those whose prayers and support

helped me through my ordeal.

ACKNOWLEDGMENTS

I am home today because so many Americans from all walks of life supported me. This book would not have been possible without you. This book is for you.

There are many people I want to thank, and I don't know how to thank them enough.

My family and I are indebted to the legal team led by Mark Holscher: Dan Bookin, John Cline, Stacy Cohen, Gregg Fallick, Edward Gerjuoy, Griffith Green, Tom Green, Heather Hersh, Brian Hershman, Nancy Hollander, Mark Hopson, Tina Hua, Kevin Marshall, K. C. Maxwell, Richard Myers, Luan Phan, and Brian Sun. Thank you so much for your hard work, protectiveness, dedication, patience, understanding, and commitment to justice. Freedman Boyd Daniels Hollander Goldberg & Cline, O'Melveny & Myers, O'Neill, Lysaght & Sun, and Sidley Austin Brown & Wood are firms which changed my opinion of lawyers. You are all generous and giving people. I will always remember the caring touch of your staff, especially Toni Adams, Melodie Baiz, Barbara Bond, Ann Delpha, Jane Sieger, and Irene Tully.

With connections from Jack Ribble, Rebecca Weinstein, and Alan Cohen, I was introduced to Mark Holscher. I couldn't even begin to imagine what would have happened had we not found Mark when we did. Thank you so much for your help and support.

In the beginning, my lawyers risked their personal and professional reputations by agreeing to represent me. They weren't the only ones who took a risk. Cecilia Chang and those who joined the e-mail list were a virtual army. Thank you to all for the concern expressed in your e-mails and the organized fundraisers, protests, and rallies. America was able to see the outrage because of your hard work. Thank you Alex Achmat, Steve Aftergood, Richard Chao, Andy Chen, Diane Chin, Chizen Chou, Nance Crowe, Kent Dedrick, Henry Der, Hugh DeWitt, Ignatius Ding, Merrillee Dolan, Gary Eschman, Hugh Gusterson, Phyllis Hedges, Marti Hiken, Chih-Ming Hu, Roger Hu, Mary-Claire King, George Koo, Ivy Lee, Lester Lee, Edward Liu, D. K. Lu, Norm Matloff, Carl Newton, Bill Sullivan, Kai May Terry, Bob Vrooman, Albert Wang, K. L. Wang, Ling-Chi Wang, Albert Yee.

My neighbors, Don and Jean Marshall, stood by me from beginning to end, from defending me publicly in March 1999, to volunteering to be my custodians at the first bail hearing in December 1999, to hosting my welcome home party in September 2000. I am so grateful and honored to have lived the last twenty years next door to your family.

Harold Agnew, Walter Goad, and John Richter also bravely came forward to provide a realistic viewpoint on the case with their expert technical testimony. I would also like to acknowledge the dozens of people who devotedly attended the numerous hearings, as many drove from Los Alamos daily, especially Bob and Kathy Clark, Bucky and Linda Kashiwa, and Ralph and Marilyn Stevens.

Jo Starling, Alberta's fifth grade teacher, approached Mark Holscher and offered to put her home toward my bail in August

2000. I am still amazed by that gesture. She is an example of America at its best.

Since my release, I have been greeted with many smiles and hugs wherever I go, whether it be at Home Depot or fishing at Nambe. Thank you, New Mexicans, for being so warm to me.

Thank you to Victor Hsi, Victor Hwang, Phil Ting, Ted Wang, Michelle Yoshida, and Helen Zia, all who led the organization of CARES, the Coalition Against Racial and Ethnic Scapegoating. I would like to thank the following organizations which helped build CARES: Asian Law Caucus, Chinese for Affirmative Action, and Organization of Chinese Americans. CARES also organized a National Day of Outrage on June 8, 2000, where nearly a dozen cities from Boston to Seattle rallied on my behalf. It kept my spirits up to read news reports of these activities from my jail cell. Thank you to Marie Weng in Detroit, Colleen Seto and Kathy Feng in Los Angeles, Alex Achmat, Carl Newton, Phyllis Hedges, and Bill Sullivan in New Mexico, Margaret Fung, Leo Lee, Jack Tchen, and Sin Yen Ling in New York, Ivy Lee in Sacramento, Pei-Tei Lien, Karen Kwan-Smith, and Kathleen Hom in Salt Lake City, Mei Ling Hsu in Seattle, and everyone who helped with the San Francisco protest.

I was happy to see groups of different backgrounds, age groups, and concerns come together to help with bringing justice to my name. Of these groups, I would like to thank George Ong of the Organization of Chinese Americans and Henry Tang of the Committee of 100. There were numerous prestigious scientific groups and civil rights organizations who wrote letters to express their outrage, and many of these people welcomed my children to speak around the country about the case and raise awareness about racial profiling. Thank you for taking care of Chung and Alberta as they flew around the country, and comforting them through this difficult time.

This book would not be possible without the excellent advice of Stacy Cohen, Brian Sun, and David Weil. Many thanks to Mark

Chait and Will Schwalbe at Hyperion for their sensitivity and passion for the book, and most of all, thank you, Helen Zia, for your infinite patience. The writing of this book took place during the difficult recovery time for my family, and I really appreciate you.

Most of all, this book is for my family. Thank you for supporting me.

—Wen Ho Lee

Many kind people across the country let me enter their lives to discuss this book's wide-ranging subjects, which somehow included nuclear weapons science and politics, radiation poisoning in Los Alamos, race relations in New Mexico, international relations with China and Taiwan, intelligence and counterintelligence, and the relative merits of red and green chilies.

I am indebted to numerous individuals whose jobs in the labs, in the Department of Energy, and elsewhere may be jeopardized if I thank them by name; some were even concerned that the government might interfere with their applications to a radiation exposure compensation program. I will mention only a few of the good people who tolerated my many intrusions: Barbara Bond, Bob and Kathy Clark, John Cline, Stacy Cohen, Phyllis Hedges, Victor Hwang, Yvonne Lee, Don and Jean Marshall, K. C. Maxwell, Carlos McEvilly, Richard Myers, Mary Norris, Jo Starling, Brian Sun, and Bob and Linda Vrooman. Thanks also to Cindy Ewing and George Arrietta, my hosts at Las Hueseras.

Special thanks to Hyperion editor in chief Will Schwalbe, for his unfailing enthusiasm and commitment to this book; and to Mark Chait, also at Hyperion, for his good-natured attentiveness.

Sydelle Kramer, my wonderful literary agent, proved, once again, that she is the best.

My heartfelt gratitude goes to the Lee family for their faith in me to help tell their remarkable story; it has been a rare privilege to know them. My deep appreciation to Wen Ho and Sylvia Lee for welcoming me into their home and for suffering through my "interrogations." I am especially grateful for the many delicious meals from Dr. Lee's kitchen.

I have my parents to thank for my involvement in Dr. Lee's story; they taught me to never accept the notion of a "Chinaman's chance."

My work on this book would not have been possible without the loving warmth and care of my life partner, Lia Shigemura.

In reliving this nightmare with the Lees, I found much strength in the spirit of political prisoners everywhere and from all those who stand up for human rights. May justice and equality prevail.

—Helen Zia

MY
COUNTRY

VERSUS
ME

INTRODUCTION

On the last day that I was shackled and chained, the chief judge of the United States District Court for the District of New Mexico apologized to me.

After 278 days of solitary confinement without benefit of a trial, on September 13, 2000, I was finally being freed. I had spent the previous winter, spring, and summer in "pretrial detention," the government's impersonal way of saying that I was such a menace to society that I should be jailed even though I was presumed to be innocent. The terrible offense I was suspected of committing: the high crime of espionage. I was not officially charged with spying, but my accusers spoke through government leaks and innuendo in the media and in Congressional hearings. According to the government officials who hoped to imprison me for life—from members of the President's Cabinet and Congress to local prosecutors—I was so dangerous that I had to be locked away under the most severe conditions they could devise.

Judge James Parker, the federal judge who presided over my "theft" of the "crown jewels"—our most critical nuclear secrets—

said in his deep and authoritative voice, with America as his audience: "I have been misled by our government."

I remember that as I stood before him and the hushed crowd of family, friends, court watchers, and reporters, I noticed how brilliant the New Mexico sun was, streaming through the high windows of the Rio Grande courtroom at the federal courthouse in Albuquerque.

Judge Parker reviewed the terms of my release under a plea bargain agreement. I pled guilty to one of the 59 counts the government brought against me: I said that I had used an unsecure computer in the Theoretical Division of the Los Alamos National Laboratory to download national defense information onto a tape, which I retained. In exchange for my plea, all other 58 counts were dismissed—including the 39 counts that each carried a life sentence for violating the Atomic Energy Act and for stealing nuclear secrets with the intent to harm my country. My sentence in exchange for the plea: 278 days in prison, the exact time I had already served.

Then, in his calm baritone voice, Judge Parker spoke to me slowly and deliberately. Throughout the many court hearings, his faint Texas drawl had always reminded me of my graduate-school days at Texas A&M, and on this day it filled the huge courtroom:

> I believe you were terribly wronged by being held in custody pretrial in the Santa Fe County Detention Center under demeaning, unnecessarily punitive conditions. I am truly sorry that I was led by our executive branch of government to order your detention last December.
>
> Dr. Lee, I tell you with great sadness that I feel I was led astray last December by the executive branch of our government through its Department of Justice, by its Federal Bureau of Investigation, and by its United States attorney for the district of New Mexico, who held the office at that time.

I could feel a stifled gasp from the packed gallery behind me, followed by complete silence. I wasn't sure if I was really comprehending Judge Parker's sincere words, so I glanced at my lawyers, Mark Holscher and John Cline, who stood on either side of me. Throughout the toughest moments of my case, when the power and might of the federal government seemed overwhelming, Mark and John and the other lawyers who defended me were as steady as the Jemez mountains. But now Mark was tilting his Boy-Scout–looking face just a bit, and though John's tall frame hovered nearly a foot over mine, I noticed that one of his eyebrows lifted by a fraction.

News reports say that Judge Parker spoke for another thirty minutes as he explained the reasons for his apology. To me, his words were a surprising but welcome end to these most horrible two years of my life. I could see the blue sky and bright sunlight from the courtroom, but as a prisoner I had rarely been out in the fresh New Mexico air, and I so missed fishing and hiking in the desert wilderness. During the whole of this year, my main "outdoor" experiences took place on court appearance days. That's when my armed escort of federal marshals picked me up from the Santa Fe jail in the early morning light to drive me the 60 miles to Albuquerque, right past some of the places I fished and hiked. I had a friendly, conversational relationship with several marshals because we spent so many hours riding in a car together on Interstate 25. Still, it was hard to forget that they carried not only the keys to my wrist and ankle shackles, but loaded handguns and an automatic rifle as well, ready to shoot me in case my dangerous spy nature emerged.

One thing I did know, more than anyone else, was that the judge and the nation were indeed terribly misled. I knew—and the other nuclear weapons scientists who watched this elaborate show knew—that the "nuclear secrets" I was falsely accused of stealing were not really secrets but were available in the open literature. Also, the files I had downloaded as part of my job as a nuclear code developer were not the state-of-the-art weapons codes that the government wanted everyone to believe. Euphemistically known as "legacy codes," they were in fact far older, more decrepit, and more flawed than the space station Mir. Had we gone to trial, these were points my attorneys would have argued. In his remarks to me, Judge Parker noted that he had seen evidence that my attorneys had not yet received—evidence that would be helpful to my case if we had gone to trial instead of taking a plea. I felt certain that I would be proven innocent if we went to trial. But that process would take many more months and cost hundreds of thousands—even millions—more dollars in additional legal expenses. The strain on my family was already too great. When the attorneys reached an acceptable plea agreement, I took it.

I have no idea how long Judge Parker actually spoke, because the moment took on a slow-motion quality in my mind. As he explained what happened in his court, it seemed that the judge was trying to make some sense of this ordeal for me, for the public, and perhaps for himself. He talked about the laws of this country that protect people from being jailed until there is a trial and a conviction—and how the accused are denied bail only in exceptional circumstances. One by one, he referred to Janet Reno, Bill Richardson, and even Bill Clinton and Al Gore as the parties in the executive branch who were responsible for the deception that led to my imprisonment. He didn't list them by name, but by title: the United States Attorney General, the Secretary of the Department of Energy, the President, and the Vice President.

Judge Parker also cited John Kelly, referring to him as "the former United States Attorney of the New Mexico District, who vigorously insisted that you had to be kept in jail under extreme restrictions because your release pretrial would pose a grave threat to our nation's security." John Kelly most certainly made me out to be a monster—I will never forget those days in court. Kelly started his prosecution of me like a vicious attack dog, and then quit his job as U.S. attorney in order to run for Congress. Maybe I was meant to be the high-profile case that would boost his campaign, but he lost the election anyway. His deputy, Robert Gorence, the son-in-law of U.S. senator Pete Domenici, enthusiastically took up where Kelly left off. Then Gorence had to step down from prosecuting me.

Some journalists reported that a personal indiscretion led to Gorence's demotion. I don't care to discuss this in my book, but there has been plenty of self-righteous hypocrisy thrown at me, from inside the courthouse and inside the Washington Beltway, by those who would condemn me, no matter what the facts showed, for a capital crime that I didn't commit. Gorence and Kelly had ordered the shackles and chains, the solitary confinement, and the other treatment I received in jail with the full knowledge and approval of Janet Reno, FBI director Louis Freeh, Bill Richardson, and, most likely, the White House.

———

As the judge talked about these things, I realized that I never paid much attention to the differences among the three branches of government, not even when I took the examination to become an American citizen back in 1974. Before all this, I never really needed to. But Judge Parker made the importance of the distinctions very clear:

> The executive branch has enormous power, the abuse of which can be devastating to our citizens. The second branch of our national government is the legislative branch, our congress. Congress promulgated the laws under which you were prosecuted, the criminal statutes. And it also promulgated the Bail Reform Act, under which, in hindsight, you should not have been held in custody. The judicial branch of government, of which I am a member, is called the third branch of government.
>
> The top decision makers in the executive branch, especially

the Department of Justice and the Department of Energy and locally . . . have caused embarrassment by the way this case began and was handled. They did not embarrass me alone. They have embarrassed our entire nation and each of us who is a citizen of it.

At the prosecution table, George Stamboulidis, the U.S. attorney in charge of prosecuting me after Gorence was demoted, took issue with Judge Parker's statement. At one point Stamboulidis objected, but the judge glared at him in silence until he sat down. The one person at that table who remained expressionless was Robert Messemer, the supervising FBI agent in my case. In his zeal to put me away as a spy, he had misrepresented and distorted the truth to Judge Parker on two separate occasions, exaggerating the "grave danger" I posed. Also on the prosecution side of the courtroom was Norman Bay, the Chinese American prosecutor who was appointed U.S. attorney for New Mexico after Kelly resigned. To me it was hardly a "coincidence" that Janet Reno would appoint a Chinese American to prosecute me.

Some reporters described my defense as a David and Goliath battle. And it was: An accused person faces a monumental uphill struggle, especially when all the "evidence" can be hidden behind classified and secret files whose existence and access is controlled by the FBI and the U.S. Department of Justice (DOJ). My attorneys ultimately exposed the lies, but it was a painfully slow process to get me out of jail. The government had fought my release up until the very last minute, even as their case against me had fallen apart.

Judge Parker was not yet done with his message to me, which he said for the whole world to hear:

I am sad for you and your family because of the way in which you were kept in custody while you were presumed under the law to be innocent of the charges the executive branch brought against you.

I am sad that I was induced in December to order your detention, since by the terms of the plea agreement that frees you today without conditions, it becomes clear that the executive branch now concedes, or should concede, that it was not necessary to confine you last December or at any time before your trial.

I might say that I am also sad and troubled because I do not know the real reasons why the executive branch has done all of this. We will not learn why, because the plea agreement shields the executive branch from disclosing a lot of information that it was under order to produce that might have supplied the answer.

I sincerely apologize to you, Dr. Lee, for the unfair manner you were held in custody by the executive branch.

Then the judge adjourned the court, and I was moments away from freedom.

I leaned over to Mark Holscher and asked him, "Is it common for a judge to talk like this?"

Mark replied, "No, Wen Ho. This is very, very rare."

Behind me, a cheer sounded and the whole courtroom erupted into a loud buzz. The members of my defense team surrounded me to hug and congratulate me on finally getting out of jail and reaching the end of this criminal prosecution. It had been a very long and bumpy road up until the bitter end. My attorneys were drying their eyes: Nancy Hollander, so tough with my jailers, gave me a watery smile. So did K. C. Maxwell, whom I had thought too young to be a lawyer, and even Richard Myers was wiping his eyes—he, the muscle man I first assumed to be a security guard. Barbara Bond and Ann Delpha, the legal assistants who worked day and night on my defense, were laughing and crying. Brian Sun, who filed a lawsuit on my behalf against the government for violating my privacy with its continual leaks about me, flashed me a thumbs-up.

In the crush of the courtroom, I found the faces of my family: My wife, Sylvia, smiled as I hadn't seen her do in a long time. Chung, my steady son who had had to struggle through his first year of medical school while I was in jail, was beaming, his happy face reminding me of the first time he caught a fish as a small boy, and not the 6-foot, 2-inch young man he is now. Alberta, who had transformed herself from my little girl into a strong, articulate woman, had tears streaming down her face. She had crisscrossed the country without regard to her own well-being—against my wishes, initially—to tell everyone who would listen about my innocence. My younger brother Wenming and his wife, Patty, had flown in from California, as had my youngest sister, Angela. We were the youngest of ten siblings who had found the way to America from our rural farming village in Taiwan. My niece Chia Huei and her husband, Carlos, had even traveled to Albuquerque with their young baby. I felt so fortunate to have the love and support of my close-knit family, from across the United States and Taiwan.

I saw many of my friends and neighbors and coworkers in the courtroom, rooting for me. To my surprise, there were also lots of people whom I had never met but who had supported me because they believed, as Judge Parker concluded, that there was something terribly wrong with the government's case against me. And then there were the reporters. So many! Some of them were wiping tears from their eyes, too.

The joy of my family and friends made me yearn all the more for home. I wanted to check on the vegetable garden that I had so carefully tended for so many years. There were my fruit trees and the lawn, all neglected, and while imprisoned, I worried about the roof leaking. I yearned to cook a real, fresh meal for myself, from vegetables I grew myself and fish that I caught in pure mountain streams, with fresh food and spices that had been part of my daily diet until I was jailed—and had never, ever found their way to the Santa Fe prison. I looked forward to seeing my friends and former coworkers from the lab, all my neighbors in the White Rock and Los Alamos communities who had watched out for my wife while she was alone during my long months of incarceration.

But I also knew that my home of twenty years would be very different now.

Once I had been a trusted member of the elite scientific corps at Los Alamos National Laboratories, where the nation's nuclear weapons arsenal is designed and maintained, where the atomic bombs that ended World War II were created. I lived and worked for more than twenty years high atop the Los Alamos mesas in the foothills of New Mexico's Sangre de Cristo Mountains. My friends and neighbors were also my colleagues and coworkers, and we raised our children together in one of the friendliest and most close-knit communities in America. Like other people who lived "on the hill," 7,600 feet above sea level, I was a nuclear scientist and a soccer dad, an outdoorsman, an active participant in this special scientific world.

That part of my life was over, a distant memory of another lifetime—the time before my government and the news media accused me of committing espionage, before I was imprisoned without benefit of a trial or even a fair hearing. Before I learned to distrust my government and just about anyone who works for it, especially the FBI. Before I learned that no one should ever talk to FBI agents without an attorney or at least a trusted witness present. Before I was branded a spy and an enemy agent—a disloyal, lying traitor, one of the most base and awful labels imaginable. I can tell you this, because I know.

———

For the first time, I walked out the front door of the courtroom, with my attorneys by my side. This time I wasn't led through a back door to change out of my suit into my prison clothes. No federal marshals came to shackle my wrists and ankles and to chain them to my waist. In these 278 days, no journalists or members of the public were permitted to see me with my chains and shackles on. From the moment that the government leaked my name to the *New York Times* back in March 1999 as "the worst spy since the Rosenbergs," they carefully manipulated the image they wanted to project of me and my so-called crimes.

Finally I could be reunited with my family. We gathered in a separate room—just us—for a few minutes, away from the pandemonium outside, our first real time together in nine months without FBI agents watching us. We didn't say much, we just laughed and cried at the same time, all hugging and holding each other at once. Then my defense team joined us. I met a few more of the people who had worked hard on my case but whom I had not been able to meet while I was jailed in isolation. People like Stacy Cohen, who looked much too young to run her high-powered public relations practice, but who had been able to counter some of the damage done to me from leaks made by the FBI, the DOJ, and the Department of Energy (DOE) at the highest levels. Heather Hersh was one of Brian Sun's associates who was working on my Privacy Act lawsuit, filed to hold the government accountable for the leaks and misinformation they used to lynch me in the media. Between my family and legal team, it seemed as if two dozen of us were crammed into the little conference room—and I wanted to thank each one personally for all they had done.

Before I could leave for home, I had one more task. Reporters from the national and international news media were waiting for me in the sunny plaza outside the courthouse entrance. I had some idea of what to expect, because for the months before I was arrested, the intense media spotlight had already begun, with legions of reporters, photographers, and TV crews camped in front of my house, completely disrupting our quiet neighborhood. But this time was much sweeter: I could speak as a free man without the weight of the entire U.S. government hanging over my head, and, as Judge Parker made clear, this time the government had some serious questions to answer.

With my legal team and my family flanking me, we marched

past the metal detectors and courthouse security guards into a crunch of reporters and the blazing summer heat, which felt beautiful to me. I waved in appreciation to the hundreds of supporters who had stood by me during these two years and were cheering me on today. A phalanx of microphones and cameras was ready and waiting for me. As a simple man whose life is dedicated to mathematics and science, I've never been one for making big speeches. But I had been waiting to say these words for a very long time: "I'm very happy to go home with my wife and children today. I want to say thank you to all the people who supported me. I really appreciate it very, very much. The next few days, I'm going fishing." At long last, I was on my way home.

All the way from Albuquerque to White Rock, news helicopters flew overhead, tracking our progress. The big white rock at the entrance to town was painted with the message, "Welcome home, Wen Ho." My wife told me that my longtime friends and neighbors Don and Jean Marshall were hosting a "welcome home" party for me and all of Los Alamos, it seemed. The way leading to my home was like a carnival, and the police had blocked my street off to allow for the crowds and the huge satellite trucks. A chorus of "For He's a Jolly Good Fellow" started up. I was truly overwhelmed by the warm and heartfelt welcome, especially when I had been so alone and isolated in prison. Mark Holscher, Richard Myers, and Gregg Fallick, my young and strapping attorneys, made a way for us through the cheering crowds to my front door.

Once inside my house for the first time in 278 days, I could see that the FBI searches and seizures had left their mark. There were blank walls where pictures once hung, shelves with empty spaces, in disarray. As I started to rearrange things, my attorneys reminded me of all the friends who were waiting next door to celebrate with me. The one thing I did was to change out of my suit into my favorite fishing outfit: my old green plaid pants and my blue striped polo shirt. I was glad to be back home.

I wish I could say that this marked the end of my ordeal, but it didn't. Maybe it was the beginning of the end, or just the end of the beginning. I was hoping to be able to shut the door on the most bizarre and surrealistic experience of my life. But not yet.

How will I ever forget this nightmare? To be an ordinary citizen one day, an unassuming engineer and bench scientist, and to wake up the next day with my name and face splashed on headlines across the country as the "spy of the century." To hear powerful politicians in Washington talk about me as though I were worse than a dog, demanding that I be imprisoned or even executed, without a shred of evidence. To see lies, half-truths, and distortions about me leaked to the media from "secret" and "classified" FBI files. Then to see those lies appear unchallenged in the news and repeated as though they were gospel. To see old friends turn away from me, unsure if the government would make them its next targets. And worst of all, to watch helplessly as my wife, daughter, and son became sick with worry and fear for our future. For a naturalized American like me, who has spent a lifetime making my chosen country safe and strong, being called a "China spy" has been devastating.

I still can hardly believe what happened to me, and I want other people to know. I want to share, through this book, how I fell into a trap, one slippery step at a time, not even realizing what was happening until it was too late. I want to tell my story as I experienced it.

Part I begins on December 23, 1998, when DOE and FBI counterintelligence officials initiated a series of interrogations of me that led to my firing from Los Alamos less than three months later. In particular, I want people to know the science that I devoted my life to, and the nuclear weapons program that I helped build for the safety of my country, but that brought so much trouble into my life. In Part II, I will share how my family and I endured my trial by media and by Congress, an ordeal that began with a front-page *New York Times* story. I will tell about the downloading of the notorious computer files that were part of my work, and how what really happened stands in stark contrast to what I was accused of doing. Part III includes details of the hysteria surrounding my arrest and imprisonment on December 10, 1999, the extreme conditions of my life in solitary confinement, and the dedicated efforts of my legal team to combat and eventually overcome the full weight of the federal government. I will share stories of my family's times in Taiwan, being born and raised in a poor farming village, losing my mother to illness and suicide, and how my family pulled together—I want America to know the humanity of the people and the communities that were so readily vilified. Most of all, I want everyone to know that if these incredible things happened to me, they can happen again, to any American.

———

Today, when I see a news headline that still describes me as the "spy suspect"—words that seem permanently stuck to me—the bad memories come rushing back. Sometimes I just close my eyes and I try to think of more pleasant things: my family and my kids, Alberta and Chung; the way the desert blooms in the spring; the last time I caught a 27-inch trout from my favorite fishing hole in the New Mexico mountains. And sometimes I think about Judge Parker and his apology.

PART
ONE

CHAPTER 1

Trouble came roaring into my safe and steady world on December 23, 1998, like the kind of flash rainstorm up in the mountains that can turn a placid fishing trip deadly. Yes, I had weathered a previous storm when the FBI came into my life 16 years earlier, but that was more like an ominous rumbling, not the full-blown thunderboomer I was staring at now. Plus, I thought that the other incident, in 1982, had been over and done with long ago. In my straightforward scientific way of thinking, once a problem is solved, it is finished and there is no need to check if one plus one might suddenly yield a different answer. But I was beginning to see how one encounter with the FBI could keep coming back to haunt me, as if their asking the same question over and over might indeed yield a new solution. Looking back, I can see that with each iteration, new and unrelated events were thrown into the mix, mutating it into a more virulent inquiry and magnifying what were once simple questions by significant multiples.

Two days before Christmas, I was called into the security office at the Los Alamos National Lab. I had just returned home from a three-week trip to Taiwan that very morning, and I went directly to work at my office in the "X Division," where nuclear weapons research takes place. It was the last workday before the lab closed for the holidays, and I had a lot of work to do. My children were coming home for the week. Chung had arrived already and Alberta was flying in that evening from North Carolina. I wanted to get home to prepare their favorite foods, something that gave me great pleasure.

Getting called in for a security check is not such an unusual event at Los Alamos National Lab, or LANL, as it is also known. Anyone hoping to work at a national laboratory like LANL knows that an extensive background clearance review is required. For classified work involving national security, it can take many months of waiting until the investigation is complete. Everybody knows somebody who is getting a background investigation done. I held a "Q clearance" for twenty years, the highest level of security clearance. While not every scientist at Los Alamos needs to have a Q clearance, most do because the majority of research done at Los Alamos is related to the design, testing, manufacture, and maintenance of nuclear weapons, the purpose behind the lab's founding in 1943. Scientists at Los Alamos also conduct major unclassified research on oceanographic and atmospheric issues, the human genome, space travel, astrophysics and other endeavors, but nuclear weapons are LANL's bread and butter.

For many years I worked in the Applied Physics Division of LANL, also known as the X Division. I was a hydrodynamics code physicist—a "code developer"—working on several of the complex computer programs that simulate the detonation of thermonuclear weapons—atomic bombs and hydrogen bombs. I can't give specific details about my work because of its classified nature. But I can say that my job was to make sure the various computer simulation programs for nuclear bombs correctly reflected the hydrodynamic changes that occur inside a bomb during a nuclear explosion. Hydrodynamics describes the changes and extreme stress occurring to the metals—such as uranium or plutonium—in the moments after a detonation, microsecond by microsecond.

I spent my career using mathematics and physics to develop the equations and computer codes that would solve problems with these simulation programs. My solutions were part of the proper functioning of our nuclear stockpile as well as conventional weapons. In my unclassified research, I have calculated the shape and force of conventional ordnance that can pierce a 6-foot-thick wall of steel, and my equations were used in the Persian Gulf War in 1992. Earlier in my career I worked on the hydrodynamics of nuclear reactor safety—to ensure against Chernobyl-type accidents, for example. My research on the numerical modeling of nuclear reactors and reactions has been used in many countries, and I was proud that my work contributed to America's safety and to global nuclear security. I enjoyed my research and took it very seriously—if I didn't do my job well, the consequences could be dire.

There was another side to being part of this nuclear brotherhood. Like every other employee working in LANL's classified environment, I consented to a high degree of scrutiny and also agreed to inform on any security infractions made by my coworkers. I gave up the right to talk about certain aspects of my work with my children, family, and friends—or anyone who wasn't Q-cleared with a need to know. I had regular security debriefings with counterintelligence officers whenever I went overseas to present a talk on my published, unclassified research or to attend a scientific conference—for which I obtained advance approval from LANL.

It is also true that for many scientists, there are times when security procedures seem arbitrary or create an unnecessary burden and interference with our research work. For example, at LANL there was the two-hour rule: If you were leaving your office for more than two hours, you had to shut down your computer. This created a bind, because some complex programs took more than two hours to finish the calculations that they were performing. In addition, infor-

mation that has long been in the open literature and printed in newspapers—for example, some of the details related to my case—are
still considered classified, and scientists are required to lock such information in vaults. Situations like these have been a regular topic of
complaint among scientists who work in classified environments,
whether at the national laboratories or among defense contractor facilities. A report by the President's Foreign Intelligence Advisory
Board that came out in June 1999 described attitudes in the labs and
the DOE as "saturated with cynicism, an arrogant disregard for authority, and a staggering pattern of denial." This constant pull and tug
between security and scientific inquiry was part of the culture of
classified research, and I was a product of that culture.

After I got the call from LANL's counterintelligence chief, I
headed to the security office. I didn't really think there was anything
unusual with the call. After all, I had just returned from an overseas
trip, and there might be some routine question that came up, even
though it was a personal trip. Or it could be a question related to another LANL employee.

I walked quickly through the long corridors of enamel-painted
cinder block and fluorescent lights from X Division to the administrative area. X Division and LANL's administrative and executive offices are located in the same H-shaped building, known as the
Admin Building, at the lab's main driveway. Other LANL divisions
are spread across 44 square miles of lab property, stretching from
the finger mesas of Los Alamos into Bandelier National Monument.

Within minutes I reached the office of Ken Schiffer. Ken, probably in his early 60s, was new at LANL. He had taken over the
counterintelligence duties not a month earlier, after retiring from a
35-year career with the FBI. His predecessor was newly retired Bob
Vrooman, a former CIA guy. I didn't really know Ken, but Bob had
questioned me about my travels several times over the years. He
had also been my son Chung's soccer coach.

Ken was waiting for me with Terry Craig, another LANL counterintelligence officer, and a third man I didn't recognize. They began questioning me about my trip to Taiwan.

They asked me why I had gone to Taiwan, who I saw, what we talked about, where I stayed, what I did, and many details about the trip. Every answer prompted another round of inquiry. I tried to be helpful and to tell them what they wanted to know. It was an unpleasant but necessary exchange, rather like a trip to the dentist spent wishing for a quick and painless conclusion. It was soon evident that this wish would not be granted.

I had gone to Taiwan on personal business, related to a terrible family tragedy. I went to enroll my 28-year-old nephew William in a Chinese Christian rehabilitation center after his mother and younger brother were killed. They were shot and murdered in 1997 during a break-in of their home in the Los Angeles area. It was the kind of shocking event that no one ever expects to happen to one's own family. William was the son of my older brother Wentou. The killings appeared to be gang related, and my siblings and I thought it would be best to remove my nephew from this negative environment and enroll him in a school in Taiwan, to keep him out of trouble. My wife, Sylvia, and my kids were fearful that I was getting involved in my nephew's problems, and were concerned that I was making such a long trip twice in one year. But my extended family is very close, and we take our responsibilities to each other very seriously. Because I was able to take time off from work, I was elected to make the trip with my nephew. We chose a rehab center in Taiwan because we felt he would be safer there and because other family members would be close by.

I was born in Taiwan in 1939, the seventh of ten children. My father had come to the island in the early 1900s when he was a small boy; my mother also was born in Taiwan. After I came to the U.S. as a graduate student in 1964, some of my siblings also immigrated to the U.S., but three still lived in Taiwan. During the twenty years I worked at LANL, I visited Taiwan periodically, especially to honor my parents' graves. My visits were spaced every two years or so. Later, when I was accused of being a spy for several countries, including possibly Taiwan, some politicians and reporters made it sound as if I had been to Taiwan an extraordinary number of times. I don't think my visits were excessive at all, but I also wouldn't have returned so soon had it not been necessary to help my brother's family through their hardship.

After I got my nephew settled at the rehab center, I visited some of my scientific colleagues. One had invited me to give a talk at the Chung Shan Science and Technology Institute, a government-sponsored research facility similar to our national laboratories. I did some occasional consulting for Chung Shan, presenting my unclassified research papers there, just like other LANL scientists who did outside consulting, with full LANL and DOE approval. I had received an honorarium and payment for expenses for previous talks I gave at the institute. But on this most recent trip to Taiwan, LANL did not approve my request to give a talk at Chung Shan Institute, and so I followed LANL procedures and did not make a presentation.

————

I sat in the LANL security office, recounting the story of my trip to Taiwan, and spent two hours going over all of this in detail with Ken, Terry, and the third man. My inquisitors were particularly interested in what I did at the institute and how much money I received. Suddenly they told me they wanted to give me a lie detector test, right away, without explanation. I was surprised and alarmed, because even though security checks were a routine procedure, polygraphs were not. I knew I must be under suspicion. For what, I didn't yet know. Though I felt anxious, I trusted the security officers to be fair with me. In all my years at LANL, I never heard of anyone getting disciplined without a lengthy and careful review, and I expected a full and fair review for whatever I was suspected of doing. Most important, I felt I had done nothing wrong and so had no cause for concern.

In a large conference room near Ken's office, the polygraph testing equipment was already set up and a polygraph technician was on hand from Wackenhut, a private security contractor that the DOE used to administer polygraph tests. It all had been planned for me. At the time, I had no idea that my interrogation was being observed from outside the room by other counterintelligence agents, including an FBI agent who was standing by, ready to arrest me. I later learned that this polygraph was ordered from the highest rungs of the DOE, by a top FBI official, Edward Curran, who recently had been appointed chief of counterintelligence at the DOE headquarters in D.C. It never occurred to me that powerful politicians in Washington were watching me, convinced I must be a spy. At the same time, it didn't seem to occur to them that I might actually be innocent.

The polygraph examiner attached the sensors to the fingers of my left hand, applied a blood pressure cuff to my right arm, and fastened wires to my waist and chest. Meanwhile, Ken Schiffer explained the topic of this test: espionage. He explained the "elements" of espionage to provide a framework for me to discuss whether I had disclosed any classified information to unauthorized people, especially foreigners; if I had ever been asked to commit espionage or to disclose information that is classified or sensitive, related to weapons, or harmful to the U.S.; if I had clandestine or secret contacts with foreigners; or if I had ever offered to do any of these things.

Being a Taiwan-born, naturalized American citizen who had attended many international conferences, both in the U.S. and abroad, I knew lots of foreigners, beginning with members of my own family but also including my friends and classmates from college and graduate school, and my colleagues at LANL and around the world. For the next six hours, I wracked my brain to remember every potentially bad or "unusual" encounter I've ever had with foreigners.

During this polygraph exam, I discussed several topics. We spent a lot of time talking about my first encounter with the FBI in 1982, when they administered my first lie detector test. I told Schiffer and

Craig about the first time I came under FBI suspicion in 1982, more than 16 years ago. It was the time when I made a phone call to another nuclear scientist who worked at the Lawrence Livermore National Laboratory, in Livermore, California, outside of San Francisco. My phone call led the FBI to me. As I later learned, this scientist was suspected of giving secrets to China about the neutron bomb, and his phones were being tapped by the FBI as part of a surveillance operation. I learned through many newspaper reports and from many Congressional hearings that this operation was called "Tiger Trap." That Livermore scientist was never charged with committing any wrongdoing, and I won't publicize his name here even though some reporters printed his name after this incident came up in my case. But his name never became as public as mine has, and I hope that he has been able to rebuild his life without a media spotlight.

Back in 1982, I didn't know that the FBI monitored Chinese American scientists. I had never even met this Livermore scientist before. But I read about him in a popular Chinese-language magazine. An article said that a Taiwanese nuclear scientist was fired from Lawrence Livermore because he gave lectures in China and Taiwan. They printed the name of this scientist. Of course this news caught my attention, since I, too, was planning to present a paper in Taiwan.

In those days, Taiwanese in America had to worry about being spied on by the military regime of the Kuomintang (KMT) Party in Taiwan. It was well known that the KMT government used many spies and informants against its own citizens and even against Taiwanese in the U.S. Their actions could be ruthless, as in the execution-style killing of Henry Liu, a Taiwanese American journalist who was shot to death in 1984 outside his home in Daly City, California, for his outspoken criticism of the KMT government.

I had never had much interest in politics, maybe because I grew up in Taiwan at a time when getting involved in politics was so dangerous. I stuck to science and math, which are much more fascinating to me and have a clear benefit to humanity. They are also far less volatile than politics. But I couldn't help wondering if someone in the Taiwan government was making trouble for the Livermore scientist for some reason, perhaps because he gave a talk. I was also planning to give a talk in Taiwan about nuclear reactor safety. Though my upcoming trip and my talk had the approval of my superiors at LANL, I was worried that what had happened to him could happen to me. I found the man's phone number in a telephone directory and I contacted him. When I reached him, he wasn't interested in speaking with me, so I hung up after a brief conversation.

It turned out that the Livermore scientist was not in trouble with the KMT but with the FBI, which had a wiretap on his phone as part of their Tiger Trap operation. The FBI monitors picked up my call to him. About a year later, in November 1983, three FBI agents came to Los Alamos. They asked me to meet them at their hotel room at the Los Alamos Inn on Trinity Drive. I met with them, and they questioned me for three or four hours about my contact with the Livermore scientist. One agent was from the Albuquerque FBI office; the other two might have been from San Francisco.

Shortly after they questioned me, the FBI wanted me to help them with their investigation of the Livermore scientist. They asked me to go to California and approach the scientist in person with some questions. Of course I felt that I should assist the FBI and visit the Livermore suspect. LANL paid for the airplane ticket to California and the rental car. In December 1983, I went to the scientist's home near Livermore in the San Francisco Bay area, introduced myself, and told him that someone was trying to frame him. I spoke with him for a half hour or so, and then I left. I reported this conversation to the FBI.

About a month later, in January 1984, some FBI agents asked me to go to the Los Alamos Inn again. They polygraphed me there in the hotel. It was the first time I had been subjected to a lie detector test, but it wouldn't be the last. After attaching sensors to my fingers, arm, waist, and chest, the polygrapher spent a half day asking me many questions. One of the questions they asked me was, "Did you pass any classified information to an unauthorized person?" I answered no. When the test was over, the FBI agents told me that I passed the polygraph with flying colors. I felt that the FBI accepted the fact that I was truthful. I believed them when they said their investigation of me was closed.

My role in the Tiger Trap investigation was over and my life at LANL returned to normal. I felt that the polygraph had verified that I had told the truth and that I also had proven my loyalty by assisting the FBI—and that was the end of the story. Until, of course, this new suspicion that I had committed espionage. Today the FBI claims that I lied to them when they asked me if I called the Livermore scientist. In many later Congressional hearings and in the news media, it was reported that I denied calling the other scientist and that this was evidence of my deceptive nature. My attorneys and I would later learn that the FBI had lost their file on me for their 1983 and 1984 meetings with me—and that they had had to "reconstruct" the information. I don't agree with the FBI version of the story, but it has been repeated many times as though it were a proven fact—and this reconstructed account would be used over and over again to justify the espionage allegations against me.

———

Now, on December 23, 1998, so many years after that first encounter with the FBI, I found myself being polygraphed again, this time in the LANL conference room. I tried to think of any other incidents that might be useful to these security officers. I told them about a strange incident that had happened only a few months earlier, in August 1998. I received a call at my office late in the afternoon from a Chinese-speaking man who was at the Hilton Hotel in Santa Fe. He said his name was Wang Ming-Li. I didn't know him. He said he was a diplomat from Beijing on vacation in Santa Fe and that he wanted to meet me. I explained that I could not meet him without lab approval. Then he told me about a Chinese American scientist named Peter Lee who had once worked at LANL. Peter Lee was not related to me. He had pled guilty in 1997 to giving classified information about submarine research to China in a lecture during his visit there in 1985. Peter Lee's case didn't receive much attention, and he was sentenced to a halfway house and to perform community service. This strange caller, Mr. Wang, asked me, "Does the Peter Lee case result in any consequences to the Chinese at the laboratory?" I told him that nothing had happened to Chinese scientists at LANL because of Peter Lee, and hung up.

The same man called me again the next day, and asked me if I had any papers or reports I wanted to give to China, because he would be willing to take them back. I told him I had nothing for him to take back. Then he gave me a Santa Fe phone number and said that if I wanted to reach him, I could call him at any time.

After I got this strange phone call, I reported the episode to the LANL counterintelligence officer, Terry Craig—the same Terry Craig who was sitting there in the conference room, listening to me retell the story to the polygrapher. I had been very upset by the call.

Looking back, I feel like a fool to have told this story to LANL security and the FBI, because it turned out that this call from "Mr. Wang" was a "false flag" operation by the FBI to entrap me. All of the people sitting and listening to me relate this confusing incident must have been laughing at me. I didn't take the bait from "Mr. Wang," but at this point, no one bothered to enlighten me. I only found out later, while I was sitting behind bars, that this whole thing had been a setup. What happened to the Livermore scientist was now happening to me, only it was much worse than I could imagine.

––––––––

My impromptu pre-Christmas polygraph test went on for six hours, past the time I would normally go home, past the time I had intended to leave to pick Alberta up at the airport. But the polygrapher kept pushing for any other events or incidents. I don't know

why or how I thought of this, but suddenly I remembered something else when the examiner asked again if foreigners had ever approached me for classified information.

I recalled an incident that occurred when I was in China in June
1988, ten years earlier. I had been invited with other scientists from
LANL and elsewhere to attend an international conference on computational physics in Beijing; I was to present a paper I had written.
It would be only the second time I had ever visited China, and I went
with my wife. I also was asked to present the same paper to China's
Institute of Applied Physics and Computational Mathematics,
China's nuclear research facility. The lab had approved both visits as
well as the unclassified paper I was to talk about.

One day, when my wife was out and I was alone in my hotel
room in Beijing, two Chinese scientists—Dr. Zheng Shaotong and
Dr. Hu Side—visited me. Dr. Zheng did the talking, and after a few
pleasantries, he asked me a question related to whether we use a
certain number of explosive detonation points in a nuclear warhead
of a certain size.

In response to Dr. Zheng's question about the number of detonation points in a certain-sized nuclear warhead, I replied that I
didn't know and that I was not interested in discussing that topic.
He just let it pass and talked about other things. Dr. Hu said nothing. When I returned to Los Alamos, I submitted a routine trip report and listed a number of the Chinese scientists I encountered,
but I did not include this incident. I didn't mention it after I returned because I remembered the trouble that followed my phone
call to the Lawrence Livermore scientist in 1982. Even though
nothing had happened in the hotel room, I was afraid that if I reported their visit, I would be subjected to the kind of FBI questioning I'd received before. But now, as I was being polygraphed on
suspicion of espionage, I told everything I could think of, so that
any doubts about me could be cleared.

Little did I realize that by telling what had happened to me in that hotel room in 1988, the fact that I hadn't mentioned it earlier became the "proof" of my suspected espionage activity. Officials at the lab, the FBI, the DOJ, the DOE, politicians in Congress, and the media would later cite my recollection of this 1988 incident as evidence that I was deceptive, a liar, and therefore a probable spy. I didn't "fail to mention it" during my 1998 polygraph in the LANL conference room—I'm the one who brought it up. Only now, the fact that I reported it would become ammunition to be used against me.

The long hours of interrogation and polygraphing were exhausting. Finally, the Wackenhut examiner asked me four specific questions.

"Have you ever committed espionage against the United States?"

"No," I answered.

"Have you ever provided any classified weapons data to any unauthorized person?"

"No."

"Have you had any contact with anyone to commit espionage against the United States?"

"No."

And, "Have you ever had personal contact with anyone you know who has committed espionage against the United States?"

Again, I replied, "No."

Within about 30 minutes, I was told that I had passed the polygraph exam. Unknown to me then, the same message was given to the FBI agent who had been waiting to arrest me in case I failed the exam. So I wasn't arrested that day, and you might even say I was cleared, but I didn't feel any particular thrill—because I had fully expected to pass. I had not done the things they asked me about, so the test couldn't show that I had lied, could it?

Despite my "passing grade," I was handed some serious and bad news. I was told that my access to X Division was being suspended and that when I reported to work after the holidays, I should report to the Theoretical Division. The T Division, as it is known, focuses on basic research questions that are not classified. I would no longer have the necessary access to work in the X Division.

I was allowed to go back to my office to clear out my things. By the time I got there I was shaken, stunned by the events of the day. What had happened to provoke this interrogation? Why was I suspected of espionage? Why was I losing my access if I passed the polygraph? Every LANL scientist knew how much office politics affected who was in favor, who was to be shunned, and who worked on what projects. And I was not the sort who could play office politics—I didn't even try. My wife and my friends teased me for being a rough country bumpkin, and I suppose there is some truth to that. In 1993 I had received a notice that I had been on a list to be laid off for an anticipated potential "Reduction In Force." To even be on this "RIF" list at all was a sign that I was out of favor; yet when a later list appeared, in 1995, I wasn't on it.

In the quiet of my office, I was filled with the anxiety of not knowing. My specialized work for the last 20 years had involved classified information. A nuclear scientist without necessary access to X Division is a fish without fins. Of course I could perform productive research in the T Division. The numerous papers I had published over the years involved unclassified applications of the mathematics I used in the classified nuclear weapons field. But T Division would not make the best use of my expertise, and I would be that much closer to getting laid off or fired.

There was another reason for me to worry about this transfer to the T Division. At Los Alamos, the classified work areas were physically set apart from the unclassified areas by a fence—a high steel cyclone fence that is topped by coiled razor wire. The fence is patrolled by an armed security force, and watchtowers keep an eye out for potential violators. Sometimes SWAT teams practiced repelling mock invaders, though, to my best knowledge, there have never been any attempts to storm the fence. People with access to

X Division, which is noted on the omnipresent ID badges we all wore, are among those permitted to work "inside the fence."

Most of the T Division, including the part to which I was assigned, was located outside the fence. This posed some immediate practical problems because so many of my own papers, books, files, computer programs—my "portfolio" and work product, to which I no longer had access—contained classified material that I could not bring with me into the T Division. Without access to X Division, I wasn't even supposed to have classified materials in my possession. As I went about the tedious process of sorting through what to take along with me to the T Division when the lab reopened after the week-long holiday break, I began to delete and destroy the classified material I no longer had the permission to possess. I will say more about this later, because these were the downloaded files that I was accused of giving to a foreign country—and the reason I was arrested, denied bail, and forced into solitary confinement.

———

It was very late when I got to my home in White Rock, the small subdivision of Los Alamos on one of the lower mesas. My daughter, Alberta, had fallen asleep on the living-room couch, but she got up right away when she heard me come in. Her eyes were round with fear. "Ba," she said to me, using the Chinese word for "Dad." "Ba, Mom says you're in some trouble at the lab." I knew that my wife was terrified about this new FBI attention, and she wouldn't be able to hide it from Alberta. I didn't know what to say to my daughter.

"Ba, are you going to be fired?" she asked.

"Mei-mei, I don't know." That's all I could manage to reply. "Mei-mei" is Chinese for "Little Sister," and it is the family name we call Alberta. I could see from the look on her face that my answer frightened her. I was the one who always had the answers in this family. She had never heard me sound so uncertain.

We did our best to celebrate Christmas in 1998. I did not grow up in the Christian tradition, but we always celebrated the holiday with our children. I'd get a tree-cutting permit and go with Chung into the Jemez mountains to find the best and biggest piñon tree; my tall, strong son would cut it down and we'd carry it home. Piñon trees are plentiful in New Mexico, and they have the most beautiful fragrance. Our home would smell like the forest for the months we kept the piñon tree because we hated to throw it away. Alberta was the artistic one in the family, and she had a special talent for decorating the tree—so that was her task. Sylvia always prepared a delicious roast duck for Christmas. That was her specialty, and it was our way of adding our Chinese heritage to our traditional dinner. On Christmas Eve we joined in with all the neighbors on our street each year by setting out luminarias along our house—the Mexican tradition of lighting the way with paper bags weighted down by sand and set aglow with candles. We had done this ever since we moved to White Rock twenty years ago. We are a close-knit family, and my kids and I could talk about anything, but this Christmas I did my best not to let the worry show.

Each year, LANL is closed between Christmas and the New Year. The official reason for this is to cut down on energy, but Los Alamos tries to foster a university-like setting for our research. That was the vision that J. Robert Oppenheimer had when he founded the lab, and it is what makes Los Alamos special among the national labs. Individual scientists can work in their offices during the holidays, if they choose.

I went back to the lab several times to try to finish moving my office. But my security swipe card no longer worked to admit me into the X Division. I needed to get in because I wanted to continue working on the scientific paper I was preparing for publication. I tried several times to get in, including late at night on Christmas Eve. Somehow I thought that the swipe card might work again at off hours. I also knew that I wasn't supposed to be trying to get into the X Division, and I was less likely to run into other people. Later, my attempts to get to my office would be used as another example to show that I was deceptive—and therefore must be a spy.

Alberta was urging me to get a lawyer. I didn't feel I needed a lawyer because I wasn't a spy and I hadn't done anything wrong. I also knew how expensive it could be to fight the lab. A friend of mine, Bob Clark, had taken LANL to court, and his legal bills were astronomical, more than what my house was worth. In fact, I had testified in court on his behalf—and was the only one at the lab who was willing to say the lab management was wrong. I wondered if that was being held against me now. But Chung agreed that I didn't need a lawyer. I thought it would all pass in time, the way my first polygraph had after I was questioned in 1984. Alberta tried very hard not to worry me, but she is the emotional one in our family, and I knew she was extremely upset by this. I tried to reassure her. "Don't worry, it will all be over soon. They'll find out the truth, and I'll be back at work like normal."

————

In hindsight, I was very stupid. I know now what a mistake it was for me to be so certain that nothing was wrong, and to keep talking to all the investigators from LANL, the FBI, DOE, and DOJ without counsel. I figured that all I had to do was tell the truth, since I was smart enough to answer their questions by myself. I could tough it out on my own. But I didn't even know that I didn't have to talk to the FBI. My wife sometimes says I am too stubborn, too proud, and too bullheaded. Some people say that Taiwanese people are known for being stubborn, proud, and bullheaded. I don't think it makes sense to generalize about a whole group of people, but it is true that I can be very stubborn.

Had I known that a trap was being set for me—had I the slightest inkling that my words could and would be twisted against me—I would have refused to participate in this cat-and-mouse game. I would not have given the many hours of voluntary interviews and submitted to the polygraphs that were still to come, even though I surely would have been fired on the spot. But I didn't know I could refuse to answer the questions, and I certainly didn't know that they were the cat and I was the mouse. So I just tried to be as helpful as possible.

I don't pay attention to any music that was produced after 1911, when Gustav Mahler died. I would fill the airwaves, elevators, waiting rooms, and shopping malls with classical music if I could. At the time, however, I found some small irony in the words of one Christmas song: "He knows when you are sleeping / He knows when you're awake / He knows when you've been bad or good. . . ."

The FBI had come to town.

CHAPTER 2

I began the New Year in the T Division of LANL, the non-secure area that was "outside the fence." The manager didn't assign me any work to do because my time there was viewed as temporary, in light of my passing the polygraph test, so I would simply work in a T Division office pending the restoration of my security clearance. I tried to continue working on an unclassified paper I had been writing, even though much of my research had been left behind in my X Division office.

On Friday, January 8, 1999 at about 2 P.M., an FBI agent by the name of Carol Covert called me. She said she was calling from Washington, D.C., but was on her way back to her office in Santa Fe. She wanted to see me on Sunday, January 10, because she was worried about me. Her call struck me as odd, but it was the FBI calling, and I didn't question her motives.

Agent Covert spoke to me in a very friendly and caring manner. An article had appeared in the *Wall Street Journal* on January 7, and was reprinted locally in the Santa Fe *New Mexican*, saying that a Taiwan-born LANL scientist was suspected of passing nuclear secrets to China about a nuclear warhead known as the W-88. The article hadn't worried me because I was sure it wasn't about me. I didn't even recognize the name of this W-88, so how could I be the suspect in the article? She said she was concerned that I might feel uneasy because of the *Wall Street Journal* story and she wanted to reassure me that the news report was wrong. She seemed sincere and I trusted her. I asked her how much time she would need; when she said 30 minutes to an hour, I suggested she come to my house on Sunday.

At the time, I didn't realize that Covert was the FBI agent in charge of my case. She was the agent who had waited to arrest me outside of Ken Schiffer's office if I had failed the polygraph conducted just before Christmas. I still had no explanation as to why my X Division access had been taken away, when I had passed their polygraph test unequivocally—a point that would be confirmed many times and just as often ignored by politicians in Washington. Top bureaucrats at the DOE and the FBI were unhappy with the polygraph results that absolved me, because of the considerable political pressure to find a spy for China, and some apparently hoped that I would be it. The FBI sent Covert to check up on me, especially after the *Wall Street Journal* article came out.

Sunday was a beautiful, bright day. Covert arrived at my house promptly at 1 P.M., in the company of another agent named John Hudenko. Carol looked to be about 40 years old; she had blond hair and wore a white dress. John was older, maybe in his mid-50s, and he had on a sports jacket. They came in and sat in my living room, Carol on my right, on the couch, and John facing me. I prepared them some green tea that is specially grown in my hometown of Nantou, Taiwan. The region of Central Taiwan where I was born is famous for its tea, and the tea from Nantou is considered one of the very best teas there is. In my home, the kitchen is my domain, and when guests come to visit, I like to offer them some of this special tea from my hometown.

My wife had gone shopping in Santa Fe, so it was just the three of us. We chatted for the first half hour. Carol took out a pad and pen from her small, white handbag. She told me that she had three bachelor's degrees—one in chemistry, one in psychology, and the last in language—and that her mother was from London. Carol said she knew French quite well and was studying Chinese. John was born in Michigan and had a bachelor's degree in Russian language from the University of Michigan; his father was from Kiev, Ukraine, he told me. John's Russian was so good that he didn't have to attend the Defense Language Institute Foreign Language Center in Monterey, California, which is one of the language training schools for the FBI and CIA.

This is what the agents told me about themselves; however, I've learned that the FBI tells many lies, so I don't know if any of this is true, or if "Covert" and "Hudenko" are their real names.

Carol began with some friendly questions, which she asked me with a big smile. John was just listening, and as the afternoon drew on, he said no more than five sentences. Carol took her notes in shorthand, and wrote down my answers.

Many of her questions had already been asked of me or discussed on December 23, during that interview and polygraph. I was learning that the FBI likes to keep asking the same questions over and over again, until there is some inconsistency that they can say is proof of deception. She asked me about my phone call to the Lawrence Livermore scientist who was suspected of giving neutron bomb secrets to the PRC. She asked me to talk again about the strange phone call I received from the Chinese man who said he was at the Hilton Hotel in Santa Fe. On that afternoon, as I recounted what happened in that incident, I still hadn't known that it had been an FBI sting operation intended to entrap me. Carol certainly knew this and was probably hoping that the memory of it might make me slip up and reveal something new.

Carol wanted to know about my contacts with Chinese scientists from the PRC and my trips to China. I told her about my first contact with Chinese scientists, during an international conference in 1995 at Hilton Head, South Carolina. That conference was about Free Lagrangian methods, a particular numerical technique that scientists and engineers use to map and compute the dynamic internal changes that take place, moment by moment, for example, when a car crashes into a wall, or when a bomb explodes.

Most of us scientists attending this conference at Hilton Head were American, with the majority from Los Alamos and Lawrence Livermore national labs. A few came from Europe, and two attendees were from China: Dr. Li Deyuan and Dr. Yu, who was sick much of the time, so I hardly met him. Carol wanted to know more about Dr. Li. I had had a friendly conversation with Dr. Li during one of the conference break times. He said that he was working on organizing an international conference on computational physics to take place in 1986 in China. He said that he would like to invite me to attend. I told him to send me information and their "call for papers." This was a typical exchange that happens at any scientific conference, just like the networking that takes place in other professions.

Not long after, Dr. Li sent me the conference announcement and its call for papers. I submitted a paper, which they accepted for presentation. Dr. Li invited me and other scientists from LANL to attend their conference in Beijing in 1986. Dr. Bob Clark, my friend and colleague from the X Division, was also invited to give a talk. I was to serve as the translator for Bob when he delivered his presentation, which also had to do with Lagrangian computational methods. LANL approved our attendance and our papers, which we were to deliver at the Institute of Applied Physics and Computational Mathematics, China's nuclear institute, in Beijing.

Bob's wife, Kathy, was going along on the trip, as were my wife and kids. Their daughters were about the same age as my kids, so we often saw their children in our home, and ours were frequently at theirs. None of us had ever been to China, except for Sylvia, whose parents had fled China for Taiwan when she was a young child of four or five. Chung and Alberta were in their early teens, and we wanted them to see China, too.

It helped that LANL was paying for Sylvia's trip expenses because they wanted her assistance while she was in China. Sylvia had worked at the lab in various jobs. The FBI had asked her to help them with some project while we were in China. Sylvia assisted the FBI several times on an unpaid basis, always at their request and related to visits by scientists from the PRC. Except for a few managers, other LANL employees had no idea that Sylvia was assisting the FBI. When I returned to LANL, I filled out a trip report, listing the people I had encountered in China, and we both had security debriefings with the lab counterintelligence staff.

My wife has requested that I say nothing more about her involvement with the FBI; I will respect her wishes. She left LANL on her own accord a few years before I was fired.

It was a very exciting trip to take as a family. Our conference hosts took us LANL visitors to see the Great Wall, the Imperial Summer Palace, and other tourist sites that I had heard about as a child. I was looking forward to seeing China's cultural wonders for the first time, and I was delighted to share the experience with my children. They behaved like typical adolescents and were not so enthused about the trip, but we insisted that they come along.

The conference hosts also arranged for some wonderful banquets for our visiting "delegation" of American scientists—sumptuous multicourse dinners with many toasts. I toasted with tea because I don't drink alcohol. Later, the FBI and news reports often referred to how the Chinese wined and dined me, insinuating that I would be willing to spy for China because they took me on a tour and gave me some nice food. That is ridiculous. At LANL, we also try to be hospitable to visiting international guests. We invite them to nice dinners and take them to see the major sites—Bandelier Monument, Taos and Santa Fe, Native American pueblos.

One of the strongest impressions I took from this trip was the very low standard of living of the Chinese. My family was very cautious about the food we ate in China, because we were concerned about quality and cleanliness. And poverty was not only visible on the streets—I saw signs of the economic disparities even at the conference, among China's leading scientists. When the conference had coffee breaks, the Chinese scientists rushed to the coffee dispensers, soon emptying the urns. It turns out that coffee was a real treat for them—because it was so expensive in China relative to their wages, they couldn't afford to buy a cup. It was sad to see these highly educated, talented scientists crowding around to get some coffee. I felt so much more fortunate than they are. But these were not the impressions of China that the FBI wanted to hear from me on that January day in 1999.

———

For some reason, Carol Covert asked me about my cancer surgery in May 1987. The cancer was detected during a routine physical at LANL. My tests showed that I was anemic, and further examination confirmed that I had cancer of the colon. The cancer was discovered on a Monday, and the doctors said I needed immediate surgery. My sister Angela, who was studying to be a nurse, recommended that I contact the Houston Medical Center. By Wednesday I had checked in for surgery with a cancer specialist. He removed about 24 inches of my large and small intestines as well as some lymph nodes, but I was very lucky—the cancer had not penetrated through the lining of my intestine, so the cancer cells had not spread to my other organs. My recovery, however, was a slow process. I was very weak after the surgery and lost a lot of weight. My family tells me that I looked so bad that many people didn't expect me to pull through. It was a very difficult time for me because I couldn't focus that well at work, and much of the time I felt as though I were in a daze. It was a shock for all of us—Sylvia had to face the prospect of raising the kids by herself, and the kids had never seen me sick before. Chung and Alberta were barely in high school. We didn't even tell them I was having surgery, or that I had cancer, until after it was all over. I don't know why Carol asked me about my cancer. It certainly wasn't out of concern, and I didn't meet any Chinese scientists while I was in surgery.

Carol was especially interested in the second trip I took to Beijing in 1988 to attend an international conference on computational physics. I was invited to give a talk related to the topic, based on a paper I had submitted, all with LANL and DOE approval. A few other LANL scientists whom I didn't know attended, too, as well as a UCLA professor who was a consultant to the X Division. I was the only Chinese American. My wife came on the trip, but Chung and Alberta did not want to go this time. We took a side tour with five other conference participants and their wives; the men were professors from Carnegie Mellon University, the University of Pittsburgh, and the University of Washington. All of us were U.S. citizens and, except for Sylvia and me, American-born and white. We were the only ones in the group who could speak Chinese. Together, we toured Xi'an, Shanghai, Hangzhou, Guilin, and Guangzhou, accompanied by a Chinese guide. We saw some of China's most beautiful natural and historic sites.

The trip was a challenge for me because I hadn't completely recovered from my cancer surgery. In fact, one purpose of this trip was to visit a doctor of Chinese traditional medicine while we were in China. I saw an herbalist while I was in Beijing and paid him $100 for a consultation—a princely sum of money in China, at least equivalent to several months' worth of income. The herbalist told me I had only three years to live, and prescribed some Chinese medicine for my recovery.

The FBI agents also wanted to know about a trip I took to Hong

Kong in 1992 to attend an international conference on continuous mechanics. That conference was organized by a well-known American professor of computational engineering sciences, Satya Atluri, of the Georgia Institute of Technology. Alberta went with me on that trip. During that visit to Hong Kong, I paid a $600 hotel bill and $100 for a sightseeing trip for Alberta. I had proof of these expenditures. Later, the *New York Times* reported that I had spent this $700 for an airplane ticket to Shanghai; Senator Arlen Specter even argued in a Congressional hearing that this supported probable cause that I had committed a federal crime. It is amazing to me how facts have been so distorted, and that otherwise intelligent people believed and perpetuated these lies!

Carol asked me again about the trips I took to Taiwan in 1998, which I had discussed during the December 23 polygraph.

Carol had two more significant questions for me: First, she wanted me to talk again about the visit that Dr. Zheng Shaotong and Hu Side had made to my hotel room during my trip to China in 1988. This was the incident I had reported during the December 23, 1998, polygraph test with Ken Schiffer and the DOE examiner from Wackenhut—when Zheng asked me the classified question that I can't repeat, about the number of detonation points in a nuclear warhead. I had already explained everything I could remember about this during the polygraph, but Carol wanted me to go over it again with her. She also asked me if I stayed in contact with any Chinese scientists. After that trip, I had received a couple of requests for unclassified publications of mine, which I did send, in keeping with LANL policies. For the few years following, I had exchanged Christmas cards with some of the scientists, but gradually the correspondence faded.

The other question was whether I had ever worked on the W-88 warhead. I answered no.

———

By now, the trees in my yard were casting long shadows. When Carol had called two days earlier and asked for this meeting, she said she wanted to reassure me about the *Wall Street Journal* article, and that this would only take a half hour. Her questions didn't reassure me one bit, and it was almost five o'clock—I had been answering questions for about four hours. But Carol and John were guests in my house, they were agents from the FBI, which I respected back then, and they said they were trying to help me resolve the security questions about me. I believed them, perhaps because I wanted to believe them. Now I know it was all lies and false pretenses, but I tried to cooperate in any way I could.

We finally took a break. At some point in the questioning, I had mentioned my fondness for classical music. Carol said that she loved classical music too, so I showed her my collection of 600 to 700 albums, tapes, and CDs of classical music. Among my favorites are Beethoven, Mozart, Chopin, Haydn, Schubert, and Liszt, but to me, Johann Sebastian Bach is the greatest. Especially his Brandenberg concerti.

The FBI agents only questioned me about my trips to China, Taiwan, and Hong Kong, but I had traveled to Europe a number of times to present scientific papers at international conferences as well, all with LANL approval. After my conferences, I liked to take a few vacation days to visit the hometowns of my favorite composers. I've been to Salzburg twice because it's the birthplace of Mozart, and I am especially fond of his opera *The Marriage of Figaro*. I admire Mozart's purpose in writing that opera.

Figaro was a servant who wanted to marry Susanna, a maid. But in 17th-century Europe, if servants married, the count had the "right of the first night," which meant he could sleep with the bride. Mozart wrote the opera as a social satire. Mozart's goal was to explain the nature of human life, to improve the human condition. His opera created such an outcry that the king modified the law to end the practice.

That's what I've wanted to do: use my science to do good, to make an improvement in human society. I wanted to make the country's defense system stronger in order to protect the citizens of the United States against anyone who might try to do harm. Unfortunately, I have now learned that the FBI, many politicians, and others in the government don't seem to believe that Chinese Americans can make this kind of contribution to America. That's why the FBI was in my house.

As I showed Carol and John my photo albums of my trips to Germany, Austria, and Hungary, I tried to convey some of these feelings. They seemed interested, but they may have been pretending. The FBI agents didn't ask questions about my conferences in Europe. I suppose that because I am of Chinese ancestry, the FBI was concerned mainly about my contacts in China. But Carol said that when the investigation was over, she would like to visit me again to talk about music.

As they were leaving, I offered them each a package of green tea from Nantou. It is hard to get in the U.S., and very costly. But they both declined, and finally left my home at 5:30 P.M., after spending four and a half hours with me. Sylvia had not yet returned from her afternoon in Santa Fe, so she never met them.

———

I was still waiting for some news about my return to the X Division. Hadn't they said that I passed my December 23 polygraph? With my sudden transfer outside the fence, into the T Division, it was obvious to my coworkers and friends that something unusual was going on. Especially after the newspaper report of a spy suspect who was born in Taiwan—out of 6,000 scientists, there were only a few dozen of us who were from Taiwan. It was a real blow to think that my colleagues of 20 years were wondering if I was a spy, when I knew it wasn't so. I kept my head up high and I spoke to only a few close friends. Thankfully, few people asked me anything.

It wasn't until January 21, 1999, that I heard from the FBI again, almost two weeks after Carol Covert and John Hudenko had come to my house. I was to meet John that day at noon, at Café Allegro in downtown Los Alamos. We refer to our two parallel main streets as "downtown," but it's really just a few strip malls along Trinity Drive and Central Avenue. John was with another FBI agent, named Mike. I'd had my lunch already, at the office, so I ordered a cup of coffee while they ate. I tried to make a little conversation with John. Since he said he had majored in Russian as a college student, I asked him what he thought about Leo Tolstoy's works and if he had a strong influence on the communist revolution in Russia. John said that reminded him of a final exam question at the University of Michigan, and he didn't know how to answer.

After they ate, John went to where his car was parked in the big strip mall lot, and moved it next to my 1980 Olds Cutlass Supreme. I had more than 160,000 miles on that car—I called it my fishing car because I could drive it on the roughest country back roads to my fishing holes. I had to tinker with the car now and then, but it was still pretty dependable. People around town recognized it, since it was one of the older cars in Los Alamos. I finally got rid of it when it seemed that I might be arrested, because I didn't want my wife to have to deal with my old car.

John and Mike brought me an 11-page typed report of Carol Covert's interrogation at my house on January 10, 1999. John wanted me to read it and sign it. The report described in detail Carol's questions and my answers. I found four minor errors and corrected them, but I was impressed by Carol's notetaking. I signed, John signed, and Mike signed. When I asked for a copy, John said no one could have a copy, not even me. His response made me feel strange—I signed it and the report was 100 percent about me. Why shouldn't I have a copy? But the FBI is the law, and the agents drove off at around 2:30 P.M. I went back to my T Division office without a copy of my statement.

I hadn't yet received word about returning to the X Division, but I was feeling pretty positive. After all, I knew I was not a spy, and I had faith that LANL internal security, the DOE counterintelligence, and the FBI agents had all realized this about me and were satisfied with their investigations. Carol Covert had told me that the investigation was almost done and that I was no longer a suspect. After all, I had passed the DOE polygraph conducted on December 23, 1998. I later learned that the Albuquerque FBI office even sent a memo dated January 23, 1999, to Washington headquarters saying that I was not the spy. The local office recommended that the FBI close the investigation of me.

Even my LANL supervisors were giving me encouragement. On Thursday afternoon, February 4, 1999, only two weeks after I signed the 11-page FBI report, Dr. Dan Butler, the acting director of the T Division, came to my office and told me that I could go back to X Division. He said that the next morning, I should first go and see Dr. Dick Burik, the associate director of Los Alamos National Lab. So on Friday morning, February 5, I went to Dr. Burik's office on the fourth floor of the Admin Building. He told me that my security problem was all cleared up and that I should return to the X Division as soon as possible.

I felt very upbeat with this news and headed directly to the X Division to fill out a form to reinstate my security access. I needed my X Division access so that I could return to my research work "inside the fence." Afterward, I headed back to work in the T Division. I remember thinking that this would be an especially good weekend because I would finally be back in my X Division office and back to normal. I was eager to get on track with my research, to put all this behind me and get on with my life.

When Monday, February 8, came around, I was in my T Division office, ready to pack up and go. At about 11 A.M., I got a call from Carol Covert, who said she was at the FBI office in Albuquerque. She had had a great idea that morning—that I could help her and John work out some problems that they had encountered in their W-88 project, which she had been working on for the last two years. Because I am so smart and have such a good memory, she said, she thought I could help her solve these puzzles. She spoke so sweetly to me, but it turned out to be poison sweetness.

I told her I might be able to help if it were only for a short time, otherwise I would have to check with my boss. But she wanted my assistance for maybe a full day each week for about eight weeks, so I offered to speak to him. Thank you very much, she said, and she would meet me at 3 P.M. that afternoon, at the Los Alamos badge office, where visitors to LANL sign in.

After lunch I talked with Dan Butler, my boss in the T Division, about moving back to the X Division, and recounted how Dr. Dick Burik told me on Friday to go back as soon as possible. To my surprise, Dan said that the FBI told him to hold my return to the X Division, because the FBI wanted to do some more investigative work on me. It seemed that FBI Agent Carol Covert had already set everything up. I began to think that she might be more like a clever fox that has a snake for a heart.

———

I went to the badge office at 3 P.M., as Carol had requested. She and her fellow FBI agent John Hudenko came walking out of the X Division, which was just past the badge office. She said that they had been talking with Dick Krajcik, the deputy director of the division, to try to understand some technical issues related to Lagrangian codes—which happen to be one of the basic numerical methods I use in developing my hydrodynamics computer codes. I suggested that we go to the nearby cafeteria, on the second floor of the Otowi Building, a facility that is outside the fence and open to the public. I knew the cafeteria would be empty at that hour. We selected a table toward the back, facing the Oppenheimer Library. Carol sat on one side of me, John on the other. She began talking about some "puzzles."

"Wen Ho, John and I have been working on this project regarding the W-88 for about two years, and now our circle of suspects looks like this." With that, Carol drew a circle, showing eight or nine suspects within the circle. "There are many people under investigation, all over this country. We have about twelve puzzles that we are trying to understand. But your mathematics is so good and your physics is so good, we think that if you can help us for a few days, we might be able to solve our problem."

I suspected that Carol was trying to butter me up with her big smiles at me, but she seemed so sincere. I told her I would help, but on one condition: only if there was nothing about this that involved me. I asked point blank, "Carol, you and John are not trying to investigate me, am I right?"

Carol moved so close to me I could even smell her perfume, and she patted me on the shoulder. "Oh no, Wen Ho, you're absolutely clear with us. Ever since you signed the 11-page statement, we know you had nothing to do with the W-88 investigation. We trust you, we're just asking you to do us a favor."

John also put on a friendly smile, and patted my right shoulder several times. Fortunately, he wasn't wearing perfume.

Based on their assurances, I offered to help. "Okay, if you're not continuing to investigate me, then I can spend some time with you on your project. Tell me what your twelve puzzles are so I can see if I may be able to help you."

Carol smiled at me in reply. "Thank you, Wen Ho, I'm very glad that you're willing to help us. You can begin helping us right now with most of the puzzles we have, but for three or four you will have to pass a test on two questions which are required by the FBI headquarters in Washington, D.C."

My alarm bells went off, and I asked what she meant by "passing a test on two questions."

She explained: "The W-88 project is one of the most classified projects, and FBI HQ insists that everyone who works on it must pass a polygraph test on two questions, which are classified, so I can't tell you what the questions are. You don't need to worry because I know you'll have no trouble passing the polygraph."

I politely declined and offered to assist with any of their puzzles that didn't require a lie detector test. Yet I was already falling for their FBI trick, their ruse to make me believe they were not investigating me, but rather enlisting my help to catch the real bad guy. They were such convincing actors that they ought to act in Broadway shows. And I believed them. I wanted to believe what they were telling me.

They were disappointed with my answer, so they huddled for a few minutes. Then Carol came back with another approach. She suggested that I just meet for coffee with the polygrapher, a Mr. Hobgood, who had come all the way from Washington, D.C. This way Hobgood could just meet me without having to do any testing, but he could assess what an honest and nice guy I am. She said that he could report all that when he returned to Washington, and then maybe the FBI in the D.C. headquarters would allow me to forego the test in order to help them with their W-88 investigation.

By the time we finished up, it was after 5 P.M. Carol said she'd call me in the morning to let me know when Hobgood would meet me for coffee. I left and went home, but I felt thoroughly confused about this game of suspicion going on around me. One moment I was no longer a suspect, and the next moment was back under investigation, and now I was being asked to help with some *other* investigation. Everyone seemed to know what was going on except me.

I was truly in the dark. I rarely watched the news or read the papers, and as I've said, I have never cared for politicians or politics. Politics always seemed messy to me, unscientific and full of people who, it seemed, might sell their own mothers for their own personal benefit. That's how it was in Taiwan when I was young, and I now know that plenty of American politicians are no better.

But my ignorance of the political realm was hurting me. Back then I was unaware that American attitudes toward China had shifted in Washington, or that political conflicts with Asia historically spilled over as racial hostility toward Chinese Americans—for example, targeting Chinese Americans as spy suspects.

Even though the tensions between the U.S. and the PRC had nothing to do with me, it felt like the investigations were turning my life into a football, as I was kicked around among various federal bureaucracies, each with its own agenda and internal conflicts. A special Congressional subcommittee investigating Chinese espionage, headed by member of Congress Christopher Cox, pointed its finger at the White House and Department of Energy for the loss of nuclear secrets. To counter those accusations, the White House needed to show that it took the China espionage threat seriously in order to combat the persistent claim that it was "soft on China." That image began before their attention turned to me, when the campaign finance scandal was hot and many Asian Americans were investigated for a presumed connection to China. But now it was the DOE counterintelligence chief who was lobbying Capitol Hill, arguing that LANL was the source of nuclear secrets to China. He found a receptive audience among politicians in Washington, who were pressuring Bill Richardson, the Secretary of Energy, to clamp down on security at the national labs—and to catch the spy, me.

Carol Covert and the FBI agents even had a name for their project to get me, the spy. It was called Operation Kindred Spirit. All of the political maneuvering in Washington was influencing the handling of my case, as I would discover later—even affecting who should be in charge of the investigation—the FBI or the DOE. By law, it is the FBI's responsibility to investigate possible espionage, but in my case, it was the DOE's chief of counterintelligence and a former FBI guy, Ed Curran, who took control, because he was unhappy with the Albuquerque FBI's inaction. Curran had ordered the polygraph by Wackenhut, the DOE contractor. But when the investigation went back to the FBI, they wouldn't accept the Wackenhut polygraph results. The FBI wanted polygraphs done by their own folks, not DOE's, even though three different polygraph experts at Wackenhut said that I had passed the polygraph by a large margin on December 23.

After the Albuquerque FBI office wrote the memo recommending that the investigation of me be closed, and after the LANL officials told me they were sending me back to X Division, they changed their minds. Carol Covert was sent to ensnare me. The whole thing was turning into a Keystone Kops slapstick routine. The joke was on me, and I didn't even know it.

CHAPTER 3

The next morning, February 9, 1999, Carol called me as she said she would and suggested we meet again at the badge office that afternoon. She would take me to see Rich Hobgood, the man from the D.C. office, for a quick cup of coffee.

At 2 P.M., I was waiting outside the badge office in front of the Admin Building. Carol drove up in her big white car and parked it illegally in front of the library. She walked over to me and said we would drive to meet Rich. We drove the short distance through downtown Los Alamos, and pulled into the Holiday Inn Express. On the first floor, just beyond the front desk, was our destination, room 102. Carol knocked on the door and a thin fellow, about 40 years old, answered. Carol introduced me to Rich Hobgood, and then she left.

I thought we were going to have some coffee, but I noticed there wasn't any. I sat on a chair while Rich sat on the bed. I told myself I would stay for no more than 30 minutes.

Rich Hobgood introduced himself—he was the father of two girls, said he lived in Fairfax County, Virginia, and told me that every

morning he crossed the Potomac River to work at the FBI headquarters in Washington, D.C. He said he had a bachelor's degree in
psychology and worked as a police department polygrapher for six
years before joining the FBI. I have no idea if any of this is true or if
he told me his real name.

According to Rich, many FBI agents were working on the W-88
project, and he had interviewed and polygraphed people across the
country, but they still had not found the real spy. He began asking
me what I knew about the W-88. I told him that I didn't know anything about the W-88, and that I thought it had been designed at
the Lawrence Livermore labs. Later, after all these questions, I
asked a coworker about the W-88 and learned that it was designed
at Los Alamos, but that's all I knew then.

Rich had a notebook with several pages full of the questions he
wanted to ask me. It looked as though he had planned his interrogation of me for many days. His questions were pretty much the
same as the ones that Carol Covert and John Hudenko had asked at
my house on January 10 and that were already recorded on the 11-
page report I had signed on January 21. Rich went through the
questions very quickly, but after more than an hour of this, I started
to realize that something was wrong. We were not having a coffee
chat so that Rich could go back to Washington and tell his FBI
bosses how nice and honest I am, as Carol had said the day before.

Then Rich changed the subject to the W-88. He asked me to
draw a picture of the W-88 nuclear warhead. I told him I didn't
know how, because I never worked on the W-88. He said, "Just do
the best you can from your imagination." So I drew a picture of an
ellipse, with two circles inside, one for the primary bomb, and one
for the secondary.

I drew it this way because this is the basic conceptual design
of a thermonuclear warhead. It is not classified and anyone can
find such drawings at the library or on the Internet. Thermonuclear weapons are really several bombs in one: The primary is the

first stage of a two-stage nuclear weapon. It's actually an atomic bomb, a sphere of plutonium that is triggered by a number of conventional explosives that are placed around the sphere. The "Fat Man" atomic bomb that was dropped on Nagasaki on August 9, 1945, had 32 detonation explosives, or "points," around the plutonium. All these explosive points made the bomb huge, about the size of a two-person submarine weighing approximately 5 tons. The Chinese scientists who asked me the classified question in the Beijing hotel room in 1988 wanted to know how many points were being used in the modern warheads.

There is another bomb in the warhead, the second stage of a two-stage nuclear weapon, known as the secondary. The secondary is full of hydrogen fuel, deuterium or tritium, the isotopes of hydrogen that are heavy with neutrons. This is in the public, open literature as well. When the conventional detonation points explode, they compress the plutonium in the primary bomb, setting off a chain reaction, and the atom bomb explodes. The intense heat and radiation from the primary bomb causes the fusion of the hydrogen fuel and the release of huge amounts of energy, triggering the hydrogen bomb of the secondary.

So I drew a very basic schematic of a thermonuclear warhead, an enclosed ellipse with a primary and secondary. Then Rich drew a diagram with a different shape enclosing a small primary and a larger secondary. He drew a third diagram, the same shape, with the primary and secondary bombs in opposite positions. I can't describe the shape in any more detail because it is classified, even though schematic drawings have appeared in many news articles. "What's the difference between these two figures?" he asked.

I didn't know for sure. I said that both designs might work. Then Rich said the code name of the primary for the W-88 and I recognized it immediately. I had been asked to run some data from the W-88 primary on "Code A." This code is a computer simulation program of what happens in a two-stage thermonuclear bomb. To test the programs, code developers like me run design data on the simulation program to see how the result compared with real test results. I had worked on this program for many years; in federal court we called it, simply, Code A. Code A was originally a simulation of the secondary stage only, the hydrogen bomb, but I had spent three years reconfiguring the code to be able to run the tests for both the primary and secondary bombs. Code A is a powerful and useful code, though it has some flaws. I used the code to run a test on the W-88's primary, which has a special project name. That primary's name is classified, so I can't repeat it here. Until I heard that name, I didn't know that the data I tested was associated with the W-88. Most of my time at LANL was devoted to Code A and another program, "Code B." Code B was a computer program that simulated the operation of the primary bomb. I had worked on these and various other bomb-related programs.

Rich asked me if I knew the missile system that carried the W-88, but I had no idea. Then he asked me, "If you wanted to design a better primary, what would you design? Please draw a diagram for me."

At that moment, I heard some loud banging in the hotel room next door, and I was startled.

"What's that?" I asked

"Oh, it's just a vacuum cleaner in the next room," he said.

A wood door connected Room 102 to an adjoining hotel room, and I was sure that anyone listening on the other side could hear our conversation. I grew very uncomfortable about discussing nuclear weapons secrets in such an unsecure location. But Rich said it was okay, not to worry, and he showed me a letter from Ken Schiffer, the LANL internal security director, authorizing us to discuss classified nuclear weapons information in the hotel. Both the DOE counterintelligence official and the FBI agent were saying that it was okay to talk about nuclear secrets in a hotel, but I still felt very uneasy and nervous.

Rich had more questions about nuclear warhead design. I asked him, "Why are we having this discussion about classified nuclear weapons secrets in an unsecure place? I thought Carol Covert wanted us to have a short conversation so that you can tell your bosses in Washington, D.C., that I don't need to take a lie detector test. Once you tell them that, I can help Carol and Hudenko with their W-88 investigation."

Then Rich dropped a bomb on me: "Wen Ho, FBI Headquarters thinks you are one of the major suspects. That is why we want to polygraph you. This test is being ordered by the FBI HQ in Washington, D.C."

I was shocked and completely unprepared for this news. This was the opposite of what Carol Covert had told me. My reaction was immediate: "If the FBI people in Washington, D.C., still think I'm the major suspect, then I want to take the polygraph right now, because I know that I am innocent."

Rich was clearly pleased that I not only agreed to submit to a lie detector test, I wanted to take it right away. I don't think he had calculated this revelation to have such a jarring impact on me. But he said it was too late to set up his polygraph machine, he was tired, and we should meet the next morning to do the polygraph.

By now it was about 5:30 P.M. So much for a 15-minute coffee break to show how honest I am. Rich paged Carol to pick me up. A few minutes later, she came into the room. I was sitting at the foot of one of the hotel beds. Carol was on my left, Rich was on my right.

I turned to face her. "Carol, you told me you wanted me to take the polygraph to test for two questions, and if I passed the two questions, then I can help you and John Hudenko solve your twelve puzzles related to the W-88. Am I right?"

"Yes, that's right. If you pass the polygraph on these two questions, then you can help John and me with our project."

I continued: "Carol, you also told me yesterday that I am totally clear and clean from the W-88 investigation. In other words, I'm not a suspect anymore, am I right?"

"Yes, Wen Ho, you are not a suspect anymore. We just want you to pass the polygraph tests so you can help me and John."

Then I turned to Rich and asked, "Rich, you just told me you want me to take the lie detector tests because the FBI people in the Washington, D.C., headquarters still think that I am a major suspect, right?"

Rich could see that there was a conflict between his story and Carol's, so he hesitated for a full minute before answering. "Yes, the FBI headquarters still thinks you are a suspect, so they want to do the polygraph test on you."

I faced Carol and said, "I don't care what kind of a game you and Rich are playing, but I do see there is some inconsistency between you two people. Can you explain this to me?"

Carol's face turned bright crimson. She paused for a beat, but quickly recovered. "Oh yes, Wen Ho, the Washington, D.C., people still think that you are a suspect. That is why we want to do the lie detector test on you."

I felt very agitated by all this—their lies, the uncertainty of who and what to believe, the revelation that I was still a major spy suspect. But I wanted to prove that I was no spy. I figured at least the lie detector machine wouldn't lie. But I forgot to factor in the people who are required to interpret the tests.

———

The next morning, February 10, 1999, I went back to the Holiday Inn Express at 9 A.M. Rich Hobgood was waiting for me in the lobby. We went back to room 102. This time I brought my own coffee, as well as a thermos of hot water, and some green tea. Yesterday, I noticed that the room was hot and dry, so I came prepared. I was still feeling upset, but I was ready to set the record straight.

We spent about 30 minutes going over the procedure. I signed a paper that said there was no video or audio recording of this test, that I had the right to have a lawyer present, and that I could refuse the test or walk out at any time. Then we started the test.

The questions included two major ones:

"Did you pass the W-88 information to any unauthorized person?"

I answered, "No."

"Did you pass the two weapons codes to any unauthorized person?"

By this, he meant Code A and Code B.

I answered, "No."

He also asked me several other unrelated questions, such as:

"Are you married?"

I answered, "Yes."

"Do you work at Los Alamos National Lab?"

I answered, "Yes."

"Do you drink wine often?"

I answered, "No."

"Do you smoke?"

I answered, "No."

"Do you gamble illegally?"

I answered, "No."

"Do you dislike black people?"

I answered, "No."

"Do you ever cheat on your publications?"

I answered, "No."

I felt hot and uncomfortable during the test, and kept drinking tap water because my throat was dry. Rich had the blood pressure cuff wrapped around my right arm so tightly that the fingers on my right hand became numb. On several occasions, my fingers jerked or jumped as I was answering questions. The wires around my thumb were also tight, and it was somewhat painful. The setup for this test was very different from the previous time I was poly-graphed, on December 23, when the room and the apparatus were quite comfortable.

The whole morning, we repeated various sets of these questions. Each set contained the two major questions, plus some combination of the other questions.

After the first round of tests, Rich said, "Wen Ho, I am sorry to tell you that you failed the test badly." I asked, "How badly?" He said that on a scale of 1 to 10, with 10 a perfect score and 1 a complete failing grade, I scored a 2 on the two major questions.

I couldn't understand how that could be possible. I had never given Code A and Code B to any unauthorized person, and I didn't even recognize the W-88 until yesterday, when Rich told me the project name for the W-88 primary. Even now I know almost nothing about the W-88's secondary. At some point in the questioning, Rich asked me what I knew about the W-88's missile system. I had no idea. There was no way I should have failed on these questions. I was quite distraught over this news.

But we continued with another round of questions, the same format with different combinations of the same questions as the first round.

Rich told me I had failed again. "Wen Ho, the lie detector is a tool. It's not absolutely reliable, they're about ninety-two percent reliable with eight percent uncertainty. From the test, I think you may have told Chinese scientists something classified by accident. Can you think one more time if you did something like that, like if you accidentally told them about the detonation points information? If you did do it, tell me and I will try to help you, because the penalty for a non-intentional mistake is very minor."

Once again, I wanted to believe my interrogators. I was so slow to recognize the pattern—they ask the questions, my answers become fodder for more questions, and around again. If I didn't give them the answers they wanted to hear, they came back again and again. I was so sure that I was right, I kept answering.

I tried hard to think of anything that could have happened that could help clarify these polygraph results, that could help prove my innocence. I thought about conversations I might have had during my conferences in China back in 1986 and 1988, more than 10 years earlier. I told Rich that, in 1986, I might have talked about jet formation after a detonation—a topic that has applications for everyday technology like ink-jet printers and oil-well drilling as well as weaponry. I had researched and published unclassified papers, with LANL approval, on the topic. I also mentioned a problem I talked about in 1988 regarding Lagrangian methods and artificial viscosity with some Chinese scientists, but I noted for Rich, again, that these are unclassified topics. Most engineering students learn about Lagrangian methods in their sophomore year in college; it is a fundamental tool, just like algebra or calculus. Artificial viscosity is an old problem in fluid dynamics, the riddle of how best to calculate a smooth course of change when a sudden shock occurs—for example, what happens to points on a tennis ball as it is slammed and compressed against a wall; how a car body crumples and changes during a crash; or what happens to a discrete particle of plutonium at the moment of nuclear fission in an atomic blast. The artificial viscosity equations create a mathematical approach to smooth over the breaks caused by the shocks.

I was having trouble explaining artificial viscosity to Rich. He asked me if I took information about artificial viscosity from the classified Lagrangian codes and then passed the information to the Chinese. I tried to show him how that would be like saying one plus one must be classified because arithmetic is used in the classified codes, but I could see that I was losing him.

At some point we took a break. I left room 102 and went a few blocks down Trinity Drive to the nearby McDonald's to pick up a couple of fish sandwiches for lunch. Then I went back to my T Division office to get some information for Rich. I wanted to help him understand the nature of my work and to show him that the science behind the nuclear weapons codes I worked on was not classified. I wanted him to know that discussing Lagrangian methods or artificial viscosity at a scientific conference is like talking about $E=mc^2$, Einstein's theory of relativity. It doesn't tell anything about the design or construction of a nuclear bomb. I found a paper I had published that I thought might shed light on the topic and brought it back to the Holiday Inn for Rich.

I got back to room 102 at about 1 P.M. and gave Rich my paper, titled, "Two-Dimensional Lagrangian Methods for Elastic-plastic Flow." Everything in the paper was unclassified and had been approved by LANL for release before publication. I brought this paper to show how Lagrangian numerical methods could be used to solve the problem of artificial viscosity—and how there was nothing classified about it. As I was talking, Rich wrote down a classified name on the paper I brought him, so I told him that he needed to treat the paper as classified.

There were no more lie detector tests that day. For the rest of the afternoon, Rich kept prompting me to remember something classified I might have told the Chinese scientists. "Wen Ho, this is your only chance for me to help you, if you admit to that now. Unless you do, when you walk out of this room, I can't help you anymore, and you may be arrested."

By now, I was sick of all this and wanted to go back to work. Just before I left room 102, at about 3:35 P.M., Rich said: "Wen Ho, I believe you are an honest man and that you didn't lie on those two questions. However, there are some glitches in the polygraph charts that indicate you may have told the Chinese scientists something you weren't supposed to. Also, I want to tell you that this lie detector test was actually requested by Carol Covert, and was not requested from the FBI headquarters in Washington, D.C. If I don't see you again, good luck to you."

This last bit was a complete reversal from yesterday's disclosure, when Rich told me that Washington had wanted the polygraph, not Carol. I didn't know what to think. Court documents and news reports would show that in fact, the FBI headquarters had ordered it, after they decided that the definitive "not deceptive" grades I received from Wackenhut were "inconclusive" and that I had "probably failed."

At the end of the day, I stopped by Dr. Richard Krajcik's office on the third floor of the Admin Building. Dick Krajcik was the acting director of the X Division at that time, and he had been the boss of my division for many years. I felt in need of some guidance to help me understand what was going on. Dick's office was not inside the X Division, so I didn't have a problem with getting access. I talked to him about what had happened during the previous two days. He shook his head and commented, "How can you people be talking about nuclear weapons secrets in a hotel room?" He suggested that I report the incident to Ken Schiffer, the counterintelligence chief.

I followed Dick's advice and went to see Schiffer the next morning, on February 11, 1999, but he was in Santa Fe, at the FBI office, discussing me. His secretary called him there, and I spoke with Schiffer, Carol Covert, and Rich Hobgood. Even as they made plans to offer me up as a spy for China, they were still leading me on. Carol tried to reassure me: "Wen Ho, Rich Hobgood, Ken Schiffer, and I are working together right now to come up with an explanation for FBI headquarters. We know you are honest and innocent, and we can help you get out of trouble. Maybe we should do another polygraph to clear you."

———

There was no word from the FBI or my superiors at LANL over the next several days. Bits and pieces of what was happening then were later reported regarding communications among Congress, the DOE, the DOJ, and the FBI, discussing their efforts to "catch" me, especially from leaked information provided by the FBI and DOE. For example, there was the "sealed" deposition of Craig Schmidt, the FBI headquarters agent who supervised Covert and Hobgood from Washington. According to a *Wall Street Journal* account, Schmidt indicated that, by discrediting the Wackenhut polygraph and ordering a new one, the FBI was able to wrest control over my case from the DOE. Schmidt even testified before the Senate Judiciary Committee that during my FBI polygraph with Rich Hobgood I made the "incredible" admission that I had helped a Chinese scientist with mathematical equations. My conversations about such basic science and math topics as jet formation, Lagrangian methods, and artificial viscosity were seen as startling evidence of my deceptiveness.

I was beginning to feel less sure of my ability to handle this, and I started seeking advice from supervisors and friends. My friends all urged me to get a lawyer, but my stubbornness and pride still made me hesitate. I spoke to lab officials about the process of regaining my Q clearance—I asked about the lab's internal appeals process. If I lost after an appeal and a hearing, I would lose my job.

It was hard to keep from thinking about the questions that the FBI and LANL security repeatedly asked of me. I wondered what they really wanted to know—was there some "right" answer I had failed to provide? Except for what I realized from my exchange with Rich Hobgood, I still didn't know much about the W-88. I asked a friend and colleague who used to work in the X Division about the W-88; he told me that the "W" in the name meant that it was a warhead, but he didn't know much more, either. On another day, while I was walking through a corridor at LANL, I ran into John Romero, a coworker in the X Division for many years. John worked on a different team from the one I worked on. I often fished near his home, and I regarded him as a friend. When I told him that I was suspected of passing secrets about the W-88, John told me that *he* had worked on the W-88. He said he knew that I had little knowledge of the W-88 and that I should give the FBI his phone number; he would be glad to tell them.

I made an appointment with Ken Schiffer for February 25, 1999, to try to find out what kind of trouble I might be in. There was much that I wanted to ask Ken, and I even made a list of some specific questions for him: What is the W-88? What did Carol Covert mean when she asked me if I ever "worked" on the W-88? What about this W-88 and China? Am I going to lose my job? What about the stress that all this is putting on my wife, my family, and me?

Ken told me that China had received some information about the W-88's size, weight, and other key data between 1986 and 1988. I would soon learn from news reports that the W-88 is the nuclear warhead used with the Trident missiles that are carried aboard nuclear submarines. This was all news to me. The W-88 was one of the smallest and newest weapons in the nuclear stockpile. Because it is relatively small, it can be launched from a submarine a few thousand miles from its target, unlike Little Boy and Fat Man, the very large and heavy atomic bombs that were dropped from airplanes flying over Hiroshima and Nagasaki. The W-88 was also much more powerful—a two stage thermonuclear bomb, with an atomic bomb primary and a hydrogen bomb secondary. The Fat Man atomic bomb weighed 10,000 pounds and had a yield of 20 kilotons, the equivalent explosive power of 20,000 tons of TNT. According to the Federation of American Scientists, the W-88 has a yield of 475 kilotons—475,000 tons of TNT—with an estimated weight of 800 pounds; it "combines a relatively high yield with increased accuracy to make it an effective hard target kill weapon."

Now I knew from Ken that the W-88 might have been the reason I was asked the classified question in the Beijing hotel room in 1988, regarding the number of detonation points used. It was certainly why the FBI was so keen on knowing about that incident. The fewer the detonation points, the smaller the bomb. The W-88 was small, a product of the design effort to create miniaturized warheads that could be delivered by missiles launched from submarines. It had the contours that Rich Hobgood drew for me during his questioning—

sketches that have appeared in many news reports. And so this was the reason why everyone kept asking about that hotel incident and any other exchange I might have had with the Chinese. Though I didn't know anything about the W-88 until Rich Hobgood told me the name of its primary, Ken Schiffer said the FBI's question would have been clearer this way: "Did you ever work on codes that were used by the W-88 weapons design experts?" Suddenly I felt insecure about my English. With what I now understood, my answer might have been "yes," but I wondered if it was *really* a "yes" since I didn't *know* I was working on W-88. As far as my questions about my job and my future at LANL, Ken wasn't so helpful. He gave me information on how to appeal the suspension of my clearance.

———————

Throughout this ordeal, I never expected to lose my job. Even just one week before I was so publicly fired in the national news, I thought that, at worst, I would stay in the T Division. Nobody ever got fired from LANL. Yes, there had been RIFs, and excellent scientists were laid off. But—fired? To my best knowledge, it never happened. I did begin to expect that I might not get my access back soon to return to the X Division. I started to look for some steady project to work on in the T Division, to ensure that I'd have a job at LANL. On Monday, March 1, 1999, one team leader said that he heard that my clearance should be resolved in a week or two, but if it became definite that I would stay in T Division, I could transfer to his group.

Later that same day, I got a call from Carol Covert, who said she was still working on questions brought up in my lie detector test with Rich Hobgood, but she would try to call me on Thursday. And she did, to set up a meeting for the next morning.

At 8:30 on Friday morning, March 5, 1999, I went to yet another meeting that the FBI set up under the guise of helping me. This time, Carol Covert and John Hudenko, together with Dick Krajcik, the deputy director of the X Division, were waiting for me in a small conference room in the northwest arm of the Admin Building.

Once again, they asked me questions about my 1986 and 1988 meetings in China. I went over each of those trips in detail, again. They had copies of the trip reports I submitted to LANL when I returned.

What did I know of Hu Side, one of the Chinese scientists who came to my room in 1988? At the time, I thought he was an expert on explosives; I had no idea that he led China's effort to miniaturize their warheads.

Why didn't I mention that hotel encounter with him and Dr. Zheng in my trip report? I had no good answer for this. In fact, I was afraid that their visit would bring me trouble.

When Hu Side visited LANL and gave a talk that I attended, why did he give me a hug? I could not remember any such hug. Why did Hu Side say to me in Chinese, in front of everyone, "Thank you for your help"? I did not recall getting thanked by him. Could it have been because I sent a copy of one of my published, unclassified LANL reports to another Chinese scientist? I also sent that report to someone in Pakistan who requested it, as well as to a professor in Taiwan who was doing work on ink-jet printers. I don't know if Hu Side hugged or thanked me, or why he would have any reason to, but the supposed incident took on a life of its own in the media and in Congress. In fact, reporters have found several photos of Hu Side giving hugs to other Americans he met on his visits to the U.S.

The questioning took on a circular quality. I had been asked the same questions so many times that the FBI was finding new ways to ask the same questions.

They asked me again: What did I know of the W-88? I didn't know anything about the W-88 before Rich Hobgood told me the code name of its primary.

Did I know the geometry—the measurements—of the primary?

No, I rarely looked at the contour geometry of the weapons whose data I ran on my codes.

Could I have known the contour geometry if I looked at it? I don't know—I didn't try.

Then there was the hunt for anything I had ever done that might be related to China.

Did I have any correspondence with scientists in China? Yes, some scientists I met sent me Christmas cards and letters, but over time, the correspondence dropped off.

Did we discuss nuclear weapons issues? No, we never discussed anything of a classified nature, but we may have had exchanges about mathematical problems.

Did I provide them any LANL documents? They requested a copy of an unclassified paper I had written, with LANL approval.

What about the summer intern I hired in 1987, the one who came from the People's Republic of China and was a college student at the University of Pittsburgh?

Why did I hire him? Because he was highly qualified.

Where is he now? I'm not sure, I believe he continued his studies at Penn State University.

They asked me to explain more about the math problems I talked about in China, the ones I brought up with Rich Hobgood. Why didn't I report my discussions about jet formation and artificial viscosity? Because these were not classified topics.

Aren't these topics used in the design and coding of nuclear weapons? Yes, but as I told Rich Hobgood, this is very basic information. I tried to explain jet formation and artificial viscosity to Covert and Hudenko. Even though this area was not Dick Krajcik's specialty and he was unfamiliar with my area of hydrocodes, I hoped he could help clarify these fundamental scientific points to the FBI agents.

They asked me about the computers I had at home. One was a Macintosh desktop, the other a Macintosh laptop. Both were owned by the lab, which routinely provided computers for technical staff to use. I told them I sometimes worked at home.

The interrogation went on until the end of the day. It was just as well; while agents Covert and Hudenko were questioning me in the conference room, other FBI agents were conducting a search of my offices in the X Division and the T Division. I had given my permission for them to do so. My laptop was at work and they took it away. I also gave them the Macintosh desktop computer from my home.

In the midst of all this, I still believed that I could prove my innocence, though it was clear that the FBI didn't believe me. I went home feeling as though I had been through the worst of it and I would soon climb out of this pit. Wrong again.

CHAPTER 4

If I actually had been a spy, I surely would have been long gone with a one-way ticket out of Los Alamos. But I knew the truth about myself. Funny thing, though, that truth also kept me in a state of denial. It was simply inconceivable to me that any rational person who had the facts could think that I was a spy. As a scientist, I thought of facts as indisputable. I clung to the simple belief that the facts would prove the truth, and that in America, a person is innocent until proven guilty. Until this happened to me, I never thought that what I look like or where I was born would affect how people saw the facts and whether they could accept the truth.

On Saturday, March 6, the day after my office was searched, the *New York Times* ran this headline on their front page: "BREACH AT LOS ALAMOS: A special report; China Stole Nuclear Secrets for Bombs, U.S. Aides Say." It was a long and sensational story. According to the *Times*, China used our nuclear technology to make a great leap in miniaturizing their newest nuclear warheads, which were remarkably similar to the W-88.

I did not read the *New York Times*—I don't read any newspapers on a regular basis because I have generally considered the news to be a waste of my time. At our house, my wife reads the newspaper and will tell me if there is something that might be of interest to me. My interests are not complicated: science and math, my family and friends, classical music, and fishing.

So ordinarily, I would have missed the article. But on that particular Saturday, my friends Bob and Kathy Clark—the ones who had traveled to China with us in 1986 as part of the LANL group—stopped by with a copy of the *New York Times* story, which they had gotten off the Internet. Bob said, "Wen Ho, you better read this. There's something strange happening. You've got to take this seriously. Something's going on."

After one look at the headline, my initial thought was, this story has nothing to do with me. I'm not interested in reading this. But then I wondered, Are they talking about me? Does anybody else fit this description? No, it sounds like it's me.

Alberta called me that morning. She had read the story in North Carolina. She was very upset and frightened. "Ba, this story is about you," she cried. "The Rosenbergs were executed for being traitors! And the *New York Times* is saying that you're worse than the Rosenbergs!"

Alberta read parts of the story to me. Unlike the *Wall Street Journal* article in January that mentioned a spy suspect at Los Alamos but gave few details, the *New York Times* was much more explicit. They didn't identify this suspect by name, but described him as a Los Alamos computer scientist who is Chinese American and who failed a lie detector test in February. It said that the "suspect's wife was invited to address a Chinese conference . . . even though she was only a secretary at LANL"—her husband was the real nuclear weapons expert. Unnamed officials leaked my personal information to the *Times* and were quoted as saying, "The suspect had traveled to Hong Kong without reporting the trip as required. In Hong Kong . . . the [FBI] bureau found records showing that the scientist had obtained $700 from the American Express offices. Investigators suspect that he used it to buy an airline ticket to Shanghai." The article said that the DOE gave the suspect a lie detector test in December. "Unsatisfied, the FBI administered a second test in February, and officials said the suspect was found to be deceptive."

I was shocked and deeply disturbed that the *New York Times* could be so definite that a suspect who fit my description had given nuclear weapons secrets about the W-88 to China. I knew I hadn't given any secrets about the W-88 or anything else, but the *New York Times* didn't bother to point out that they had no proof of any of the allegations, nor did they ever suggest that I could possibly be innocent. If they could accept these falsehoods as fact, what else did they get wrong? They quoted Paul Redmond, the CIA's former counterintelligence chief: "This is going to be just as bad as the Rosenbergs. . . . This was far more damaging to the national security than Aldrich Ames." On what did this Redmond, this so-called expert, base his extreme claims? Did the *New York Times* even try to substantiate such an extreme comparison?

I'd heard of Ethel and Julius Rosenberg, the couple who were put to death for giving secrets from Los Alamos to the Soviet Union in the 1950s, during the McCarthy era. That happened before I came to America. I didn't know of this Aldrich Ames, but I found out soon enough that he worked at the CIA and for 10 years sold secrets about America's spy apparatus to the Russians; his treachery led to the deaths of many CIA and FBI sources. Now the *New York Times* was painting *me* as worse than the Rosenbergs and Ames.

I could not understand how such a powerful and influential newspaper could be so one-sided. As Judge Parker pointed out in his courtroom apology to me, the case against me was built on misleading sensationalism, and this newspaper let itself become a conduit for those lies and leaks about me. Maybe that's how they sell newspapers, but it came at the expense of my family and me. The *New York Times* ought to have apologized to us, because their article pushed Congress, the DOE, the FBI, and LANL over the edge. According to their article and the people quoted in it, there was no room for doubt: China got its nuclear technology by spying on America, the spy was from Los Alamos, and I was it. Yet not a single one of these assertions has been proven true.

The article made me sound even more suspicious by printing false information—outright lies about me that could have been easily checked. I never took a secret trip to Hong Kong. My trip to the conference in Hong Kong in 1992 had full LANL and DOE approval. I paid the $700 for my hotel room and a tour for Alberta with my credit card—there was no secret ticket to Shanghai or anywhere else! *New York Times* Pulitzer Prize–winning reporters who wrote these lies could have found the facts, had they bothered to question any of the information leaked to them by the lab, the DOE, and the FBI.

In time, it would become almost routine for me to find vicious, unsubstantiated lies about me in the news, leaked by politicians and bureaucrats, all presented as though they were verified facts. I was learning that the truth is not as simple as I believed.

But the *New York Times* also gave me some clues as to why Carol Covert, John Hudenko, and the FBI headquarters people were after me. For the first time I learned that I had been a suspect for a few years, but the FBI/DOE hadn't had enough evidence to fire or arrest me—though some people in Washington really wanted to put me away. One of those people, a man named Notra Trulock, was mentioned many times in that *New York Times* article. I had never heard of him before, but he was in charge of counterintelligence for the entire DOE, including LANL. The *New York Times* said that Trulock was the source of the theory that China had a spy at Los Alamos. Trulock, the story said, went from agency to agency in Washington—from Congressional office to special Congressional hearings—presenting his charts about the Chinese spy threat and naming me as his prime suspect. He had conducted an investigation of me, which was called Operation Kindred Spirit—a name that offered an obvious insight into how some people in the DOE felt about Chinese Americans and the PRC.

Apparently not everyone agreed with Trulock: According to the *Times* article, the CIA did not agree that China's nuclear weapons designs could only have come from the U.S. It seemed that there was a conflict between the DOE security and the CIA, between the FBI and the DOJ, and between Congress and the White House, over how to proceed with Trulock's assessments, with me as his central spy figure. I would later hear from Trulock, when *he* filed a lawsuit against *me* while I was in jail, because, he claimed, *I* defamed *him*.

But, more telling for me, the recently appointed Secretary of Energy, Bill Richardson, accepted Trulock's recommendations— and the big effort to get me. Richardson would later give Trulock a $10,000 award, from taxpayers' dollars, for his "successful" investigation of me.

Up until now, I had felt sure that I could handle my problems by myself. Suddenly I realized that all these big, powerful people in these huge bureaucracies were after me. I was just Wen Ho Lee, one person. How could I fight the politicians in Washington—the ones in Congress, the top brass at the FBI and the DOE, and even the White House? If they all wanted to squash me, to kill me, how could I stop them? I was no longer sure at all.

In the midst of all this, Carol Covert called me. I wondered how she had the nerve to call. Incredibly, she said she had some good news for me, that the FBI headquarters in Washington was sending her a package about me, and that she felt very optimistic. So she wanted me to meet her and John Hudenko at the El Dorado Hotel in Santa Fe the next day, Sunday, March 7, 1999, at 2 P.M.

———

That day, a little after 12 noon, Bob and Kathy Clark stopped by on their way home from church. Kathy said they wanted to see if I was okay. I hated to ask anyone for help, but I was so unnerved by the

New York Times story and yet another call from the FBI that I asked Bob to go with me to meet with the FBI in Santa Fe. I asked him if he would be my interpreter in case I didn't understand their questions clearly. I felt so insecure now, and I remembered how I didn't quite understand their question, "Did you *work* on the W-88?" I was afraid that if I made any mistake now, I'd be lost. I also knew that it was a lot to ask of Bob. Why would anyone want to get into the middle of an FBI espionage investigation?

Bob said yes, he'd go with me. I am so very thankful to Bob and Kathy Clark, for being such good friends. On that particular Sunday, I really needed my friends.

When Bob and I arrived at the El Dorado Hotel at 2 P.M., John Hudenko was waiting for us. I introduced them. John explained that Carol was still at the FBI office in town, about a five-minute walk from the hotel, along the north end of the Santa Fe Plaza. John didn't want Bob to come along to the FBI office with me, but I insisted I needed Bob as an interpreter to help me better understand their English. When we got there, John told Bob to wait at the post office next door because he couldn't sit in the FBI office unattended. I went in alone.

Carol was on the phone, without the usual smile on her face; it seemed as though she was arguing with someone—I guessed that it was about my case. When she got off the phone, she said that the package had arrived from Washington with the results of my February polygraph with Rich Hobgood, along with the "reinterpreted" results of my December 23 polygraph. According to the FBI headquarters people, I failed both the DOE test and the two questions of the FBI polygraph.

"You failed, Wen Ho!" Carol shouted. "You failed everything!"

For the next hour, Carol and John tried to intimidate me. This time, they focused only on my 1988 visit to Beijing and what I said to Zheng Shaotang and Hu Side in the hotel room. They wanted me to say that I gave the Chinese scientists details about the detonation-points question. But I could only answer what had truly happened.

Once again I told them that I said to the scientists, "I'm not interested in discussing that question."

They asked me the same questions over and over again. The gist of their questioning was this: "Wen Ho, why don't you admit you were a spy?" But I could not say this because I was *never* a spy. I think their FBI bosses in Washington told them, "This is your last chance to make him admit that he did something." The FBI used a hidden video camera on me, taping me through the whole interrogation. Of course, they never told me about the camera, but my lawyers eventually got a transcript of what happened at the FBI office that afternoon, of how they threatened me with the loss of my job, my future, my children's futures, my friends—even the electric chair, like Ethel and Julius Rosenberg. The transcript doesn't identify which FBI agent asked each question, but Carol Covert, the sweet and smiling agent who had wanted to help me, did most of the questioning. The FBI also deleted some names and references from their transcript, which I restored in brackets. I've included part of that official transcript here because, even today, I am so appalled by what happened in the Santa Fe FBI office that day, under direct orders from Washington, D.C.:

AGENT: Look at it from our standpoint, Wen Ho. Look at it from Washington's standpoint. . . . You have an individual that's involved in the Chinese nuclear weapons program. And they come to your hotel room, and they feel free and comfortable enough to ask you a major question about [detonation points—author added].

LEE: Uh, mmm.

AGENT: And then in 1994, they come to the laboratory and they embrace you like an old friend. And people witness that, and things are, are observed, and you're telling us that you didn't say anything, you didn't talk to them, and everything points to different than that.

LEE: Well . . . (sighs).

AGENT: So, you know, I mean, it's, it's, it's, it's an awkward situation that I, I can understand, you know, where, where these things could happen. I mean, you were treated very nicely in 1986 when you went to China.

LEE: Uh, hum.

AGENT: I mean, they were good to you. They took care of your family. They took you to the Great Wall. They had dinners for you. Then in 1988 you go back and they do the same thing and, you know, you feel some sort of obligation to people, to talk to them and answer their questions. . . .

LEE: No, no, no.

AGENT: You gotta understand this is the way it is. . . . You're being looked at as a spy!

LEE: Yes, I know, I know what you think, but all I'm saying is, uh, I have never say anything classified. I have never say anything.

AGENT: It might not be that, Wen Ho. It might not be even a classified issue. It might just be something that was said, but Washington is under the impression that you're a spy. And this newspaper article is doing everything but coming out with your name. I mean, it, it doesn't say anything in there that, that it's Wen Ho Lee, but everything points to you. People in the community and people at the laboratory tomorrow are going to know. That this article is referring to you. . . .

LEE: Let me ask you this. OK? If you want me to swear with the God or whatever, OK? I can swear if that's what you believe. I never tell them anything classified. I never told them anything about nuclear weapons. . . .

AGENT: What happened, Wen Ho? Something else had to have happened in that motel room. Something had to have happened when they came to your room. Because it's, it's just logical. . . . We know how the Chinese operate . . . we know . . .

LEE: What do you mean, what do you mean?

AGENT: Something happened in that room that you're not telling us?

LEE: This is what I'm saying. You know, we may chat something social, OK? I don't remember what we have said in that room in the hotel, OK? . . . All I can remember is when they asked me this question [about the detonation points—author added], I told them I don't know and I, I am not interested in discuss. And then we switched to different conversation. I don't even remember what we said before or what we said after. I mean it's such a long time, but I know it's nothing to do with the technical. OK?

AGENT: Do you know what's in the package that I got today and the phone call that I got from Washington? You failed your polygraphs. You couldn't pass it. When they asked you questions and they got down to issues about code issues, and they got down to weapons questions. You couldn't pass your polygraph.

LEE: That, that, Washington, D.C., polygraph. They did not ask me anything about codes. . . .

AGENT: Whatever they asked you, you failed. . . . All the analysis that's been done in Washington! You failed Wen Ho! . . . There's a black line and there's a white line. You either passed or you failed. You failed. . . .

LEE: (Sighs).

AGENT: You are a scientist, a nuclear scientist. You are going to be an unemployed nuclear scientist. You are going to be a nuclear scientist without a clearance. Where is a nuclear scientist without a clearance going to get a job?

LEE: I cannot get any job.

AGENT: You can't! Wen Ho, you gotta tell us what went on in that room. You got to tell us why you're failing these polygraphs! Washington is not going to let you work in a laboratory or have a clearance!

LEE: I can retire, to tell the truth, I'm fifty-nine and something. . . .

AGENT: You know what, Wen Ho? If you retire and the FBI comes in later on down the road. A day, an hour, a week, and we come knocking on your door, we have to arrest you for espionage! Do you really think you're going to be able to collect anything?

LEE: No, no, but look, look, look . . .

AGENT: They're going to garnish your wages. . . . They're not going to give you anything other than your advice of rights and a pair of handcuffs!

LEE: But, but . . .

AGENT: And now, what are you going to tell your friends? What are you going to tell your family? What are you going to tell your wife and son? What's going to happen to your son in college? When he hears on the news . . . "Wen Ho Lee arrested for espionage." What's that going to do?

LEE: But I'm telling you, I did not do anything like that. I never give any classified information to Chinese people. I never tell them anything relating to nuclear weapons, uh, data or design or whatever, I have never done anything like that.

AGENT: Pretty soon you're going to have reporters knocking on your door. They're going to be knocking on the door of your friends. They're going to find your son and they are going to say, you know, your father is a spy?

LEE: But I, I'm not a spy.

AGENT: But Wen Ho, something else must have happened for you not to be able to pass these polygraphs.

LEE: I don't know, I don't know what to explain. I did not tell them anything about [the detonation points]. I told them, I say, I . . . let's see. I don't know and I'm not interested to discuss this question. That's exactly what I told them. . . .

AGENT: What if they polygraph [Sylvia]? What if they decide, okay. We're going to go polygraph your wife.

LEE: On what? On what subject?

AGENT: On this subject. Your wife went to China with you.

LEE: But she's not in the room.

AGENT: What difference does it make? Husbands and wives tell each other things. Don't you think they're going to go knocking on your door here pretty soon. If they don't knock on your door with a pair of handcuffs, they're, they're going to knock on your door with another polygraph person to polygraph [Sylvia]. And then what's that gonna look like to the kids? What's your son going to think when your, your wife gets polygraphed? And what are the people that you work with gonna think of? What are they gonna be saying tomorrow morning? This is in the newspaper. It's in the Los Alamos paper.

LEE: Well . . .

AGENT: You know what I believe? I believe that you're not telling me the truth. I believe something else happened in that room and that's why you're failing the polygraph. And unless you can come up with what happened in that room, part of a conversation that's causing you problems, you're never going to pass a polygraph. And you're never going to have a clearance. And you're not going to have a job. And if you get arrested, you're not going to have a retirement.

LEE: Well, OK, let's, let's stop here, 'cause I'm very tired, OK, I'm, I'm . . .

AGENT: Wen Ho, this is serious. What are you going to do tomorrow when all the people that you used to work with come in and start talking to you about that newspaper article? What are you going to tell the scientists when they say Wen Ho, they're accusing you of spying. . . . They're not going to be your friends, Wen Ho, tomorrow morning.

LEE: Beg your pardon, OK. Uh-mm, I have to go because I'm very tired.

AGENT: Wen Ho, if you walk out that door today, that's it. I can't do

anything for you. I can't do a thing for you! If I don't have
something that I can tell Washington as to why you're failing those polygraphs, I can't do a thing.

LEE: Well, I understand.

AGENT: I can't get you your job. I can't do anything for you, Wen
Ho. I can't stop the newspapers from knocking on your
door. I can't stop the newspapers from calling your son. I
can't stop the people from polygraphing your wife. I can't
stop somebody from coming and knocking on your door
and putting handcuffs on you.

LEE: I mean, whatever. You people want to do, like I, what you
just said, go ahead do it. 'Cause I, I don't know what, I
don't know how to handle this case. I'm an honest person
and I'm telling you the truth, and you don't believe it. I—
that's it.

I was trying to leave the FBI office, the questioning was upsetting
me, and by now I was repeating myself over and over again. But
Carol kept coming up with a new onslaught of questions to keep me
from walking out the door, telling me how her bosses in Washington, D.C., would not accept my explanation of what had happened
in the hotel room. I told them about my memory problem after my
cancer surgery in 1987, and that I had experienced a memory loss
before, when I was 16. I had had my appendix removed and was
hospitalized for a week; afterward, I lost parts of my memory. I completely lost my English vocabulary, and I couldn't remember subjects that I knew well. I forgot everything, and it wasn't until more
than a year later that I regained that memory. But Carol and John
didn't want to hear about this; my story only seemed to irritate
them. Then Carol talked about the Rosenbergs.

AGENT: Do you know how many people have been arrested for espionage in the United States?

LEE: I don't know. I don't pay much attention to that.

AGENT: Do you know who the Rosenbergs are?

LEE: I heard them, yeah, I heard them mention.

AGENT: The Rosenbergs are the only people that never cooperated with the federal government in an espionage case. You know what happened to them? They electrocuted them, Wen Ho.

LEE: Yeah, I heard.

AGENT: They didn't care whether they professed their innocence all day long. They electrocuted them. OK. Aldrich Ames. You know Aldrich Ames? He's going to rot in jail.

LEE: I see.

AGENT: OK? John Walker! Okay, he's another one. He was arrested for espionage. OK? Do you want to go down in history? Whether you're professing your innocence like the Rosenbergs to the day that they take you to the electric chair? . . . Do you want to go down in history? With your kids knowing that you got arrested for espionage?

LEE: I don't . . .

AGENT: The Rosenbergs professed their innocence. The Rosenbergs weren't concerned either. The Rosenbergs are dead.

LEE: I'm just telling you. I believe truth and I believe honest, and I know, I know myself, I did not tell anything . . . OK? I told you more than ten times . . . eventually something will be clear-cut, OK?

AGENT: Do you know what bothers me? You're going to have this kind of reputation. You're, you're a person who came to this country, OK, because you had a feeling that you wanted to live here. And you have a lot to offer the United States.

LEE: Yes.

AGENT: And you came here, and you're a nuclear scientist . . . and, and you are a wonderful scientist.

LEE: I'm sorry I'm really tired. I have to go.

AGENT: Wen Ho, you know what's going to happen?

LEE: Let me, let me go, please.

AGENT: You know what's going to happen, Wen Ho? People are going to read this stuff, and they're gonna think you're not a loyal American.

LEE: I know. My daughter already told me this morning. She reads the *New York Times*. She read the *Washington Post*. She read the *LA Times* and she know I didn't do it. . . . I'm innocent, but I don't know what can I do. I'm, I'm, I'm, I tell you how I feel, I feel, how you call that? Hopeless, OK.

AGENT: It is hopeless, Wen Ho. . . . You could live another 20 years, but the problem is, it's going to be bad.

LEE: I know, I don't know what to handle this.

AGENT: Your kids are going to have to live with this, OK. You're going to have to live with it. Your wife is going to have to live with it. This is going to eat away at them like a cancer. Just like the cancer that you had, but all the way . . .

LEE: Probably worse than the cancer.

AGENT: That's right, it is worse than cancer. We can't do anything if somebody knocks on your door tomorrow. I can't do anything.

LEE: [Carol and John], I really appreciate your kindness and your efforts, try to help me out to clean up this stuff and I've been try the best I can to work with you every time you call I say yes, and I really appreciate your time, OK? I really appreciate . . . in my mind, I appreciate. I want to say thank you.

AGENT: There's nothing more we can do for you, Wen Ho.

LEE: Well, it . . . my life. I accept it, OK. I will try to do the best I can, and I, I believe, eventually, and I think, God, God, will make it his judge, judgment.

AGENT: I wish I had your confidence, Wen Ho, but I don't. You know what I see? I see a lot of problems for you. I see no job. I see no clearance. I see no way to pay your bills. I see no way to keep your son in school. I see your family falling apart. All because of this.

LEE: Yeah, I, I don't know what to do. I, all I can say is that I, keep in my mind I appreciate both of you, OK. I, I will say thanks if I don't see you again. I appreciate it, I really appreciate it, OK. Thank you.

When I finally left the FBI office, I was shaking. I found Bob, who had waited so patiently for me outside. I was grateful that he was there, because I'm not sure if I could have driven the 30 miles back up the hill. I couldn't even begin to explain to Bob or my wife or anyone what had happened. I just wanted this nightmare to end.

———

I went to work on Monday morning, March 8, 1999, as usual. At about 11 A.M., Dan Butler, my boss and acting director in T Division, walked into my office with two other men, one from the security office and another who was probably from personnel. Dan handed me a memo, firing me from LANL. The memo stated:

This is notification that your employment with the Los Alamos National Laboratory is terminated effective immediately. The reasons for this termination include:

1. Your failure to properly notify Laboratory or DOE personnel about your contact with individuals from a sensitive country;
2. Your failure to properly mark and store viewgraphs containing classified information in a secure location, but rather leaving the documents in a cardboard box;
3. Keeping your classified password in one of your notebooks which also included directions on how to access a classified computer system; and

4.   Engaging in an apparent effort to deceive Laboratory man-
      agement about these and other security issues.

The four issues noted indicate a pattern of disregard for security
policies, procedures, and applicable DOE Orders, and it further
demonstrates your inability to maintain classified information
securely.

———————

The memo contained a few other personnel-related instructions.
Without discussion, Dan asked me to sign the paper, which I did.
Then he asked me if I was planning to sue the lab. I thought that
was a strange question, but I said no, I'm not interested in a lawsuit.
He told me to leave my office immediately. I said fine, let me get my
things together. Dan said no, you can't take anything but your car
keys, and you can't go anywhere in the labs except for the personnel
office to finish processing your termination.

I said fine. I took my lunch with me and walked out to my car,
escorted by the security guard. I sat in my car. I wasn't sure what to
do, so I ate my lunch in the car and stared at the memo.

Item 1 referred to the encounter at the hotel, which I had explained so many times.

Items 2 and 3, I learned, were infractions discovered in the
search of my office in the X Division the previous Friday, March
5th. I had deleted the classification marks from three documents
that I used frequently. One was a chapter of a reference manual; another I had photocopied without the classification marks; and on
the third, I had cut the classification marks off the top and bottom
of the page. These were common, routine acts—done by many
other scientists at the lab—that might get a verbal reminder or
warning, but nothing more. Item 3, writing my password down, was
an infraction, but not cause for termination. In any case, I kept all
these items in my locked X Division office, which I could only enter
after passing through the security checkpoints.

Item 4 astonished me; I had met with the LANL security, the FBI, and DOE every time they asked, without a lawyer, and I had tried to answer every question to the best of my ability. In fact, friends would later tell me that I was apparently too forthcoming with my interrogators.

Before I headed home, I went to the personnel office and signed more papers. After 20 years of service, my career at LANL was unexpectedly and abruptly over.

I drove the short distance to White Rock and thought about what I would tell my family. Given all the recent events, it would hardly be a surprise to them. But even as I walked into my house, I could hear the telephone ringing. Reporters were calling, they wanted to know what I thought about being fired, about being a spy! The lab and the DOE had leaked my name out to reporters before the ink was dry on the termination memo I signed! The lab never treated anyone this way. LANL's official policy was to keep information private about security infractions or any kind of investigation, because they knew that false accusations could ruin a scientist's reputation and career.

Sylvia and I just let the phone ring on and on, once we realized that reporters from all over the country—even from other countries—were calling us. It rang all day and night, while the news reports blasted, "Spy Suspect Fired at Los Alamos Lab" and "U.S. Fires Scientist Suspected of Giving China Bomb Data." The next day, we changed our phone number, the one we had had for 20 years. I spoke to Alberta and Chung. My daughter was in tears. "Mei-mei, you were right," I said. "I have to get a lawyer." But I didn't know where or how to find someone who could help me, and I was afraid it might be too late.

PART
TWO

CHAPTER 5

"Surreal" is the word that comes to mind when I think of how my sheltered life in White Rock was transformed overnight into an international headline and media circus. There were times when I would chuckle at the absurdity of it all, only to learn of some new and more outrageous falsehood about me. In my darker moments, Carol Covert's voice would come back to haunt me: "Do you know what happened to the Rosenbergs?"

It's sort of like watching a play or opera unfold, only to realize that it's all about you, it has everything and nothing to do with you, and it's completely out of your control. Even before I was fired, the *New York Times* had my name, and now they printed it. So did everyone else—every major newspaper, television news show, radio station, and Internet news site. News media outlets all over the world had my name and face, which they all linked with the word "SPY."

My peaceful neighborhood turned into a media encampment. Only 12,000 people live in the town of Los Alamos, with another 6,000 in my subdivision of White Rock. Overnight, our street sprouted reporters, TV satellite trucks, photographers with giant

telephoto lenses, TV crews shouldering their heavy cameras—
blocking the street, knocking on my door, peeking into my windows—everyone on the prowl for some new piece of me that would
make their bosses happy. They trampled my yard as well as my
neighbors', and asked every hapless passerby what they knew about
the awful Wen Ho Lee and his family.

CNN blared, "CIA Measures Damage Following Leaked Nuclear Secrets," while headlines on ITN interactive broadcast network in the United Kingdom ran, "Suspected Chinese Spy Fired by
U.S. Energy Department." Throughout all the interrogations, I
somehow thought people would realize how weak the China connection was for me, since after all I was from Taiwan, not China,
and had only been in China twice in my life for LANL official business, both trips with lab and DOE approval. But nothing seemed to
be "normal" with my situation. Even the way I was fired, with the
announcement on television by the Secretary of Energy, was totally
unprecedented and contrary to the standard employment practices
at LANL. With stories like the *Wall Street Journal*'s "GOP Eager-
ness to Find Security Lapses Under Clinton Could Chill Ties to
China," I was getting a quick education from the news on how
much my fate was dictated by politics in Washington and by tensions between the U.S. and China.

On the evening of the day I was fired, some reporters were
walking on my street. A *New York Times* reporter accosted my next-
door neighbors, Don and Jean Marshall, and asked, "Do you know
your neighbor is a spy?"

Don was so unnerved by the encounter that he couldn't sleep
that night. He called the reporter at the Los Alamos Inn late that
night and woke him up to tell him that he had the wrong man. The
Marshalls were not only my dear neighbors, but they were both scientists in the X Division. We first met when the houses in our White
Rock subdivision were under construction. It was December 1979,
a year after I had been hired at the lab. Don and Jean were check-

ing on their house, and they saw that I had tacked a picture of my family onto the fireplace of my house, which didn't even have the framing up yet. Jean remembers that I introduced myself: "Hi, my name is Wen Ho, like Santa Claus, Ho, Ho, Ho." My kids say that my jokes are corny, but Jean always laughed. She taught piano to Alberta and Chung when they were small. Their son and daughter were schoolmates of my children.

Don and Jean have told me they were certain that the accusations were wrong because they'd known me as a neighbor and coworker for so many years, they knew my routine and habits well, and they could see how my family went about our lives. In fact, the Marshalls were so sure that I wasn't an agent for a foreign government that they put up their home as collateral toward my bail when the FBI and Department of Justice said I was too dangerous to be released from jail. My family has been blessed with such wonderful neighbors. And while I have been truly fortunate, these kinds of close community ties are among the many things that make Los Alamos special.

———

Los Alamos is not the kind of town where neighbors can keep secrets from one another. I suppose there's an irony in that, considering that the whole town was built as a secret scientific encampment, and almost everybody works on classified information. Theoretical physicist J. Robert Oppenheimer, the lab's first director, and Major General Leslie R. Groves, the military commander, had two criteria as they searched for an appropriate site to create an atom bomb: one, it had to be a large enough area in a climate that would allow outdoor work in the winter; and two, the site had to be far removed from both coasts in case of attack. They selected this secluded mesa not just for its natural beauty, which Oppenheimer felt would serve as an inspiration to the scientists, but because it met the military's security requirements—there was only one way to get in and out of the remote location. During the Manhattan Project days, when some two thousand young scientists/professors were barracked, military style, in a race to build the atom bomb, the secret town had Santa Fe Post Office Box 1663 as its address. Birth certificates for children born here listed the P.O. Box as their place of birth.

Back in 1943, in the earliest days of LANL, Oppenheimer advocated intellectual exchange and the free flow of ideas, while the brigadier general who administered the Manhattan Project wanted to keep movement and communication as restricted as possible. The result was something like a military fortress to the outside world, complete with barbed wire and watchtowers looking over the makeshift labs and bare-bones living quarters. It was so stark and prisonlike that the immigrant scientists from Europe said it was reminiscent of a concentration camp. Some of the world's leading physicists were among the foreign national scientists of that period, including Enrico Fermi, Niels Bohr, Hans Bethe, John von Neumann, Leo Szilard, Edward Teller, and Emilio Segré.

Oppenheimer insisted that inside the Manhattan Project, there would be few restrictions, and he recreated the kind of university atmosphere fostered at the University of California at Berkeley's school of theoretical physics, which Oppenheimer had founded. Even today, the University of California is the employer of record at the lab, not the DOE or the government, but the university acts more like an absentee landlord. When I was fired, it was strange that DOE Secretary Bill Richardson, not my University of California employers, announced my employment termination to the world.

Still, this principle of sharing of ideas across disciplines allowed the scientists to solve problems that had never been attempted before. How much uranium or plutonium would be needed to produce the desired bomb yield? What are the hydrodynamics of fission—that is, what happens when things blow up? Could critical mass be achieved by imploding—compressing—the nuclear explosive against itself?

In those days when Los Alamos was known only for a private boys' school and the homesteads of a few Hispanic families, the scientists and military engineers were creating the project from scratch. They had to clear the space in the mesa's forests to build the laboratories; to construct the buildings for the cyclotron, accelerator, and other equipment vital to nuclear research; to make the machine shops that would build the prototype bombs—not to mention housing, schools, roads, stores, and so on, all under the cloak of secrecy.

This tension between secrecy and openness persists today. It also changes depending on who's in Washington and who the big bosses at the lab are trying to please. The politics of the labs never interested me, but now I know what a big impact politics had on what happened to me.

When I first came to Los Alamos, I was one of the "Cold Warriors," using my scientific knowledge for nuclear deterrence, the theory that "assured mutual destruction" will prevent nuclear war. I worked to keep America safe. Once Alberta came home from her high-school debate class and asked me how I could work on weapons of mass destruction. I told her that we need to have a strong nuclear stockpile to prevent anyone from ever using nuclear weapons against us. And that is what I have done for 20 years of my life.

The computer codes I developed at LANL also helped us win the Cold War. It is sad to see how the contributions I've made to my country can be so readily discounted, or not even considered at all, because of my Chinese ancestry. Others have been accused of similar deeds, like John Deutch, the former CIA director, or the National Security Agency advisor at the White House who moved classified information to an unsecure computer, or the LANL X Division scientists who were involved with the missing hard drives—an incident I probably would have been blamed for, had it not taken place when I was in jail. Or any number of other incidents. They were all excused because they were assumed to be good Americans. No such courtesies were offered to me. But none of the others was Asian.

In the Cold War years, security at the lab was tighter and the rules were clearer. When the Soviet Union fell, in 1989, many things changed. Support from Washington for our nuclear weapons research was no longer guaranteed. Layoffs—or RIFs, in government jargon—were announced and projects now had to be marketed inside and outside the labs in order to get funding. With the diminished threat of nuclear war, the DOE and LANL took on a more open approach. Exchanges with foreign scientists, including Chinese from the People's Republic of China, were already taking place, and I received lab approval to attend international conferences, just like so many other LANL scientists. With the end of the Cold War, we were encouraged to collaborate with private corporations and to publish our research, which I did. Our nuclear secrets were declassified on a massive scale, making formerly classified documents available to anyone. What's more, the files I was later accused of stealing were not even formally classified "Secret" then—they were only classified Secret after I was fired.

But once you've been admitted into this elite company town, which has more Ph.D.s per capita than any other community in America, you're pretty well accepted. At least, I always felt I was, until I became a spy suspect. The clearance check required to work at the lab is very stringent, with reviews of your background, personal finances, and medical exams, and requirements for regular drug tests, so you feel a sense of security, knowing that your neighbors and coworkers had to pass. Until all this happened to me, I never locked my house or my car, and I never worried about it. No one did, because crime is virtually nonexistent in Los Alamos.

The one robbery I've heard of in the last 20 years was a break-in by some teenagers. Within minutes of being called, the local police set up a roadblock at the main route out of town. The boys tried to run, and one actually fell into the canyon and had to be medevaced out.

If your kids stay out too late and you're not sure where they are, you can call the Los Alamos Police Department to help find them. Years ago, when Alberta was home from college and out with friends late at night, Sylvia got worried and called the Los Alamos police. An hour later, Alberta arrived home with a police escort. That might have been embarrassing for her, but incidents like this gave me some peace of mind while I was locked up in jail—at least I knew my wife would be safe when she was home alone during those nine months. In fact, when I was imprisoned, the Los Alamos police even called Sylvia to see if she was OK and to remind her to call if she was ever frightened.

Some people say they find the close nature of Los Alamos to be stifling. Old-timers greet newcomers with the knowledge that they'll either love the place or hate it, with no in-between. It's a great community to raise children in, because kids and their education are everybody's number-one priority, and being surrounded by so much natural beauty offers a lot of wholesome outdoor activities. But the town shuts down after eight o'clock, and being watched by the LANL security patrols and Los Alamos police can be disconcerting. Then there are the observant eyes of neighbors. As in other small towns, people exchange the latest gossip at the supermarket. There's even a running joke that if you're thinking of having an affair in Los Alamos, you'd better rent a car, because everyone in town knows who drives what car. Wives—and husbands—of lab scientists tend to be as highly educated as their scientist spouses, and if they can't find challenging work at the lab, life on the hill can be pretty dull.

None of these complaints ever bothered me. Our family life centered around Chung and Alberta—their piano lessons, soccer games, tennis and volleyball practice, German club, and student council. On weekends, there were the Chinese language classes taught by Chinese parents like me who volunteered with the Los Alamos Chinese Cultural Association. I wanted my children to be able to speak Chinese as well as English, because I believe that speaking more than one language is important; at least Sylvia and I could give them the gift of another language. People in Los Alamos value multilingual ability, and it was not considered unusual or negative for us to speak Chinese at home. I also love the outdoors and would spend every spare moment fishing and hiking through the mountains if I could. Nightlife to me is staying home and listening to my classical music records and CDs. Los Alamos was a pretty good fit for me and my family.

What brought me to Los Alamos was my dream of working at this top research facility with some of the best scientific minds in the country and, indeed, the world. My journey to Los Alamos National Laboratory is not particularly unusual as a career path of a young Ph.D. in pursuit of a way to practice his or her science. Back in 1964, when I was a doctoral student at Texas A&M, my advisor did a lot of work for NASA, and that's how I first learned of these national laboratories. My field was fluid dynamics—hydrodynamics—creating mathematical models of what happens to particles over time, when they are subject to some kind of change or stress. There is an elegance in the motion of a liquid or a gas—how air is able to lift airplanes, or what happens when boiling water turns to steam. You can describe the changes with very well-defined mathematical equations. Every college science student learns to use Lagrangian, Eulerian, and other numerical methods, but the FBI and Congress seem to think these are state secrets. The particles in motion could be gas molecules, liquid ink in an ink-jet printer, solid metal of a car when it crashes, or substances in a bomb that explodes, or they could be subatomic neutrons and so forth. When you describe the physics, it's really quite beautiful. My doctoral thesis examined the flow of air between two vertical hot plates—a simple problem, but I wrote a computer code to solve the velocity of the flow field in two dimensions. Today, of course, almost everything is solved using computer codes, and very few problems are attacked with pencil and paper. Back in 1964, it was a very new thing to use computer codes to solve engineering problems, and I was in on the early stages of this novel approach.

I enjoyed my time in Texas, even though College Station was kind of ugly—no mountains, no ocean, lots of cows and cowboys. But Sommerville Lake was nearby, and I caught a lot of bass there. I found people in Texas open and friendly. The occasional Texan would throw eggs at me when I rode my bicycle to campus—some folks in Texas didn't like foreigners, but I knew I was in good company since anyone from out of state was considered a foreigner. Tuition was very cheap, and my scholarship covered my expenses if I was frugal. In the summers, I worked. I went to San Francisco and worked as a busboy at a fancy private club in the Ferry Building— the chef there taught me how to cook. I also went to New York to work as a kitchen aide at a Jewish restaurant-resort in Hempstead, Long Island. Some journalists reported that I had worked at Chinese restaurants, which I never did. They probably assume this because I'm Chinese. The best thing about my jobs was the sightseeing I did by Greyhound bus. I was very adventurous, and visited friends who were students in Boston, Buffalo, and Chicago. I enjoyed meeting new people and seeing this beautiful country. My trips made me realize that America is a very complicated place, with lots of contrasts and many different kinds of people.

By the time that I received my doctorate, in 1969, I had saved enough money to buy a car—a brand-new Mustang. It was blue and it gleamed. Growing up as a farm boy in a rural village of Taiwan, I had never dreamed of owning such a car. I drove it to Los Angeles to watch the Rose Bowl Parade. That's how I met Sylvia, who was there with friends from her church, and I offered to give them a ride home. Sylvia and I hit it off, and within a few months we were engaged. I already had a job lined up to teach mechanical engineering in Singapore, but Sylvia wanted to stay in the U.S., so I did.

We got married at the courthouse in Los Angeles. We had no

money for a ceremony. Engineering jobs were scarce in southern California then, and I thought I'd have better luck in New York. Sylvia stayed in LA, where she had a job. I took the Greyhound to New York because I'd heard it was bad to have a car there. I found a cheap place to stay and within a few weeks landed a short-term job writing computer codes—developing computer programs to make die-cast molds from blueprints. These were the very early days of using computers for industrial processes.

After a while, I found a steady job in New Jersey that would pay me about $1,400 a month, and I went back to LA to get Sylvia. We packed up the Mustang—all we had were some suitcases of clothes, no furniture—and we took our time driving cross-country. By October of 1970, we had decided to have a wedding reception at a fancy Chinese restaurant off Central Park, on Manhattan's East Side. Several of Sylvia's classmates from her high-school days lived in the New York area, and I had made some friends. We had a great party. Afterward, I gave a ride to one of our guests up Broadway and left my car for only a few minutes; when I returned, my car had been broken into and four boxes of unopened wedding gifts had been stolen.

Within a couple years, Chung was born, and we would go picnicking with friends to New Jersey's parks and lakes. One hot Sunday afternoon, we were hanging out by a lake with some other families. I found some tangled fishing line and decided to see if there were any fish in the lake. I didn't have a pole, but I came across a long branch. After looking around the shore, I found a rusty hook. Now I had a pole, about 6 feet of line, and a hook. I stuck a piece of ham on the hook and dropped the line in the lake, about 2 feet from the edge. I caught a fish right away. It wasn't very large—like a sand dab. I dropped the line again without even using any bait and caught another fish. Within an hour, I had more than fifty fish.

Fishing is the most fun for me. I forget everything else except how to improve my cast, how deep to drop my line. I actually have many fishing secrets—the FBI didn't ask me about them. I have a way of knowing where the fish are. I have a rule: If a fish bites three times and I pull but don't catch it, I let it go, because that's a smart fish. Trout are smart fish, and that makes them much harder to catch. In my experimental findings, trout are smarter than catfish, and female fish are smarter than males. New Jersey fish are not very smart. On that especially memorable afternoon, we split the catch with our friends and I spent the rest of the day cleaning and scaling.

By 1973, I was ready to leave the New York/New Jersey area. I felt that people there did not like Chinese or Asian people. When I walked on streets in northern New Jersey, people made nasty comments, racial comments. At work, it was obvious that if you didn't look a certain way, or have the right face, or speak English with an American or European accent, you would never get promoted. Once my car was hit by another car while I was at a toll booth, and a police officer and several people saw the accident. The police officer said it wasn't necessary to have witnesses, but when I took the matter to court, the police and the people who struck me testified that *I* had put my car in reverse and hit them! I don't know if the fact that they were all white and I was Chinese made them stick together and lie, but I knew I didn't want to raise my family there. So I started looking for work elsewhere, and got a job in San Diego as a fluid dynamics scientist, studying air pollution and smog—how the organic particles form and flow through the air. The company paid for my relocation; we still didn't have much furniture.

Once again, we packed our clothes into my blue Mustang and took a leisurely drive across America. This time we drove down to Florida, where we happened to watch the launch of an Apollo rocket. It was magnificent! I was so excited and proud to see what scientists and engineers could accomplish. As we sat outside Cape Canaveral, the warm, moist air and scenery of the South reminded me of Taiwan, especially the pecan trees, their branches loaded down with bunches of nuts. In Taiwan, longan fruit also weigh heavy from the trees. I hadn't been back to Taiwan since I left for grad school in 1963. For the first time, I saw the beautiful plantations, just like in *Gone With the Wind*, but I also saw how black people were treated like dogs. It reminded me of how I had felt, living in New Jersey.

We stopped at Texas A&M along the way, to visit my professors and to show off my baby. My sister Angela was attending nursing school near Houston, so I had a chance to spend time with her. We even did some sightseeing at the breathtaking Carlsbad Caverns in New Mexico, not knowing that we would end up living in the state. All along the way, I was struck by the vast natural beauty of this country and how friendly most Americans are. I felt very proud to be here and believed Americans to be honest and trustworthy. I really didn't see the ugliness until all the lies, deceptions, and false accusations came into my life.

The following year we learned that we were going to have another baby. I was working with a San Diego company to study the air and water pollution associated with nuclear power plants. Around the time of the baby's due date, the contract for the project wasn't renewed with my company. On the evening Alberta was born, I was in the delivery room and saw the baby come out. It was such a miracle. The next day, I got a pink slip. I waited three days before telling Sylvia. By Monday I was hired by the company that won the contract for the same air pollution project I had been working on— but I would have to commute to Los Angeles, a two-hour drive. I developed computer models of the fluid dynamics of the pollutants. Computers then were very slow; if I ran a program asking what the pollution level would be in an hour, it might take four to five hours to get the answer, and by then we already knew. The worst part was that I had to get a small apartment until I could move the family into a house in LA. I hated to leave Sylvia with the two children. It was a hard time for us, but I wasn't worried. There's a saying in Chinese: "When the boat reaches the bridge, it will naturally line up straight," in other words, no matter how difficult the situation is, everything will be okay.

It helped that Chung and Alberta were such good babies. They never kept us up at night, and within the first week of coming home, both babies slept all night long. We were very lucky with our children. As they grew up, I would tell them that because they gave us no trouble, we treated them quite well.

By 1974, I had become a U.S. citizen. After living here for more than ten years, I was finally a full-fledged American. For my citizenship test, I was asked how many colors there are in the U.S. flag; the examiner had a flag right behind him. There was a lot I didn't know about the Constitution and the two-party system that I since have learned because of my case. I wish I had paid more attention to these things then. But I clearly understood that if my country ever went to war and needed me to fight, I was willing to do so. America was our home now. With our two Chinese American babies, this was where our future belonged.

Being an American citizen also meant that I was eligible to work at the national laboratories. It was well known among scientists that the national labs had better computers than private industry. I wanted to do research, not just work on solving engineering problems. I applied for a job at the Idaho National Engineering and Environmental Laboratory, which was run by the Department of Energy. I was hired, and in 1975, I started work at Idaho Falls, writing computer codes relating to nuclear reactor safety. I wrote computer programs that modeled the water and heat flows in light-water nuclear reactors, which are used to generate electric power. My computer codes helped keep the reactors cool and ensured that a Chernobyl-type disaster would never happen here.

I enjoyed my work in Idaho, and Sylvia became an American citizen there. Idaho Falls was a friendly place, and it was also heaven for fishermen. I experienced the best fishing of my life. I'd go fishing after work and come back home in time for dinner with my catch of ten big trout—I always caught the limit. There was lots of great fishing, and I brought home plenty of trout to feed Alberta and Chung. That's why they're so tall—Chung is 6 feet, 2 inches, and Alberta is 5 feet, 10 inches. They're tall in any crowd, but especially among Chinese. I'm 5 feet, 4 inches, so it must have been the fish.

Chung was still a preschooler then, but when he turned five years old, we became concerned about the quality of the school system. At the end of 1977, I applied for work at Argonne National Labs in Chicago and at Los Alamos. Both Argonne and LANL had reputations for being strong research institutions, more physics oriented, while Idaho Falls was engineering oriented. I received offers from both LANL and Argonne. But the job at Los Alamos was only a verbal offer, and because of some kind of management disarray, it seemed that the job wouldn't come through. I took the job at Argonne and we moved to Chicago. My work still focused on nuclear reactor safety, but at Argonne I worked on fast breeder reactors for the Nuclear Regulatory Commission, not the commercial light-water reactors I studied at Idaho Falls. The principles of the cooling system were the same, with a primary cooling loop and a secondary loop, but a fast breeder reactor uses liquid sodium to cool the nuclear core, not water, which is used by the light-water reactors. Sodium cools the nuclear pile more efficiently, but it's also more dangerous, since the sodium can explode in the air spontaneously. There are only a few fast breeder reactors in use around the world—France uses them to generate electricity, and Japan had two, but shut them down.

Shortly after I joined Argonne, I got a real job offer from LANL. I talked it over with my boss, and decided to stay in Chicago for a year, then move to Los Alamos. I regretted staying such a short time at Argonne, but LANL was the number-one research place in this country, and it had the top scientists in my field. I wanted to be among them. I especially admired Frank Harlow, whose work I had studied at Texas A&M. His solutions to fluid dynamics problems were ingenious—and he worked at LANL. Plus, the town of Los Alamos had a top-notch public school system, as good as any private school on the East Coast. Seventy-two percent of the students from Los Alamos High School go to college, and because LANL employees work for the University of California, children pay in-state tuition. We were very happy with the chance to work and live there.

Once again, I went to my new job ahead of my family, leaving Sylvia with the kids in Chicago until I could get us established while I waited for my security clearance. The security application forms asked for all sorts of information: every place I ever lived, worked, and stayed. Did I participate in any Communist organization? Did I ever belong to a group advocating the overthrow of the government? Did I drink alcohol? Do I smoke or take drugs, had I ever been arrested for drugs? My answer to all these was no. The FBI then had to check on all my addresses, contacts, and answers—that process usually took months to complete.

I was hired at LANL in December 1978, and I went to work at my new job in Q Division, working on light breeder reactors and their cooling problems. The job paid $50,000 per year and it was very similar to the work I'd been doing at Idaho Falls. My job was to develop the code related to transient reactor accidents, a computer program that can predict what will happen, say, if a pump breaks down. Heat would be generated in the reactor core. That's what happened at the Three Mile Island nuclear plant. Lots of accidents occur with nuclear reactors, but with the help of our computer programs, they don't turn into Chernobyl disasters. You don't need a computer program to know the consequences of a Chernobyl, where so much radiation is released.

Each part of the cooling process has its own computer program, a subroutine that analyzes what happens, moment by moment, in the event of an accident. I was involved in developing the codes and calculations to ensure nuclear reactor safety. My work was recognized; even before I came to LANL, I was invited to various conferences to present papers and to talk about reactor safety issues.

After working for two years in Q Division, I applied for a position in X Division. Most of the work at Los Alamos has to do with nuclear weapons, and those jobs are more steady. In the Cold War days, the nuclear weapons projects were well funded, whereas in Q Division it was always a struggle from budget to budget. I figured my future would be more secure if I worked in the weapons area; I didn't want to be caught in the kind of budget or contract layoff I had experienced in San Diego. At LANL, jobs are posted, and if you want to apply for one, you go to the personnel department and fill out a form that is similar to a resume. If they're interested, you get called for an interview. I applied for a job for "a hydrodynamicist who knows computer codes." It was very similar to my work in Q Division, except that it involved nuclear weapons codes instead of nuclear reactor safety codes. I went to work in X Division in 1980, and soon after, I received my Q clearance.

Until Sylvia and the children moved to Los Alamos, I rented a room in the inexpensive dormitory-style housing that the lab maintains. A lot of visiting scientists who are separated from their families end up staying there. I had made good use of my days as a busboy—I learned how to cook at the swanky club in San Francisco—and I did the cooking for myself and another "single" scientist in the building. As soon as my family arrived, we moved into a rental apartment until our house in White Rock was completed. I don't think the other guy ate as well after I left.

When we finally moved into our brand-new home in the spring of 1980, I felt that we had reached the American dream. My family was settling down in this wonderful town, I had a secure job at a highly respected institution where I could do research with a community of scientists dedicated to making a contribution, in this setting of great natural beauty. I was very proud and content to devote the next 20 years of my life to keeping my country out of harm's way by helping to build our nuclear stockpile. But then it all started slipping away. Within these few weeks of 1999, my American dream spiraled down, until it completely shattered.

CHAPTER 6

As I sat in my home trying to ignore the reporters in my driveway, I asked myself why this was happening. It seemed that everything I worked so hard for had collapsed suddenly, like a nuclear implosion, a black hole. One day I was helping the FBI and they were saying that I wasn't a suspect, the next day I was fired and my name was plastered around the world. Now, reporters were all over my yard, my street, my neighborhood. Somehow my dream had gone terribly awry.

Sylvia and I tried to stay in the house, to ignore the knocking on our door and the faces that peered through our windows. The only good thing about the media blitz was that everybody now knew my name, and the hunt for a lawyer took on a whole different attitude.

The week before I was fired, I asked Alberta to try to find a lawyer. I finally realized that she had been right all along, but my stubbornness kept me from opening my eyes. She made many phone calls. One of her friends was attending law school in New York. The friend had a contact through one of her professors with O'Melveny and Myers, one of the biggest law firms in the country.

That contact gave Alberta a phone number. When Alberta left a voice message on the cellphone of attorney Mark Holscher, she was near tears. "You know the headlines about the spy for China? That's my father, except he's not a spy. He's innocent and he needs a lawyer, can you help us?"

Mark Holscher was at the airport in Salt Lake City when he listened to Alberta's message. He was there because of the bribery case of the Salt Lake City Olympic Organizing Committee, and he already had more work than he could handle. Mark says there was something in Alberta's voice that made him return the call. Right away he had this advice: "Turn off your phone. If the FBI contacts you, tell them you have a lawyer. Try to avoid the reporters, and come to Los Angeles to meet me."

The next day, March 11, three days after I was fired, I got up very early. The reporters had turned in for the night hours ago—my case had created a business boomlet for the hotels in town. At 5 A.M., I backed my car out of the garage without incident, to make the two-hour drive to the Albuquerque International airport. From there I caught a flight to LA, to meet Mark Holscher. I hoped he could help me.

Before this, the only time I needed to hire a lawyer was to prepare my will. That simple task cost me $200, which I thought was an exorbitant charge for such a small matter. It's not as though I had many possessions to account for. When I was fired from LANL in March 1999, my pay was $82,000—a decent salary that had risen over my 20 years at the lab through strong performance ratings and merit increases. LANL bench scientists knew we could make more money in private industry, or if we went into management at the lab, but I liked my work, and it allowed Sylvia and me to enjoy a nice, middle-class life as well as help pay for our kids' education. I was careful with my hard-earned money and wasn't inclined to part with it for nonessentials like lawyers. Their work had always seemed dis-

tasteful and seedy to me—making money off other people's misfor-
tunes. Not pure and high-minded like working in the sciences—
that's what I thought before these troubles began.

I have to laugh at myself when I think of the simple view of the
world I held then. It was easy to be so self-assured when I lived in
the safe, secure cocoon that Los Alamos provided, until that cocoon
broke open. Riding the elevator up to the 15th floor of the O'Melveny and Myers law firm in downtown Los Angeles, I could see
from the impressive offices that I would have to pay a lot more than
it took to draw up a will. I didn't have a lot of money, which I tried
to convey to Mark Holscher, the attorney I met. He was a clean-cut,
athletic-looking young guy, about 36 years old, and he made me feel
comfortable talking to him. I told Mark that I was innocent, and
that I believed this should all go away soon. Even then I had no concept of what I was facing. Mark said he only knew a little about my
case—what had been in the newspapers—and he wanted to listen
before he could say whether he could be my lawyer.

We talked for a couple of hours. I did most of the talking, while
Mark listened and took notes. He seemed smart and was very
friendly. He had grown up in Southern California and attended college and law school at Berkeley. His father was a retired scientist in
the aerospace industry.

I came back to their office the next day to talk more. This time I
met another lawyer, Tina Hua, a young Chinese American who was
tall, like Alberta. She could speak Chinese, so we exchanged some
greetings in Mandarin. It still wasn't clear whether they would take
my case. Mark told me that his firm had more than 700 lawyers
around the world, and that some of their work involved the University of California and the Department of Energy, which might affect
whether he could represent me. He asked me to come back a third
day, while he discussed my case with his firm's management committee. Later he told me that not everybody in his law firm was convinced they should represent me. I knew there were reasons—after

all, the newspapers said I was a spy, I didn't have much money, and my lawyer would have to fight the FBI, the labs, and the government.

When I went back to the law firm the next day, Mark had good news—the firm had decided to take my case. He said that I clearly needed a lawyer to get between me and the government. This was an immense weight off my shoulders, since I had no idea what to do. It was clear that my cooperation with the FBI, DOE, and LANL security thus far had only brought me more trouble. However, there was a limit to how much the firm would initially commit to my case. Mark would represent me for now, but if the government decided to indict me and we would have to prepare for a trial, the firm would reevaluate its commitment to me; to defend me in a trial for espionage could cost millions of dollars. I wrote the firm a check for $10,000 to retain their services, which was a great deal of money to me, but I'm sure it was very small by their standards. Beyond this retainer, O'Melveny and Myers would work pro bono, without any additional payment. Mark, Tina, and other lawyers in the firm then began clocking long hours to learn the case and to start preparing my defense.

For the next few weeks, I stayed in Los Angeles, visiting Mark and Tina twice a week to go over the latest in the scores of wild accusations about me appearing in the news and to discuss what the real story was about. I stayed at my sister Angela's house, taking long walks, going grocery shopping, and preparing dinner for her family when they came home from work and school. Sometimes, when I walked into a store or a restaurant, the TV would be showing news about me, with my home in White Rock in the background. The reporters were still camped outside my house, waiting for me, without a clue; they had no idea that I was watching them from LA!

Most of the news that followed my firing was disturbing, even frightening. A rare exception came in the form of a letter to President Clinton, sent on March 17, 1999, by four national Asian American organizations, a week after I was fired. The letter included these words:

Dear Mr. President:

On behalf of the undersigned Asian American organizations, we implore you to speak out forcefully and clearly against the reckless and racist media attacks against the supposed "disloyalty" of Americans of Chinese descent arising from the current controversy at the Los Alamos National Laboratory. Please use your upcoming weekly radio address and issue an official White House statement to counter these negative comments. . . . [I]t is reprehensible to label and viciously sterotype an entire ethnic group in America, which comprises millions of loyal, hardworking, law-abiding citizens, permanent residents and non-immigrants who are making positive contributions to this society. You must not allow all Americans of Chinese descent or any other Asian Americans to be singled out and tainted by this current smear campaign. Political leaders who failed to speak out in 1941 allowed 110,000 loyal Americans of Japanese heritage to be incarcerated behind barbed wire for years.

The letter was signed by Henry Tang, chairman of the Committee of 100; George Ong, president of the Organization of Chinese America; Herbert Yamanishi, national director of the Japanese American Citizens League; and Nancy Gee, president of the Chinese American Citizens Alliance. I didn't think that other Asian American people would care about my situation; I didn't even know such organizations existed. But I appreciated that they would write such a letter, especially when many—perhaps even most—people presumed that I was guilty, as the New York Times story seemed to conclude.

The bulk of what I saw in the news was pretty terrible, as the government leaked out bits of information about me, my family, and my employment history that would normally have been kept private. The New York Times wrote headlines like "Los Alamos Scientist Admits Contact with Chinese, U.S. Says" and "Though Suspected as

China Spy, Scientist Got Sensitive Job at Lab." But I never denied that I had contacts with Chinese, and I had worked in sensitive jobs at the laboratory for most of my 20 years at LANL. What was new about this stuff? Every day there was some new story with my name, saying that Wen Ho Lee is a dirty spy. After a while I felt numb when I looked at the news, and I would say to myself, Okay, what lie will they tell today?

————

My sudden life as a refugee from Los Alamos didn't suit me. For 20 years, I had followed an orderly and well-established routine, the steady life of a scientist. On a typical day, I got up and fixed my breakfast. When Chung and Alberta were school age, I fixed their breakfasts, too—oatmeal, French toast, or pancakes—and packed their lunches. I stopped making them lunch when, as teenagers, they began to complain that my lunches were boring.

I always arrived at work by 8:30 A.M. My office in the X Division was on the second floor, in the wing that was closest to the Otowi Building, the building outside the fence, where the cafeteria and administrative offices are. To get into the X Division, I first went past a badge reader, then a handprint reader, and through a one-way turnstile gate. I took the stairs to the second floor and passed through another checkpoint, a badge card swipe, and unlocked the door to my office. I turned on my computers—one that was connected to the open, "green" network; for the other computer, I had to reconnect the cable to the classified, "red" system. Then, while the computers initialized, I made myself some tea and ate the breakfast I had packed.

For the first hour or so of my day, I worked on my research. I wrote math equations and ran calculations on my equations, then I'd use the output to make graphs of the equations. LANL allowed scientists to spend up to 20 percent of their time working on non-lab research, which they encouraged us to publish, as part of the big

push, in the early 1990s, to find commercial applications for our
codes and to encourage LANL collaborations with private industry.
In the post–Cold War era, the lab hoped that non-weapons applications of our work would be useful to get funding for lab projects,
particularly since Washington was no longer inclined to write blank
checks for the labs.

Before I went to the X Division, I published a lot about nuclear
reactor safety, but of course we couldn't publish anything about our
classified work. So I worked on my papers and research on shaped
charges—that is, conventional explosives designed in a particular
shape. Some of my research was used in the Persian Gulf War and is
applicable today to the use of shaped explosives in drilling oil wells.
All of my research and publications were approved by LANL,
though most lab supervisors paid no attention to what we were doing. I would give them copies of my papers, but I doubt they read
them. When some lab managers reviewed my published papers on
shaped charges so the government could prosecute me, they thought
my paper was about nuclear bombs. It shows how little these supervisors know about the science in the laboratories they manage.

I spent the bulk of my days working on the hydrodynamics
codes of nuclear weapons, the most important problem to solve in a
nuclear bomb, because the codes examine what happens inside
when the bomb blows up and the metals liquefy. Other scientists,
weapons designers, might ask me to run some data on my codes to
see how the computer-simulated results compared with actual test
data. The X Division was about evenly split between designers and
code developers like me. The job of weapons designers is to come
up with new, more powerful, and more efficient weapons. They
would bring those design specs with their desired results to code
developers, who would try to work out the physics and mathematics
to produce a computer code that would simulate the bomb action,
once you light the match. The simulations save millions of dollars in
testing costs for each design. The computer codes that I and others

developed are the alternative to spending millions to make a bomb prototype and millions more to blow it up in Nevada—using lead or some metal other than plutonium.

If I wasn't working on a designer's request, I would try to make some improvements in the codes. Many codes or their subroutines are more than 40 years old, and the guys who wrote them are in heaven or hell. Some codes are impossible to refine because nobody knows what the original programmer was trying to do. To figure it out, you have to read the code in FORTRAN line by line, to try to understand the underlying mathematical picture—and these codes are hundreds of thousands, even millions of lines long. Once some-one found a bug in the code and removed it—but then the code wouldn't work. So they put the bug back in, even though no one knew why the program worked that way.

As a LANL code developer, I was responsible for codes related to both the primary fission bomb and the secondary hydrogen bomb. In order to do my work, I accumulated a collection of com-puter literature related to both parts. Oftentimes other code devel-opers and scientists would stop by my office to look up some obscure code information, because they knew if anyone had some background on these codes, I would. It was my job to know these codes, not the sneaky or nefarious activity that the government and the newspapers constantly insinuated.

Around 11:30, I'd eat my lunch at my desk. I packed my lunch with leftovers from dinner the previous night and I warmed it in the office microwave. After lunch, I locked my door and went for a walk in the woods behind my office. Lots of other LANL people would be doing the same thing, walking or running along the trail through the ponderosas. It was good exercise and very peaceful, with lots of birds, sometimes rabbits, deer, and elk, or even an occasional rattlesnake.

Within a half hour or so I was back at my desk, working on the weapons code. For years I had been saying that we ought to throw away some of the ancient legacy codes and start over rather than

continue to patch the buggy old codes up. I referred to one particularly bad code—which the court designated as Code B—as
garbage. They were certainly *not* the "crown jewels" that LANL
manager Stephen Younger declared them to be and that the news
media accused me of stealing. But some of our nation's weapons
designers must be lazy—if we threw away these old codes, they'd
have to do a lot of rewriting. I'd made this point many times while
I was at LANL. Nobody listened, but I wonder if speaking the
truth about our codes also contributed to the lab's poor treatment
of me.

Unless I was working late on a project, I shut down my computers some time after 5:30, disconnected my secure computer
from the red system, closed and locked the door to my office, and
headed home. Then I'd go to work on my garden or my lawn. If it
was one of the long and beautiful summer evenings that New Mexico is famous for, I might even go fishing, usually hiking three or
more miles to get to my special fishing spots. I would also cook dinner. Sometimes Sylvia would cook, but most often I did the cooking,
because the kitchen was my domain. Before Chung and Alberta left
for college, we always had dinner as a family. It was one of our
household rules that the kids had to be home for dinner. Often their
friends came to visit and stayed for dinner, too. Later in the evening,
I would go over their math and science homework with them. For
the rest of the night, I listened to classical music, and maybe spent
some time working on a paper or reading.

This was my steady, daily life at LANL, and I liked it very much.
There were few disruptions, and as a code physicist, I required un-
interrupted time to work through the codes. Code developers are
described as loners, and in fact we might work alone for months on
our particular code problems. The teams I was assigned to hardly
ever had meetings. In my division, we rarely had to prove we were
working on anything at all. I wouldn't be surprised if some people

spent their days asleep at their desks. But I cared about my work and took pride in the research I had published.

———

After I was fired, I no longer had my daily work routine and hadn't even spent enough time at home to contemplate a new one. I flew back to New Mexico on April 7, 1999, after spending almost a month in Los Angeles.

Soon after I arrived home, the FBI had yet another surprise in store.

I was home just two days when they showed up with a warrant to search my house. Early on the morning of April 10, as I started to prune the fruit trees out in back, they rang the doorbell, waking Sylvia up. She still has nightmares about being awakened by the FBI. Suddenly, nearly a dozen FBI agents were swarming over my house. I had met one of them before, Michael Lowe, on March 5, 1999, during the search of my T Division office. That seemed like ancient history to me, so much had happened since then. The FBI agents told me to sit in my kitchen as they rummaged through my house, but I asked them if I could work in my garden.

As I headed to my yard, I encountered the FBI agent who was now in charge of my case, Robert Messemer. Unlike the other FBI people, who didn't mind showing a little bit of their humanity, Messemer was cold and seemed intent on making sure I knew that he was the master. He towered over me, watching me intently, like a vulture circling a carcass. I thought I'd try to add a little friendliness to this unpleasant situation.

"What's your name?" I asked him.

He said nothing.

"Are you from Albuquerque?"

Again no answer.

"Where are you from?"

I looked directly at him. This time he responded, his eyes hard and his voice scornful.

"I'm not going to tell you."

I simply shrugged my shoulders and went back to my gardening. Months later I would sit in court and listen to this FBI agent lie about me to Judge Parker. Eventually he would have to recant his testimony and admit that he made "misstatements" to the judge. Messemer was one of the government witnesses who misled Judge Parker into keeping me in jail for nine months.

For the next several hours, the FBI agents combed through every drawer, every box, every item in my home, like government-sanctioned looters. They made a list of items that they took from us. They listed 47 items, but in fact they took hundreds of my family's personal possessions, many of which they grouped together as one item, for example, "Box of Misc. Documents" or "Letters, photos, Slides, Reels of Tapes."

Among the items they took:

Computer manuals, including Microsoft Word
Computer software for off-the-shelf retail computer programs
Albuquerque telephone directory
Santa Fe/Los Alamos telephone directory
All address books and business cards
Phone listings for the Los Alamos Chinese Cultural
     Association
Member directory of the Los Alamos Chinese Cultural
     Association
Four Plays, by Tennessee Williams
Selected Short Stories, by Guy de Maupassant
Several photo albums, including ones belonging to Alberta
A diary written by Sylvia's mother
Several notebooks marked as Alberta's
A high school math notebook belonging to Alberta

A manila envelope addressed to Alberta

A notebook belonging to Chung

An airline ticket belonging to my nephew

Old computer hardware components, including an Apple
     hard drive

Computer programming books

Computer printouts and documents related to my research and
     published papers

Various notebooks

A map of China

Newspaper clippings

Loose photographs

Boxes of computer floppy diskettes

Any item related to computers or computing was supposed to be seized, as well as anything that had notations written in Chinese. I had apparently made a few margin notes in the book by Guy de Maupassant (Alberta had a note with her doctor's phone number in *Four Plays* by Tennessee Williams). But Chinese was my first language, and it was the language we used at home. Now, writing in Chinese was treated as evidence of some kind of crime. Some of the items in Chinese had precious sentimental value and were irreplaceable, like the keepsake book of messages written by Sylvia's mother to her every year on her birthday, or the newspaper clippings about Sylvia's father when he was a young engineer. Only a few of these items have been returned to us.

Why was the FBI suddenly interested in my household possessions? They were still desperate to find any evidence that I had committed espionage for the People's Republic of China. By the time my house was searched, there were some 60 or so FBI agents assigned to my case, and soon there would be even more, all at work to prove that I was a spy. And this was just their most recent effort. I had been an unknowing suspect for fifteen years, ever since I contacted the Taiwanese American scientist at Lawrence Livermore labs, whose phone was being tapped. Yet for all the time and expenditure by the DOE and FBI and their Kindred Spirit investigation, they had found nothing. They couldn't even identify a motive. It was enough that I was a nuclear weapons scientist, that I had been to China and had networked with Chinese nuclear scientists, and that I was a Chinese American. It didn't matter that many other nuclear scientists had contact with Chinese counterparts, nor did it seem to matter that I had been born and raised in Taiwan, a country at odds with China. As some of their own counterintelligence people concluded several times, I was the wrong guy. Even the news reporters were writing that Kindred Spirit was a bust. The *Los Angeles Times* ran the headline, "FBI unable to build case against scientist linked to China leaks, espionage. Officials try to determine if Wen Ho Lee passed along classified information. But evidence is hard to come by, they say."

But there was a new reason for their hunt as well. During the search of my offices on March 5, they found a printout of my computer directories and files that were in the X Division. Back in 1993–94, I had copied some classified files into a directory on the green, open computer system. I placed the files under three levels of passwords. These files had not been classified as Secret or even Confidential, but were labeled PARD, which stands for "Protect as Restricted Data." PARD was a category created to help the labs cope with the millions of files that might possibly contain something classified but were known to be 99 percent unclassified. PARD data was treated as a lower security level than Secret and Confidential on the LANL computer system. In fact it was just above the Unclassified level, and the handling of PARD files was far less stringent than the handling of Secret documents. For example, PARD documents did not have to be locked up in a vault at night, whereas documents marked Secret and Confidential had to be secured at the end of each day.

After I was fired, these files were classified Secret or Confidential, and I was accused of mishandling Secret information; the indictment against me would wrongly say that I moved and copied fifteen Secret and four Confidential files. Of course they announced this to the world and said that I "stole" these files. But none of that was true. It was sickening to see people believe the government's propaganda that I "stole" files that I worked with every day for years, yet nobody even whispered that John Deutch "stole" the many CIA files he downloaded and took home, because people said he worked on them. So did I, but then again, I was a Chinese American, and he was a "real" American.

The reason I downloaded these files was very simple and mundane: I wanted to protect them from loss in the event that LANL changed the computer operating system again or experienced a computer crash—both had occurred in the past, causing serious problems for me. During those incidents, I lost some important computer codes that I had written.

In spite of what the government said about my downloading in official statements and leaks to the news media, there was nothing clandestine or hidden about my files or tapes. I gave the files very obvious filenames that reflected the computer codes I worked with in my years in the X Division. I knew that the LANL computer security unit could—and did—monitor my file transfers. I called the LANL help desk for advice on how to download and make the tapes on a number of occasions. I had a notebook that I labeled "How to download files," and listed all the files I had downloaded and made into tapes. The FBI had this notebook—which is how they found my downloads and learned that I had made tapes. In my T Division office, they also found some computer tapes—somewhat comparable in size and capacity to present-day Zip disks. These tapes had no classified information on them, a fact that the FBI and lab computer analysis verified.

There was good reason for me to worry about losing my files. In 1993, I lost several files as a result of a computer system conversion at the lab. Losing my work made me lose confidence in the LANL computer system. This is a bit technical, but I want to explain what happened when the LANL computers were converted from one operating system to another, and then converted to yet a third. In 1988 or 1989, LANL changed its computer operating system from LTSS, the Livermore Time Sharing System, to a new operating system called CTSS, or Cray Time Sharing System. Cray is the supercomputer hardware we used for what was then the fastest computer system in the world. Changing operating systems is what happens when you switch your personal computer from a PC to an Apple. You then have to figure out what to do with all your files, documents, and computer programs that were written for the PC operating system. How do you fix those files so that they can run on the Apple operating system? Without a conversion method of some sort, it would be impossible to run an Apple program on a PC, and vice versa.

LANL came up with a procedure to convert, or "port," my LTSS programs into CTSS programs, but it was extremely tedious. I had to take each file I wanted to convert and go through a long series of time-consuming, manual steps to make it readable to the Cray operating system. As if that wasn't bad enough, I worked with hundreds of files that needed to be ported and manually converted. So did other code developers. We spent many months in X Division porting files because of the operating system change—almost no code development took place during that time. But then LANL changed to yet a third operating system in 1992, the UNICOS operating system. That meant I had to go through the same laborious steps all over again for each file, only this time converting from CTSS to UNICOS.

Then I discovered a problem: I hadn't converted about a dozen files from the LTSS system to CTSS back in 1988–89, so that meant I had to find a way to convert them from LTSS to UNICOS. But I couldn't find any way to do it. Every file I still had in the LTSS format was lost. One of the codes I lost was about nuclear reactor safety, which I had developed at Argonne National Laboratory in Chicago. This was an important code, and it was gone.

I worried that the lab might change to yet another operating system in a few years. So I thought the best way to prevent a similar loss was for me to put all my files onto tapes and to keep them in my X Division office with other classified material I worked with, behind the fence, behind all those security checkpoints.

As a code developer, it was important that I have my own copy of *my version* of the codes I worked on. That's because other code developers worked on other parts of the code at the same time that I worked on the hydrodynamics portion. For example, others were responsible for codes that model the movement of radiation, of neutron transport, of shock physics. If they made changes to the code, it could affect the way my subroutines operated on the code. What I wanted to do was to save a snapshot of the code at a certain time. It wouldn't help me to have a copy of the code after months or years of additional work had been done on it, because I would have to reconstruct all the changes to all the subroutines that might have affected my part of the code. I might be able to reconstruct everything, but it would be a great waste of time, possibly years, when it was so simple just to have a tape as documentation of the program.

In 1993 and 1994, after I lost my codes, I decided to make some backup tapes, but I didn't have my own tape drive. So I asked a colleague-friend who had a tape drive if I could use his. He worked in the T Division, outside the fence, in the unsecure area. I told him I needed to use his tape drive to download some files. I didn't tell him that they were classified files because he didn't have a Q clearance. It was not a simple process—it took me several weeks to copy my files onto the tapes.

My friend gave me his password so that I could use his computer. With my colleague's knowledge, I would go to his office when he wasn't there, so that I wouldn't be in his way. The government made it sound as though I was sneaking into his office to hide my activities, and that's how it was blasted out all over the news. But it wasn't true. I knew that the computer monitoring system would be tracking the file downloads I did. Later, in the course of my case, when LANL managers presented the court with what they knew of my downloads, I learned that my file transfers were indeed noticed by the monitors, but I was never admonished for the downloads. If I had been told to stop, I would have.

FBI agent Robert Messemer, the one who was so cold to me, lied about this particular episode to Judge Parker. He said repeatedly that I had told my friend I wanted to download "my resume," and that this was evidence of deceptiveness. I never said that, and my colleague confirmed that I only said I wanted to "download some files." Messemer was caught misleading the judge, but in the meantime I spent nine months in jail and these lies were all over the news.

It is not illegal or a violation of security to make tapes of PARD or even Secret codes or programs at LANL, as long as tapes of classified material are kept in a secure location. In the mid-1990s, I was given a tape drive by the lab. Had I been able to make all my tapes in my own office, inside the fence, it would not have been necessary for me to download to the green, open system. Then the lab and the FBI would have had no security violation to pin on me.

But it was a security violation for me to make classified tapes outside the fence and to leave the PARD files on the green, open system. And the FBI and DOJ made it sound worse by saying I left Secret files on the open system, which they were not at the time I downloaded. Once I moved the data from the red, closed system to the green, unclassified system in order to make my tapes, I decided to leave them on the green system. I felt it was secure because I put three levels of passwords on the files. I left them there as another backup, for my convenience—not for any espionage purpose. I knew it wasn't proper. That's why I deleted the files off the green system when I lost my access to X Division and was transferred to the T Division outside the fence on December 23, 1998. I knew I wasn't supposed to have these PARD files anymore, and I was able to delete them from my T Division computer because I had access to the green system. I wasn't hiding my actions; I even called the LANL help desk for instructions on how to delete the files, and these actions, like the creation of my files, were being monitored.

I wasn't the only scientist who, rightly or wrongly, made an exception to security rules that seemed arbitrary and impeded my work. From the day that this nightmare began, other scientists have said that they had committed or knew of others who had committed security violations. They've shared this information with me, my family, and my lawyers. Understandably, almost all have chosen to remain anonymous.

I felt that there was virtually no risk that anyone could break through my three passwords and gain access to these files. Anyone trying to get into my computer directory is allowed only three attempts to enter the correct password. Without the first password, a user cannot log on to the LANL network. Without the second password, there is no access to the separate computer system a person would need to read the files I downloaded. The third password required knowledge of the exact filename to be accessed. I did not treat these files carelessly, as FBI, LANL, and DOE officials repeatedly stated and the media has broadcast.

Some LANL people have asked, Why didn't I make backups on my hard drive or some portable storage device? I didn't have a hard drive or a floppy drive, and at the time, I didn't have a tape drive. My computer system was a Sun SPARC workstation, a dumb terminal. Others wonder why I didn't ask the staff in C Division, which is a computer support division, to make the backup copies for me. I didn't want to ask them to do it, because it was simpler for me to do it myself. I didn't want to spend time explaining which parts of which files I wanted to save or how I wanted them organized, nor did I want to wait for the weeks or months it would take them to make my backup tapes. I wanted my files kept in a certain way—just as I kept my office, my music, my tools, and my kitchen organized just so.

I knew I had committed a security infraction for making my tapes outside the fence and for leaving my PARD files on the green system, and I deserved to be punished for it, like anyone else who violated security rules. But before me, no one was ever fired for this. I certainly didn't deserve to be arrested, thrown into jail, placed in solitary confinement for nine months, and accused of espionage.

At the time that my house was searched, I didn't know that the lab and the FBI were in a frenzy over my files. I didn't know that the lab shut down the LANL computers for two weeks while they did a forensic search for any "damage" I may have done. The FBI has said it was the largest computer forensic search in history. I really didn't think what I did with my files was such a terrible thing, since I kept everything secure. But then I never anticipated that I'd become a front-page spy suspect, and that my every deed would become magnified. Politicians were blowing up my security infractions into a federal case of espionage, all because they wanted to hang "a spy." The facts didn't seem to matter.

All of this was just beginning to unfold before my stunned eyes. By the time of the search, it was very clear that *something big* had changed, because now we had a 24-hour, around-the-clock FBI watch over us. If the media encampment was bad, the new, intensified FBI surveillance of my family was hell.

CHAPTER 7

Sylvia and I became virtual prisoners in our home. FBI agents now were trailing us wherever we went—to the grocery store, the library, the gas station. At least 10 or 12 FBI agents followed us in four, five, or six cars, making for a little wagon train. I finally had achieved "team leader" status—a basic supervisory level at LANL that I never would have made, because promotional opportunities for immigrant Asian Americans were so limited. But I was leading a team of FBI agents, not scientists.

I stopped visiting friends—anyone I spoke to got a follow-up visit from the FBI: What did we talk about? How did they know me? What was the nature of our relationship? And so on. We didn't want to bring trouble to our friends, especially since everyone worked at the labs, and the file that the FBI most certainly created on them could possibly hurt them the way that my phone call to the Taiwanese American scientist at Lawrence Livermore lab had damaged me all these years.

It wasn't just my family that was subject to this scrutiny—our entire close-knit neighborhood was under siege. Our neighbors were being watched, their activities monitored. Many phones in the neighborhood were acting strangely, with odd clicking sounds. Every time I spoke to Mark, we began the conversation with "This conversation is privileged; it is protected by the attorney-client privilege," because we believed my phone was tapped. Mark Holscher's and Brian Sun's telephone records were subpoenaed by assistant U.S. attorney Bob Gorence. My neighbors down the street told me they saw people working on the phone utility poles in their yard, and they thought their phones were being bugged, too. It was embarrassing, humiliating—which was surely the government's intent.

I tried to use my "house arrest" productively, and began writing a college-level mathematics textbook about differential equations and how to apply them to a variety of engineering problems. But I was constantly interrupted. Every day, reporters knocked on my door. They came with cameras, asking, "Can we talk with you?" Of course, I said nothing. My lawyer told me not to say anything, and there was nothing I wanted to say to them about this craziness. Reporters would stand at my kitchen window, taking pictures of me washing the dishes. I felt that it was not gentlemanly to take pictures like that. There were many times when I wondered, why is this happening to me? I kept telling myself that this could not last forever; someday it would all be over.

After two weeks, I said to my wife, this is too much. I had only just come back home from Los Angeles, but I needed to escape this madness. I decided to go back to LA to my sister's home, and this time Sylvia came with me. The FBI came along, too. My sister Angela's house was near a mall. Sylvia and I walked there every day, with the FBI tailing along behind us, driving their cars like snails. It was a two-mile walk. We'd have coffee at the mall to kill time, and come back a few hours later, FBI in tow. At least in Los Angeles, we could be anonymous.

We watched the news and read the papers—every time I looked at a newspaper I saw my name—and all the lies. It reminded me of the book *The Hunchback of Notre Dame*, by Victor Hugo, one of my favorite writers. In it, Quasimodo joins in a party, a play where he is anointed Pope of Fools. I felt as though I were living through some play full of fools, too. That was my daily life. It was so stifling, like being crushed by a heavy stone, but not so bad that it kills you. You just wake up the next day and go through it all over again.

About twice a week I visited Mark Holscher and Tina Hua at their law office in downtown LA. On the day that *Los Angeles Times* reporter Bob Drogin wrote that I was going to be arrested within 10 days, Mark introduced me to another attorney, Brian Sun, who was a friend of his and also a former U.S. prosecutor. Mark had asked Brian to help on the case by representing my wife, Sylvia, in case she became a suspect, and Brian offered to do so on a pro bono basis. Brian was Chinese American, an ABC— American-born Chinese. He could speak some Chinese, and told me he was willing to help. Later, Brian would represent my other relatives who had to appear in court, as well as taking up my civil suit against the government. Mark would remain the lead attorney in charge of my case.

It wasn't clear whether the government was going to indict me, even though the *LA Times* said I was going to be arrested. We were following my case in the news, just like everyone else. More than a month had gone by since energy secretary Bill Richardson ordered me to be fired, and still there was no let-up in the "spy story" coverage about me. The politicians in Washington all seemed to be clamoring for me to be arrested. I watched a program called "The NewsHour" one afternoon. The news anchor, Jim Lehrer, asked Bill Richardson three times, "Why hasn't that man been arrested?" Neither Lehrer nor Richardson—nor any other politician or reporter— seemed to consider that perhaps I had not committed a crime, or that in the United States, people who are accused of a crime are innocent until proven guilty.

In Washington and on the news I was guilty, guilty, guilty. In

Congress there were numerous hearings that recirculated the lies about me and created new ones. Notra Trulock, the DOE counter-intelligence head who had made me the prime suspect of the Kindred Spirit investigation, was a star witness at many of the hearings, the great hero who had found the Chinese spy. Several government reports on China's spying, including a Congressional report by Congressman Christopher Cox, were in the process of being released—and so many of these hearings, reports, and news stories declared that Wen Ho Lee was a spy.

They hadn't electrocuted me, "like the Rosenbergs." Not yet. I was still free to walk around, leading my FBI team. Energy Department head Bill Richardson was on the defensive for not producing enough evidence to put me away. Some news stories, like the one in the *Washington Post*, "FBI's Spying Probe Proves No Easy Task," even suggested that the investigation into my supposed espionage was foundering and would be difficult to prove. That story also gave me more information about the W-88 warhead that I was accused of "stealing" for China. I learned that in 1995, a PRC double agent walked into the CIA office in Taipei and turned over 74 pages of documents. Most of these papers were not significant, but one was a 1988 Chinese government document. It had diagrams with dimensions of several nuclear warheads, including a diagram with some of the dimensions of a warhead that was very similar to the W-88.

I didn't know those dimensions, and I later learned that detailed descriptions of the W-88 were available at other national labs besides LANL and aboard submarines, and were sent to 548 recipients throughout the government, military, and defense contractor companies. But Kindred Spirit focused on me even though plenty of others at LANL and elsewhere fit the profile and had the same information, access, and opportunity as I had. No one has been able to explain why this PRC double agent would "give" this information to the CIA, or why he would choose Taipei as the drop-off at a time when the PRC was firing missiles off the coast of Taiwan. Even more puzzling was why Notra Trulock, the FBI, the DOJ, and Congress would so readily accept the walk-in "gift" from a known PRC double agent on face value as the basis for investigating and prosecuting me. If the PRC's purpose was to create turmoil and confusion in Washington and our national labs, they did a good job.

The politicians in Congress continued to accuse the government of inaction, and "unnamed officials" leaked out more and more about my life and my job, trying to make me seem as suspicious as possible. The DOE and FBI dribbled out lies and "classified, secret" information from "unnamed sources" into the media. Many reporters were only too happy to recycle the leaks without criticism or any follow-up investigation. James Risen, one of the original *New York Times* reporters whose article characterized me as "worse than the Rosenbergs," continued to print wrong information about me. For example, he wrote that in 1997 I had hired a post-doctoral student as an intern who was a citizen of the People's Republic of China. That much was true. I hired him, with approval from my supervisors and LANL officials, because he was a top student at the University of Pittsburgh. He performed only unclassified work. The reporter could have readily obtained this information from the lab, if only he had asked. But then the *New York Times* said:

> The research assistant has disappeared. Even as the bureau tries to find him to question him, government officials say they are wondering whether he played a role in a Chinese intelligence operation at the heart of America's program. . . . He returned to the University of Pittsburgh, officials said. They said they were not sure whether the assistant, who was in the United States on a student visa, was still in the United States. [March 24, 1999]

In fact, the former intern was studying mechanical engineering at Penn State, where his name was readily available on the university's web site. He was even listed in the telephone directory. Risen could have found him by asking LANL officials how to reach him, had he bothered to check. Instead, the *New York Times* again published, without question, what their unnamed government sources had leaked, casting me once again in the most suspicious and negative light possible.

Then came the stories about how I downloaded my files from the red, closed computer system to the green, open system. Again, those two guys from the *New York Times*, Risen and Gerth, printed leaks from those unnamed officials:

> The data—millions of lines of computer code that approximate how this country's atomic warheads work—were downloaded from a computer system at the Los Alamos, NM, weapons lab that is only open to those with top-level security clearances, according to the officials. The scientist, Wen Ho Lee, then transferred the files to *a widely accessible computer network* at the lab, where *they were stored under other file names,* the officials said. . . . American officials said there was *evidence that the files were accessed by someone* after they were placed in the unclassified network. Other evidence suggests that this was done by a person who improperly used a password, the officials said. [April 28, 1999, emphasis added]

Those unnamed officials knew that I had put three passwords on my files, but the *New York Times* made it sound as though I made the files freely available to everybody. And the officials knew from their massive forensic computer search of the LANL computer system that no one had accessed my files. The *New York Times* even intimated that renaming my files was a suspicious, deceitful act, when in fact it was standard computing protocol—and the names I gave clearly indicated the contents of the files.

Washington Post reporters Vernon Loeb and Walter Pincus wrote about the same story, but they gave a more complete picture:

One senior administration official . . . said that *a password was needed to access the information even after Lee transferred it* from the classified computer system. The unclassified system allows investigators to determine when and whether the data was accessed, the official said, and initial indications are that the material was accessed "at least a little bit.". . .

Another high-ranking official reported *no indication that the information was compromised.* He denied a published report of evidence showing that a password had been misused to gain access. He also denied that the FBI had been derelict in not searching Lee's computer at the beginning of the espionage investigation in 1996.

At the time, FBI agents from the bureau's Albuquerque field office wanted to search the computer but were told they needed a search warrant from a secret federal court under the Foreign Intelligence Surveillance Act. The warrant was denied, the official said, because of *a lack of evidence showing that Lee was engaged in acts of espionage.* [April 29, 1999, emphasis added]

Other reporters, too, occasionally looked more critically for an explanation. Bob Drogin of the *Los Angeles Times* asked opinions of other LANL scientists who were not working on prosecuting me:

But one scientist who has followed the case closely said Lee still may have a reasonable explanation.

"If he's the greatest spy of the 20th century, why is he still out there mowing his lawn?" the scientist asked. "In the old days, when the super-spies got wind of the feds coming, they disappeared and showed up years later in Moscow."

Other questions are equally puzzling. The FBI only discovered the pilfered nuclear weapon files, for example, because Lee gave them permission to examine his personal computer after he was fired. [April 30, 1999]

It was rare to find any acknowledgment that I had voluntarily provided most of the information that had been twisted and turned against me. Still, I had not "pilfered" any files.

––––––––––

I told Mark that I didn't think he should answer questions from the *New York Times*, because their stories were so unfair. He agreed and stopped answering phone calls from Risen and Gerth. Supposedly they were the star reporters of the paper, but they were doing a hatchet job on me, and a sloppy one at that. An editor at the *New York Times* called Mark to try to get him to change his mind, telling Mark that he must talk with them because they were the most important paper in America. Mark scolded the editor, saying that the paper was arrogant and careless, potentially putting my life at stake for the capital crime of espionage. He wouldn't talk to the newspaper as long as Risen and Gerth continued to cover my case. Later, when other *New York Times* reporters began to write about my case and the stories became more balanced, my lawyers resumed answering their questions.

I spent my days at Mark's office, working with him and Tina Hua on a statement we would make to the media. I wanted to tell the public that what they were hearing about me was not true. We were buried under an avalanche—how were we going to fight the government and fight the media when every TV station, every newspaper, was running these lies? It was all such a big pressure on all of us, a huge stress. Tina and Mark worked many long days and nights to produce our media statement. It is quite long, but I want to include the whole statement, which we issued on May 6, 1999.

Dr. Wen Ho Lee has dedicated himself to the defense of this country for the last 20 years. His work, much of which is classified, has led directly to the increased safety and national security of all Americans, and he is responsible for helping this country safely simulate nuclear tests.

In 1986 and 1988, Dr. Lee went to Mainland China to present papers at two technical conferences. Dr. Lee's participation in these conferences was pre-approved and encouraged by the Los Alamos (National) Laboratory and the Department of Energy. These same entities also cleared the texts of the papers given at these conferences, which covered mathematics and physics topics.

The press has incorrectly reported that Dr. Lee made "several" trips to Mainland China and also failed to report that his two trips were approved in advance by the Los Alamos (National) Laboratory and the Department of Energy. These two approved trips were the only times Dr. Lee has ever traveled to Mainland China. These false press reports do a disservice both to Dr. Lee and the Los Alamos (National) Laboratory.

The press reports also fail to include the fact that Dr. Lee presented similar papers at conferences in several countries throughout Western Europe and other parts of the world. The false insinuations that Dr. Lee went to Mainland China in the late 1980s with an improper purpose are unfair. Not only did Dr. Lee go to Mainland China to present a technical paper, his and his wife's attendance were with the full knowledge and approval of the Federal Bureau of Investigation.

COOPERATION WITH THE FBI

There have been inaccurate press reports regarding the circumstances surrounding Dr. and Mrs. Lee's cooperation with the government. Mrs. Lee agreed to the FBI's request that she assist it as a volunteer without pay in the FBI's efforts to monitor Chinese scientists. She agreed to help the FBI with the full knowledge and approval of Dr. Lee and continued to do so for a number of years.

At the request of the FBI, Dr. Lee's wife attended the 1986 conference with him, where she voluntarily provided background information on Chinese scientists. Dr. and Mrs. Lee supported and agreed with the FBI's request that Mrs. Lee assist it in obtaining background information on Chinese scientists. It simply defies logic for critics to now allege that Dr. Lee was engaged in improper activities in Mainland China while he and his wife were there.

At no time during or after the pre-approved 1986 or 1988 trips did Dr. Lee ever provide any classified information whatsoever to any representative of Mainland China, nor has he ever given any classified information to any unauthorized persons. As was anticipated and approved by the U.S. government, Dr. Lee and his wife socialized with Chinese scientists. It was fully understood by the Department of Energy and the Los Alamos (National) Laboratory that the conferences included social events with the participants.

For over three years, government agencies have investigated Dr. and Mrs. Lee's 1986 and 1988 trips to Mainland China. To date, these investigatory agencies have not found any evidence that Dr. Lee ever disclosed any classified information to anyone in Mainland China. Dr. Wen Ho Lee is a loyal American, and has always fully cooperated with the government's investigation. He has submitted to four interviews with government representatives regarding his activities during this period, and continues to cooperate with the United States Attorney's Office for the District of New Mexico. In addition, Dr. Lee continues to inform Justice Department officials of his whereabouts and provide them with other information to prove that he has not and will not ever provide classified information to anyone.

In helping the FBI, Mrs. Lee put herself and her husband

at risk, with no possible benefit to herself or her husband. Mrs. Lee never requested any payment from the FBI for her help, although the government paid her expenses to travel to Mainland China with her husband and offered to pay her expenses for entertaining Chinese scientists who visited the Los Alamos laboratory. The FBI also gave Mrs. Lee inexpensive gifts as tokens of its appreciation for her work.

Both Dr. and Mrs. Lee were briefed by the FBI before their 1986 trip to gather background information regarding Chinese scientists. While there, they followed the FBI's instructions and after this trip, Mrs. Lee briefed the FBI. Upon returning from their 1988 trip, Mrs. Lee provided a written report to the FBI. In addition, Mrs. Lee agreed to the FBI's request that she permit an FBI agent to monitor her communications with Chinese scientists in her role as Los Alamos (National) Laboratory's liaison. For several years, Mrs. Lee forwarded translated copies of all correspondence with Chinese scientists to FBI agents.

LAWRENCE LIVERMORE NATIONAL LABORATORY

Dr. Lee assisted the FBI in its investigation of suspected espionage activity at the Lawrence Livermore National Laboratory. In 1982, Dr. Lee spoke briefly with a Livermore scientist who was rumored to be facing disciplinary action for delivering a scientific paper in Taiwan. Dr. Lee, who was considering delivering a scientific paper in Taiwan, called the scientist. Due to its interception of that call, the FBI questioned Dr. Lee and gave him a polygraph test to ensure that his contact with the Livermore scientists was for an innocent purpose. Dr. Lee was told he passed the polygraph test.

The FBI then asked Dr. Lee to help them by flying to Lawrence Livermore National Laboratory to meet with the Livermore scientist about the scientist's involvement with China.

Dr. Lee readily agreed to help. The FBI paid for Dr. Lee's travel expenses to Lawrence Livermore National Laboratory. Dr. Lee received instructions from the FBI before the meeting, met with the scientist and then briefed the FBI after the meeting.

COMPUTER CODES

Press reports incorrectly state that Dr. Lee mishandled his Los Alamos (National) Laboratory computer files. Dr. Lee has never given classified files to any unauthorized person. In fact, Dr. Lee took substantial steps to protect his computer files, and we are confident that federal investigators will also conclude that no third party could have or did access his protected computer files.

Like other Los Alamos scientists, Dr. Lee was expressly permitted to spend 20 percent of his time on projects unrelated to his classified activities. Contrary to recent press reports, Dr. Lee's computer files contained dozens of nonclassified codes, which include several hundred thousand lines of code. Dr. Lee's changing of file names on nonclassified computer codes to reflect improvements he made in nonclassified codes is not only proper, it is accepted and recognized as standard procedure when revising computer codes. It is irresponsible for the press to falsely portray any unclassified codes as containing classified information and it is equally irresponsible for the press to fail to disclose that it is accepted procedure to change file names to reflect improvements or additions to codes, whether classified or nonclassified.

CONCLUSION

Both Dr. Lee and his wife have lived and will continue to live the modest life they have led in New Mexico. Dr. Lee will not be a scapegoat for alleged security problems at our country's nuclear laboratories. Nor should he be used to further the political agendas of those who are illegally leaking confidential information concerning the details of the government's investigation. Upon receipt of proper security clearances, Dr. Lee's lawyers will present specific evidence of his innocence confidentially to the United States Attorney's Office for the District of New Mexico.

Like the former head of the CIA and a former security officer for the Department of Energy, whom the press claims to have improperly handled classified information, Dr. Lee is entitled to fair treatment by the government. Misleading press reports fail to note that thousands of government employees could be subject to this type of investigation regarding the storage of protected files on government computers.

We are not aware of a single instance where a government employee was ever prosecuted for saving protected files on a federal government computer system. In fact, many other government officials, who have actually taken classified national defense information to their homes or left this classified information in public places, have never been fully investigated, much less prosecuted.

Literally hundreds of foreign scientists have visited the Los Alamos (National) Laboratory each of the last several years. Thousands of e-mails and other communications went to and from Los Alamos (National) Laboratory and foreign scientists during this time period. United States nuclear scientists also took hundreds of trips to foreign countries during this time period. It would be improper and unfair to scapegoat Dr. Lee for any security lapses that may have occurred during these two decades as a result of these activities.

It was a relief to get this statement out. I hoped it would set the record straight. But we hardly noticed a change. I had said these same things many times to the government, and my attorneys spent a lot of time repeating themselves to reporters. But even with our statement, the same questions always came back, with some new government twist, like a viral mutation. Many politicians in Congress simply ignored the information that Sylvia and I had assisted the FBI.

Mark and Brian continued to handle the media swirl, which seemed to intensify as time went on. Two days after my media statement, the U.S. accidentally bombed the Chinese embassy in Belgrade. That event had nothing whatsoever to do with me, but it added to the anti-China fever that was burning around me and inflaming my life. Just reading the biased stories about me made me sick. But I had to follow the news, because it was the only way for me to find out whether the government might prosecute me—and for what. One story said that the government's case was crumbling, while another said I was going to be arrested within 10 days. Yet another story denied my imminent arrest and suggested that I might be charged with the lesser offense of mishandling classified information. All of this was extremely upsetting to me, especially knowing that other LANL employees who had violated security rules were never treated like this. Unlike them, I was threatened with the death penalty by my FBI interrogators with the apparent support of my LANL managers, the head of the DOE, many members of Congress, and even the White House.

Mark said that my case was a moving target. I believe *Newsweek* magazine described my situation accurately: "Though the case against Lee may be crumbling, the Feds appear determined to get him on something. 'I think the case will just linger and keep spiraling down,' says one top FBI official. 'Then we'll find that he spit on a sidewalk, and we'll charge him with that.'"

———

Sylvia and I stayed in LA almost until the end of May. During this time, the news was incessant, partly fueled by endless Congressional hearings about China's espionage and me. In the three months since I was fired, there were more than 20 separate hearings about my terrible acts of "espionage." By the end of the summer there would be more than 40 Congressional hearings. So many of the politicians in these hearings reminded me of the "night soil" handlers in the undeveloped country villages of Taiwan where I grew up—the collectors of human waste whose function was to keep stirring the excrement.

Here are just a few of the Congressional committees, along with their hearing dates, that were using me as a soapbox:

Senate Armed Services, and Energy and Natural Resources, March 16, 1999; House Appropriations Subcommittee on Commerce, Justice, State, and Judiciary, March 17, 1999; Senate Select Intelligence, March 17, 1999; Senate Armed Services, March 25, 1999; Senate Energy and Natural Resources, April 14, 1999; House Armed Services Subcommittee on Military Procurement, April 15, 1999; House Commerce Subcommittee on Oversight and Investigations, April 20, 1999; Senate Select Intelligence, April 29, 1999; Senate Judiciary, May 5, 1999; House Committee on Energy and Commerce, May 5, 1999; Governmental Affairs, May 20, 1999; House Science, May 20, 1999; House International Relations Subcommittee on East Asia and the Pacific, May 26, 1999; Governmental Affairs, June 9, 1999; Senate Banking, Housing and Urban Affairs, June 10, 1999; and so on.

Every politician in Washington seemed eager to show off how they were helping to catch a spy named Wen Ho Lee.

Several people who understood politics better than I did explained to me that Republicans in Congress had been criticizing President Bill Clinton's China policy for a long time. They said that the Republicans tried to embarrass Clinton by accusing Chinese American and Asian American campaign donors of being spies for

China or somehow acting for the PRC. I heard that many people, mostly Asian Americans, were investigated by the FBI because they had Asian-sounding surnames. Only a handful were found to have committed campaign violations, while the vast majority of the Asian Americans who came under investigation had done nothing wrong. Their accusers were never able to find a spy, and they were desperate to show that the Democrats allowed Chinese spies into the country. That's why I was being singled out, according to some of my friends and colleagues.

Before I was accused of being a spy, I didn't pay much attention to Republicans and Democrats. Now I was a football being kicked between them. Back then, I had never heard of this word "scapegoat." But I learned what it meant. The dictionary defines scapegoat this way: "One that bears the blame for others; one that is the object of irrational hostility." I was getting a crash course in American civics, and I felt that the dictionary taught me something important: I had become a scapegoat.

More night soil was stirred when Congress announced several reports on China's espionage and security at the labs. A special damage report on how much the PRC might have benefited if they got the W-88 design was released in April 1999. It was headed by the Director of Central Intelligence jointly prepared by the CIA, DOE, Defense Department, Defense Intelligence Agency, FBI, the National Security Agency, the State Department's Bureau of Intelligence and Research, the National Counterintelligence Center, and nuclear weapons experts from Los Alamos, Livermore, and Sandia national labs. Chaired by retired admiral David Jeremiah, this was known as the Jeremiah Report. Among its findings: It was unclear whether China used American documentation or blueprints for the W-88, and China benefited from information obtained from lots of sources, including the open literature as well as its own research efforts.

My attorneys also told me about the report from the President's Foreign Intelligence Advisory Board that came out in June 1999. Called the Rudman report, after its chair, former senator Warren

Rudman, it harshly criticized the security at the nuclear labs, citing numerous security problems and calling the DOE "a dysfunctional bureaucracy that has proven it is incapable of reforming itself." It blasted the "culture of arrogance" at the labs, how lack of cooperation by scientists undermines security efforts—I certainly wasn't alone in my attitude toward security.

Most important for me, the Rudman report said the investigation into the loss of nuclear secrets to China was too narrow—it focused only on the W-88, when the PRC double-agent "walk-in" gave details on six other warheads, and it looked only at a small sample of scientists during a brief window of time. That narrow investigation turned up only one spy suspect: me. Like the Jeremiah Report from the Director of Central Intelligence, the Rudman report questioned whether China's nuclear weapons program was based on stolen U.S. secrets: "On one end of the spectrum is the view that the Chinese have acquired very little classified information and can do little with it. On the other end is the view that the Chinese have nearly duplicated the W-88 warhead. None of these extreme views holds water."

In July, former Senator Jack Kemp issued a report, prepared by nuclear physicist Gordon Prather, that also questioned how much China's nuclear program depended on espionage against the U.S. But this report's main focus was on the security policies of Clinton's first energy secretary, Hazel O'Leary. During O'Leary's time, millions of pages of classified documents were declassified and put into the open literature as she tried to reorganize the unwieldy and esoteric classification systems. She was secretary from 1993 to 1997, the same period that I did my downloading from the red partition to the green. As a cost-saving measure, she instituted another level of security—the L clearance—that had less access than the Q clearance. Background checks for each Q Clearance cost $5,000, while the L clearance was only $50. At first the Q and the L badges were different colors, but then O'Leary mandated that they should be the same color so no one would feel like a second-class employee. Decisions like these contributed to some confusion over security dur-

ing that period, and made it hard to take some of the security measures seriously.

Mark and Brian and the other attorneys read all these reports
carefully and noted how they pointed to many flaws in an espionage
case against me. That much was good news.

But none of these reports got the dramatic media attention accorded the Cox Committee report on U.S. National Security and
the People's Republic of China, the unclassified version of which
was released in May. Named after Representative Christopher Cox,
the report painted a worst-case scenario, that China systematically
stole nuclear secrets from the U.S. on every advanced thermonuclear warhead. "No other country," said Cox, "has succeeded in
stealing so much from the U.S."

The multi-volume report claimed that every one of the 80,000
Chinese who travels to the U.S. each year is tasked by the PRC to
find high-tech tidbits, and that 3,000 U.S.-based "front" companies
have hidden Beijing connections. The report described the episode
with the walk-in agent in detail, showing the path that led to Los
Alamos and me, the prime spy suspect, and even mentioning the
summer intern I hired—the one that the *New York Times* reporter got
all wrong. "Walk-in" was defined in the report, as cited in the *Ency-
clopedia of Espionage,* as "An unheralded defector or a dangle, a
'walk-in' is a potential agent or a mole who literally walks into an embassy or intelligence agency without prior contact or recruitment."

The other reports had directly criticized the findings of the Cox
Report as too extreme, but this of course was just more juice for the
media. The talk shows presented it as the outrageous truth, and it
was headlines for the news. According to the report, I was the spy
who stole the design information for the W-88 Trident D-5 thermonuclear warhead, and this allegation again reverberated through
the echo chamber. *Time* magazine's cover featured an eye with the
Asian epicanthal fold peeking through a red star cut-out, with the title, "The Next Cold War?"

I knew something about the Cold War of the 1950s, even though I didn't come to the U.S. until 1964. As an American nuclear scientist, I helped fight and win the Cold War. But I also had read the book *Thread of the Silkworm*, by Iris Chang, about the career of Tsien Hsue-shen, one of the most brilliant students in all of China, who in 1935 was selected in a national competition to go to college in the U.S., to MIT. He became one of America's leading physicists, helping to pioneer our nation's space program—but then he came under suspicion during the Cold War. Accusations of ties with the American Communist Party and threats of a McCarthy trial and deportation destroyed his reputation and ended his teaching career at Caltech and MIT. Tsien was arrested and jailed in an INS detention prison, where a bright light was flashed on him every 15 minutes, 24 hours a day. The constant pressure and surveillance of Tsien during the McCarthy period drove him to leave his home in America and to go back to China—where he became the "father" of the Chinese ballistic missile program. Tsien's life and the treatment he received in America is a well-known tragic story among Chinese American scientists.

From Chang's book about Tsien, I learned more about the Rosenbergs and about the ordeal of other scientists, like J. Robert Oppenheimer, the founder of Los Alamos National Labs, who had his security clearance revoked after being accused of Communist ties—after he built the atom bomb. I also read that, during the 1950s, Chinese Americans became targets of suspicion. FBI director J. Edgar Hoover had federal agents tap phones in Chinatowns from New York to San Francisco and monitor Chinese newspapers and organizations. Signs seeking FBI informants were posted throughout those Chinatowns. The posters announced a "confession" program offering immigration amnesty to any Chinese who reported on others they believed to be Communists.

Knowing all this, I was surprised to find out that the Cox report blatantly distorted this history. Christopher Cox's committee report declared, "After being accused of *spying for the PRC* in the 1950s, Qian [Tsien] was *permitted* to return to the PRC. . . ." [emphasis added.] This wasn't true. Tsien was never accused of being a spy for the PRC, but was suspected of having ties to the American Communist Party. These suspicions were never proved. The Cox report deliberately lied, clearly insinuating that Tsien stole U.S. secrets for China—which was exactly the accusation against me. The report even used Iris Chang's book as a citation in three separate places to suggest that Tsien was a spy, even though her book drew the exact opposite conclusion. That lie wasn't the only misrepresentation in this official government report, which was so widely quoted and used against me.

The Cox committee, those *New York Times* reporters, the FBI, and the people who wanted me prosecuted as a spy and a traitor were so quick to label me "as bad as the Rosenbergs." Maybe they are as bad as McCarthy.

My father, Yi-Mei Lee, built our adobe house and much of our furniture. He was also a farmer who grew rice, vegetables, bananas, and yams, and maintained a tilapia fishpond. When I was a child, my brother and I swam in the pond, and fish would jump out of the pond to the banks. Fishing then was very simple — I would just pick up fish from the banks and place them in a bucket.

My mother, Shen Ko Lee, had a natural talent in math and a good memory. She liked to tell me beautiful folk stories and fairy tales. She and my father had ten children.

I was born in this house that my father built in Taiwan in a process very similar to the historic method of making adobe homes in New Mexico. (The boy in the photo is Chung in 1977.)

I graduated from National Cheng Kung University in 1963 with a Bachelor's Degree in Mechanical Engineering.

My graduate school office at Texas A&M University. While I was there, I learned that Texas had six flags — the last flag was made when "the United States joined Texas."

The mathematics department building at Texas A&M. I spent a lot of time in this building, in Professor Kent's mathematics classes and Professor Kettleborough's fluid dynamics classes.

Chung, Alberta, and Sylvia. At about the time this picture was taken, we went to the San Francisco Opera and sat near the front. While the soprano was singing Mozart, Alberta was snoring, and the two made a good duet.

Our first Christmas (1979) at an apartment in Los Alamos, waiting for our house to be built.

December 1994. I'm glad my children didn't inherit my height.

Although I worked at LANL full-time for over twenty years, fishing has been my lifelong job.

The results of a day at the river: eight fish, ranging from twelve inches to twenty-seven and a half inches.

Although I was at first worried about Alberta's safety as she crisscrossed the country speaking out about my case, I am very impressed by and grateful for her strength and perseverance. I am struck by how sad and angry she looks in these pictures. They remind me of how she would constantly say to me, "How can this be happening to my father in my country?"

The many protests and demonstrations in support of my case moved me very much. They made me appreciate how important it is to have and to use our right of free speech. These people worked so hard for me, devoting so much of their time to writing letters, organizing, and protesting on my behalf.

There were protests around the country: (clockwise from top) Sacramento, San Francisco, New York, Albuquerque.

September 13, 2000. Awake from the nightmare. I left the courthouse with my family and legal team. Here I am with my lawyers, Mark Holscher (next to me) and Nancy Hollander (behind me, with glasses), and Alberta and Chung.

Thank you, White Rock, New Mexico. I will always remember your warmth.

At our neighbor's house in White Rock, New Mexico, September 13, 2000. It's great to be back home.

CHAPTER 8

The media whirlwind was still gathering momentum. Mark and the other attorneys were a great comfort to me, a true shelter from the fury. Still, I couldn't hide out in Los Angeles forever. I thought the worst would be over as soon as the truth became known, but I didn't realize how strong the political crosscurrents were, or what an important symbol I had become to so many politicians eager to play the China card. After a month of living this nightmare and hoping that I'd soon awaken, it was time to come home and face the prospect of living under this cloud indefinitely. I was glad that our neighbors had a small break from this nonsense, because in the middle of May, I was bringing the FBI and the media back home to Los Alamos with me.

Our neighbor down the street, Mary Norris, walked her big half-collie, half-chow dog past my house twice a day. She often stopped to talk about neighborhood things—the block parties, whose kids were graduating. She and her husband had moved to White Rock in 1980. He was a chemist at the lab. After their daughter was born, Alberta and Chung took some candy to the baby, as though she could eat it. When Mary's husband died, the whole neighborhood reached out to support the Norris family. I prepared some food and brought it to Mary and her daughter.

Mary's dog patrol gave her a pretty good idea of what the FBI was up to. She observed five or six FBI cars parked throughout the neighborhood, with agents on their stakeouts, watching and photographing the goings-on in quiet White Rock. Of course, they were easy to spot in their flashy, late-model rental cars, when in Los Alamos the usual vehicle is an old truck or station wagon. They sat and watched through blistering days and long nights, speaking to no one, not even offering a hello. The neighbors watched them in return, as the agents took pictures and monitored phone calls. Every two hours, the FBI changed shifts. The cars would leave, and different cars with fresh agents would take their place. Every shift rotation set off the neighborhood dogs, and we would all hear a new round of barking and howling.

Mary told me that the news media stalked the neighborhood, looking for people who would tell them "Wen Ho Lee, evil spy" stories. They refused to listen to her and other neighbors who wanted to talk about "Wen Ho Lee, good neighbor and family man." No reporters wanted to hear it. Mary said a journalist from a national news magazine knocked on her door and asked, "What kind of vegetables does Wen Ho Lee grow in his garden? Are they all *Chinese* vegetables?" Actually, I grow all kinds of vegetables, and fruits, too. Some of my vegetables are "Chinese"—but what does that prove? Even so, Mary concluded that the FBI was worse than the media presence. Agents parked right outside her teenage daughter's bedroom window, all day and all night. Her daughter was frightened and felt like she was being watched at night. I knew the feeling myself, because I had trouble sleeping when FBI headlights would shine in my windows at night. I even asked my doctor for sleeping pills. Finally, Mary gave them a taste of their own medicine: She went up to the car parked by her daughter's room and snapped a photograph of the FBI agent who was sitting in it. The agent panicked and called for backup—and soon there was a gang of FBI agents surrounding Mary. The Los Alamos police chief, who lived in the neighborhood, had to intervene on behalf of the neighbors.

The FBI parked a big RV in the police chief's yard and used it as its base. If someone got a new car, or if visitors came to the neighborhood in an unfamiliar car, they were followed and checked out. I heard that some of the neighbor kids were afraid to go into their family's outdoor hot tub because they were being watched. Other neighbors said that there was so much electronic surveillance going on, they had trouble logging onto the Internet. I couldn't tell, because my computers had been removed and I didn't want to get any replacements, since they would surely be confiscated during the next FBI incursion. But I felt awful that this curse was now afflicting my close-knit neighborhood.

Sylvia and I tried to go about our lives in the best way we knew how, always with a half dozen cars in tow. One day we took a drive through the scenic northern New Mexico countryside I loved, to go eat at Rancho de Chimayo, one of my favorite spots for New Mexican food. We had a big party for Chung there once, when he was still in high school. The agents followed us into the crowded dining room and stood there, waiting and watching us until we finished eating and left. That day I decided to drive through the winding mountain roads to Cordova, to visit some wood-carving galleries there. When nature called and we had to make a pit stop on the small two-lane road, all the FBI cars stopped too, to watch as Sylvia did her business behind some bushes. I made light of it and told Sylvia the video would be on the evening news that night. We had a good laugh. But it was all very degrading.

Sometimes I took the "kids" fishing with me. I say this because my FBI shadows were not much older than my own kids. I heard that it made them happy when I went fishing in the mountains— they got a nice break from sitting all day in a hot car in White

Rock. Often I drove to the nearby Nambe pueblo reservation, where you have to pay a fee to enter. Each year I bought a season pass, and the Nambe Indians knew me as a regular. They were glad that I brought them so much business, with each FBI car paying an entry fee whenever I fished there. These young FBI agents would huff and puff as I hiked for miles up and down the mountains to my favorite fishing spots along the Rio Grande. When I dropped my line, they relaxed. Some would sit and sunbathe. A few asked me to pose with them for pictures—me, the celebrity spy. I lectured them, telling them all to go back to school and study computers or something with a real future, because this job they had was no good.

I worried, though, that some FBI or government agents might plan to hurt me. I no longer fished alone in the New Mexico wilderness. What if one of these people tried to kill me, and make it look like an accident? What if they tried to set me up, to make it look as if I were trying to escape to China? It seemed possible. Now when I went fishing, I told Sylvia exactly where I was going, what river, what part. I put a note in my car with a list of the license plates of the FBI agents who were following me. At the Nambe reservation, I told the Indians, If I get killed, please call my wife—it's the FBI who killed me. Now I always fish where there are other people around, so there will be witnesses. It's really a shame, because I love the pristine wilderness, but I feel that I have to watch out for people following me.

One day an elk darted out from the Ponderosa pines in front of Sylvia's car, and she crashed. Thankfully, Sylvia wasn't hurt, and the elk ran off. Another motorist gave her a ride to the hospital. Of course the FBI was right there, too, just watching. After I checked on Sylvia, I drove out to see the car. It was gone. While I was trying to figure out what to do, one of the FBI cars silently signaled for me to follow, and led me to the garage that had towed the car. The FBI knew everything.

When Chung came home for a visit from graduate school, he

helped me put up a fence along the side of our house to keep all the watchers from wandering into our backyard. Of course, Chung and Alberta became "team leaders" too—they were followed by the wagon train, same as Sylvia and me. Chung would try to shake his FBI tail, turning sharply off the windy roads of the Los Alamos mesa—roads that he knew far better than they. Or he might stop suddenly in the middle of the street. Nothing too wild—Chung is a lot like me, steady and even-tempered—but he wanted to let them know what he thought of them. Unlike Alberta, who was very alarmed by what was happening, Chung and I both felt this would soon blow over, and he would try to calm Alberta's fears.

Some people said that the FBI office in Albuquerque was trying to prove itself with me because they had lost Edward Howard, the CIA employee-turned-spy, while they were tailing him; he defected to the Soviet Union in 1985. But I had had plenty of opportunities to leave the country, if I'd wanted to. The FBI agents watched me, and I watched them, writing down descriptions of them. There were more than ten different cars to keep track of. I tried to think of it as a game, but it wasn't very funny that they questioned my friends when they stopped by to visit or when I went to their homes to give them vegetables from my garden. Each year, as the days stretched into summer, my garden yielded bountiful crops of cabbage, eggplants, stringbeans, chives, and Chinese vegetables like bok choy—pretty much anything I planted provided several harvests. I always shared my good fortune with my neighbors, friends, and coworkers, bringing them bags full of whatever was ripe.

Because of my FBI "team," I hesitated taking my homegrown vegetables to my friends. I stopped by a colleague's home one day, Jen-chieh Peng. Jen-chieh was one of the top physicists at LANL, working in the Theoretical Physics area as a Lab Fellow—a very prestigious status. His work was unclassified, not involving nuclear weapons, and he didn't have a Q clearance that could be jeopardized by contact with me. His wife, Tzehuey, also had a Ph.D., but didn't work at the lab. So I thought it would be okay to stop by his house, as I did every summer, to drop off some vegetables. After I parked my car at their house, the line of FBI cars kept circling around their narrow street.

Sure enough, when I left their house, the FBI agents paid them a visit, asking what I gave them, what we talked about, and so on. Many of the Chinese Americans at LANL were interviewed two or three times by the FBI. My whole ordeal began because I made an innocent call seventeen years earlier to someone who was under FBI surveillance—the Lawrence Livermore scientist, who was never charged with wrongdoing. I felt concerned that my Chinese American friends and colleagues might now face similar repercussions from a vindictive lab or the FBI. So I stopped visiting our friends and became a recluse, which was really not my nature. It is also out of concern for these friends and colleagues that I am not mentioning more of their names in this book.

Occasionally, some friends would run the FBI gauntlet to our house—to check up on us, to see if we were OK. Jen-chieh Peng came by one day to give me a book, *The Dialogues of Plato*, because he thought it described my situation. Plato wrote about the arrest, trial, and execution of his teacher, Socrates, who was accused of being impious and corrupting the young people of Athens. Socrates refused to ask for forgiveness for charges he believed to be unjust and invalid—and instead accepted the death sentence.

The Pengs and many of our friends belonged to the Los Alamos Chinese Cultural Association. So did the other Chinese Americans who came to live and work in Los Alamos in the late 1970s and early 1980s. When I first came to Los Alamos in 1978, there were only three or four other Chinese families, but in the 1980s there were a couple dozen. Our number was so small that we all knew each other. Most of us came from Taiwan, with a few from Hong Kong. No one in our small community back then was from the PRC, though a few, like Sylvia, had immigrated to Taiwan from the Mainland in 1949 as young children to escape the Communists. Their parents were members of the Kuomintang party, which fought against Mao and lost. A few of the Cultural Association members were like me—born in Taiwan and raised speaking the Taiwanese dialect, not the Kuomintang's Mandarin.

The Cultural Association was exactly that. We had a New Year's party in the late winter, and a Harvest Moon party at the end of summer. We gave lucky red envelopes and tasty Chinese sweets to the kids. Chung and Alberta loved the moon cakes and would eat so many I was afraid they'd get sick. Sometimes we had musical programs, often performed by our own members. Our biggest challenge was to run a Chinese language class on Saturdays for our children. We, the parents, were the volunteer teachers. My kids complained about going, especially when I was teaching. But Sylvia and I insisted that they should not only learn to speak Chinese, but to read and write as well. We were not very successful on that front.

Politics was not a part of our association's purpose or function. But sometimes it seeped in. Once there was tension between the families who had close ties to the Kuomintang and its secret police and those who felt that Taiwan should be independent and democratic. As a native Taiwanese, I sympathized more with Taiwan independence; I was not, however, interested in being political. None of this had anything to do with the PRC—but I'm sure the FBI has gone through the membership list of the Chinese Cultural Association with a fine-tooth comb and interviewed all of its members. I'm sorry that they have FBI files now too.

————

Being among the other families from Taiwan would remind me of my own roots and why I get such pleasure from gardening and fishing. I grew up in the rural countryside of central Taiwan. My parents were subsistence farmers—we ate whatever we grew or caught. We lived in a dirt house, like the adobe brick homes on the pueblos, with dirt floors and none of the modern amenities, like running water or indoor plumbing. The climate was always hot and humid, so I went barefoot, with only a thin pair of shorts for clothing until I was in middle school. That's when I got my first pair of flip-flops—real shoes came much later. Every day, my brothers and I went fishing in the streams and ponds for frogs, shrimp, and snakes as well as fish. This supplemented the rice we grew. Without it, we'd have no protein.

Not many of the other scientists in the Los Alamos Chinese Cultural Association were from backwater villages like mine. But we had a shared history of growing up in post-World War II Taiwan, after the fifty-year Japanese occupation, living under KMT rule, struggling in the shadow of Communist China. We had a common culture and language—and the experience of coming to the United States as students, the first pioneers of the brain drain from Taiwan in the mid- and late 1960s. So Sylvia and I were active in our small cultural association, going to dinners and playing bridge. It had always given me great pleasure to share my fish and my vegetables with my friends.

Then there was another reason for my garden—my cancer. As I've said, the surgery for colon cancer in 1987 left me feeling pretty weak and mentally foggy for a year or two. I had had a strong reaction to the anesthesia and didn't fully regain my memory until 1989. It was up to Sylvia to delve into the available cancer research and join cancer support groups to find out how I could improve my chances of survival. We completely eliminated red meat, eating instead my fresh-caught fish, as well as organic chicken that Sylvia bought from a special store in Albuquerque. We began eating only the freshest organic foods—with my garden as the primary source. We drank only bottled water. Sylvia instituted the rule that we would eat no foods that had been grown in another time zone. If the food came from another time zone, it wasn't fresh enough.

Sylvia's regimen was an abrupt change for the family. No more stir-fried flank steak, one of my specialties. The children were just teenagers, and they missed their McDonald's and Sonic Drive-In burgers. But Sylvia's new diet worked for me. Back then, I didn't know if I had two months or two years to live. I worried about Sylvia raising the kids by herself.

After my two-year milestone passed with no recurrence of cancer, I told Sylvia, "I think I'll be able to see the kids through college." When I reached my seven-year milestone with no cancer, the doctors said I was in the clear. By then, my kids were in college, and I began to feel more comfortable about the future. Only now, with the FBI surrounding me, was my future again uncertain.

In May, a significant letter about my case appeared in the *Wall Street Journal*. Harold Agnew, one of the revered nuclear physicists of Los Alamos who started with the Manhattan Project and retired as lab director, wrote a letter debunking some of the rhetoric about China and the W-88. During his tenure as LANL's director, Agnew oversaw the design of the W-88. On May 17, 1999, the *Wall Street Journal* printed the following:

In my opinion those who are screaming the loudest in Washington have little knowledge or understanding with regard to the issues at hand. The Chinese nuclear establishment, most of whom have studied in the West, are extremely competent. They may indeed be curious as to what the U.S. has developed with its technology, but we have also been curious as to what they have developed and fielded. From time to time they have been in our kitchen looking for recipes and we have poked around theirs. Our general public has no knowledge as to how successful we have been, and their population is also in the dark with regard to their successes. . . .

As long as any nation has a demonstrated nuclear capability and a means of delivering its bombs and warheads it doesn't really matter whether the warheads are in a little smaller [*sic*] or painted a color other than red, white and blue. I suspect information published in the open by the National Resources Defense Council has been as useful to other nations as any computer codes they may have received by illegal means.

Being able actually to use information from any of the national laboratories' codes requires a great deal more knowledge than following a cake recipe. It's even questionable as to whether the Chinese computers are compatible with the weapons codes at our national laboratories. . . . Ideas are welcome, but copying seldom, if ever, occurs.

The design of the W-88—the most advanced U.S. nuclear warhead, used in the Trident system—is actually quite old. The basic test was done by the Los Alamos Scientific Laboratory (not National Laboratory) when I was director, and I retired 20 years ago. It is a "delicate" and neat package. Having a computer printout as I remember them would give the general idea, but actually being able to manufacture the total system from a computer code is a different matter. No nation would ever stockpile any device based on another nation's computer codes. Maybe for security reasons the originator has a "virus" that would result in a dud if the codes were to be followed exactly. Not an unreasonable concept.

In any event, whether or not China or any other nation has profited from this information, if indeed they have received it, will be known only if they conduct a nuclear test in the right yield range. If China doesn't resume testing, no harm will possibly have been done other than to our egos.

Harold Agnew's letter was a welcome voice of reason at a time when the murky politics surrounding my case seemed more like an out-of-control nuclear breeder reactor. My attorneys and I hoped it would slow the hysteria in Washington. Here was an undisputed, respected expert on nuclear weapons, and one who had been an advisor to presidents on nuclear policy, casting doubt on the wild claims of the Cox Commission. I had said all along to Mark and the attorneys that my brief conversations with the Chinese scientists at the 1986 and 1988 conferences were inconsequential to weapons design. Even if the codes I downloaded with password protections had somehow fallen into China's hands, they would be of little use. Agnew made the point crystal clear.

Several other scientists also came forward to critique the Cox report and its frightening claims. The prestigious Federation of Atomic Scientists began to talk about my case on their website, calling out the wild inaccuracies in the claims that were being made about nuclear science. The Federation was founded by nuclear weapons scientists from the Manhattan Project, and it had been monitoring my case from the beginning. Its website, *www.fas.org*, posted news and documents about my case and discussed the dangers of bad policy decisions that could make security so tight that scientists wouldn't be able to do their jobs. These scientists didn't know me, but they were speaking up for the scientific truth. They also warned against the racial targeting of the many scientists of Chinese or Asian descent who work for our nation's defense, especially when politicians like Senator Richard Shelby, chairman of the Select Committee on Intelligence, were calling for a moratorium on all foreign visitors to the labs.

Alberta and my lawyers gave me articles printed from the Internet and the FAS website. These provided me with a lot more information about the W-88 warhead I was accused of giving to China. In the May 1999 issue of the *Bulletin of Atomic Scientists*, Stephen Schwartz, a physicist and the executive director of the Educational Foundation for Nuclear Science, described China's nuclear weapons outlook. He said China's nuclear arsenal is much smaller than ours and that their limited arsenal is suitable for their needs. According to his report, China has a total of some 400 warheads, with only about 20 capable of reaching the U.S. This is in contrast to the 8,300 operational warheads of the U.S., almost all capable of hitting targets in the PRC. China's long-range ballistic missiles carry a single warhead and take longer to launch because they use liquid fuel, while all 982 U.S. ballistic missiles, including the W-88, have multiple warheads and use fast-loading solid fuel.

I had never paid much attention to the specifics of international nuclear weapons policy, but I found the FAS articles to be helpful in unraveling the misinformation directed against me. From them, I learned more about the forces and issues that had a stake in me. Schwartz explained that China did not need the expensive, high-tech warheads:

In any event, it takes only a few nuclear weapons—or perhaps just the capability to manufacture them—to achieve deterrence. Anything beyond that is irrelevant from a security standpoint unless one seeks a nuclear war-fighting posture, something China has not shown any interest in. During the Cold War, the United States built 70,000 warheads and spent more than $5.5 trillion (in constant 1996 dollars) on nuclear weapons and weapons-related programs, figures that no country could or would want to match. China's estimated total annual military budget is $35 billion—about what the United States spends each year on its nuclear weapons programs alone. . . . Whatever the final outcome of this case, Americans must guard against turning the national laboratories—and the country—into a fortress against threats both real and imagined. They must avoid, in Henry Kissinger's words, a "nostalgia for confrontation." Warns former defense secretary William Perry, "If we treat China as an enemy, it will surely become one." If that happens, American society and science will be the big losers.

Of course, these weren't the only interpretations of the Cox Commission report. Many articles and talk shows banged the drum against the insidious spying techniques of China, which characterized Chinese Americans as potential, and easy, espionage targets. This kind of derogatory reference to Chinese people and culture, which appeared in the *Washington Post* two weeks after I was fired, was common: "China's spying, they say, more typically involves cajoling morsels of information out of visiting foreign experts and tasking thousands of Chinese abroad to bring secrets home one at a time like ants carrying grains of sand. The Chinese have been assembling such grains of sand since at least the fourth century B.C., when the military philosopher Sun Tzu noted the value of espionage in his classic work, *The Art of War*."

I hoped that the voices of Harold Agnew and other highly respected American scientists would counter the sensationalism of news reports poisoned by leaks and lies and political grandstanding. Their reasoned perspectives and expertise seemed to have an impact, providing reporters with the information that could help them look more critically at the FBI's Kindred Spirit espionage investigation.

I learned later that there were other developments at work. Further critiques were being made of Trulock's Kindred Spirit probe. At some of the Congressional hearings held during this time period, counterintelligence officers familiar with Kindred Spirit and my case were asked to provide testimony. One of those counterintelligence officers was Bob Vrooman, who had worked at LANL. Vrooman was the security official who had debriefed me on my 1988 China trip.

Bob Vrooman later would make a public statement about my case, but as early as May 1999, he was testifying as to what he saw, even when it didn't match the official government "party line." He wrote the following letter to Senator Conrad Burns, of Montana, where he moved after his retirement from LANL; the letter was later entered into the court record of my case as an exhibit:

[dated May 11, 1999]
Dear Senator Burns:

I am a new constituent and noticed that you are on the Energy and Natural Resources Committee, which recently held hearings on Chinese espionage at the DOE Laboratories. I recently retired from Los Alamos National Laboratory, where I was the chief counterintelligence officer from 1987 to 1998.

I found the tone of the hearings very upsetting. Senator Murkowski implied that the Los Alamos National Laboratory should have fired or removed Mr. Lee from access as soon as he was suspected of espionage. He suggested that Los Alamos did not take the Lee case seriously until it was leaked to the *New York Times*. The answer to this allegation is brutally simple. The administrative inquiry (AI), done by Mr. Trulock's staff at DOE that identified Lee as a suspect was seriously flawed and lacked intellectual rigor. There was no evidence in this AI that Lee had passed any classified information to the Chinese.

In my 30-year intelligence career I have done many administrative inquiries involving counterintelligence issues. I am also familiar with other counterintelligence investigations. The single distinguishing feature of the AI that identified Lee was the complete lack of evidence that he committed espionage. I, of course, can not comment on the details of the AI because it is classified. I can, however, note that ethnicity was a crucial component in identifying Lee as a suspect. Caucasians with the same background as Lee were ignored.

My staff and I worked closely with the FBI agent assigned to this case. One of our major concerns was to protect Mr. Lee's civil rights. We were particularly concerned because the case against Lee was so weak. . . . I have dealt with scientists for many years, and there is nothing more precious to a scientist than his reputation. . . . It is very important in a scientific institution like Los Alamos to protect reputations and keep derogatory information confidential.

It is also important to allow the FBI to conduct espionage investigations without interference from partisan politics. The FBI agent assigned to this case has a law degree and was concerned about the lack of evidence. In my opinion the FBI conducted this investigation entirely appropriately. . . .

The ethnic issue also surfaced in comments made to us by some people in the DOE's Office of Counterintelligence that ethnic Chinese should not be allowed to work on nuclear weapons.

I have also noticed the ethnic issue in some comments made in congressional hearings. During several hearings that I have either participated in or have watched, the issue of espionage committed by a U.S. citizen with legal access to classified information leads to the conclusion that there should be a ban on foreign visitors to the Labs. The logic of this escaped me until I realized that the connection was not logic but race. I hope that you will vote against any effort to stop foreign visitors to the DOE laboratories.

In the late 19th century, Alfred Dreyfus, a Jewish French artillery officer, was accused of espionage. The evidence was weak but he was convicted. His conviction included a mass media campaign, which divided France. The Dreyfus affair was the prelude to the horrible anti-Semitism of the 20th century. It is my hope that the Lee affair is not the prelude to a 21st century that includes rampant anti-Chinese racism.

For the record, I am not a Sinophile. I have a long record of serving the U.S. both in combat in Vietnam and as a CIA case officer. I was also a conservative Republican, but have registered as an independent since moving to Montana. Our party's scare mongering regarding the Chinese disgusts me.

Bob Vrooman's wasn't the only testimony that cast doubt on Kindred Spirit. U.S. Attorney General Janet Reno appeared before the Senate Judiciary Committee regarding the espionage case against me. The DOJ did not pursue a search warrant of my X Division office because they did not have enough evidence to show probable cause that I had committed a crime to justify the warrant. Some members of Congress were demanding Reno's resignation, in part because she wouldn't bow to political demands that weren't supported by law. From everything she had seen, Kindred Spirit had not produced enough evidence for her to support the probable cause necessary for a search warrant, let alone to charge me with the capital crime of espionage.

It was apparent to my attorneys that there was a shift in the wind. Kindred Spirit and the espionage case against me seemed to be self-destructing. But without ever admitting their blunder, without acknowledging that I was innocent of espionage, or at least could never be so charged, the FBI and DOJ began to shift their focus on me, looking instead at the downloaded files. We soon learned that Kindred Spirit had morphed into a new investigation called Operation Sea Change. It was a hybrid change—they could keep the insinuation of espionage without the cumbersome need to produce real evidence. As Mark Holscher had said, I was a moving target.

If for one moment I harbored the notion that the abandonment of espionage charges might signal an end to this madness, the FBI ripped that hope from me on June 9, 1999. That was the day they swooped down, dragnet-style, on the closest members of my family as though they were dangerous criminals or racketeers. Simultaneously, across the country, FBI agents issued subpoenas and demands for immediate interrogation to my children, my brothers and sister, and my niece. From the East Coast to the Midwest to the West Coast, the FBI knocked on the doors of my loved ones, hoping to interrogate them all at the same time.

It was about 11 A.M. eastern standard time on Wednesday, June

9, when Alberta's boss's boss called her into his office. Her own supervisors weren't in, so the top manager called her to say that the FBI was there to ask her some questions. The FBI agents told her, "You should talk to us—your father is in very serious trouble." Alberta started crying and shaking and told the FBI that she had a lawyer. Then they slapped her with a subpoena to appear before a grand jury in Albuquerque on June 14. Alberta immediately contacted Chung in Ohio to warn him not to speak to the FBI—they were knocking on his apartment door as she phoned him. She notified attorney Brian Sun, who had represented Sylvia when the FBI attempted to subpoena her in May. Brian had sent the government a letter on Sylvia's behalf, asserting spousal privilege, which protected Sylvia from testifying against me because she is my wife.

Within a few minutes, the FBI also contacted my sister Angela and my brother Wentou in Los Angeles, and my brother Wenming and his wife, Patty, in Northern California. My siblings all spoke briefly with the FBI agents, submitting to short interviews, not knowing they could refuse. They, too, were subpoenaed to appear before the grand jury.

It was even more distressing to learn that FBI agents also bothered my niece Lori, in Minnesota. Lori is three years older than Chung, and she is the older sister of William, the nephew I took to Taiwan. It was her mother and younger brother who died in the horrible home invasion only two years earlier. Her father—my brother Wentou—had been injured in the attack and was not doing well. I was very distressed to think that my problems were now adding to her family worries. Lori was a very bright student and had a master's degree in electrical engineering. LANL had hired her as an intern for two summers while she was a college student, and she lived at our home in White Rock during that time. Lori was now married and working in Minnesota. We found out too late that the FBI came to her house at 10 A.M. central daylight time. She also didn't know that she could refuse to answer their questions. Agent Robert

Messemer, the one who gave "mistaken" testimony to Judge Parker about me, traveled to Minnesota to interrogate my niece. For five hours, Messemer and another agent questioned Lori in her home. When they left, they seized her home computers.

My family members were subpoenaed to appear before a grand jury in Albuquerque on the following Monday, June 14. Brian Sun agreed to represent all these relatives pro bono. He was able to get Robert Gorence, the Assistant U.S. Attorney, to delay the grand jury for a few days, until Friday, June 18. In those few days, Brian met with my relatives to determine what the FBI asked them and what the grand jury intended to focus on. Though I felt terrible about this sweep of my family, I didn't talk to any of them about these events. I wanted to tell them how sorry I was that my troubles were spilling into their lives, but my lawyers felt it would be better for me not to discuss any of this with them. They wanted to see if the government planned to prosecute any of my family members—or to use them as witnesses against me.

Much later, I learned from my family that the FBI dragnet and the grand jury on June 18 had focused on issues related to my downloading of the files and the tapes that I made. The FBI wanted to know if I had ever given any computer-related materials to my relatives; if I had asked them to store anything for me; if I used any storage lockers; if I had asked my family to ship or mail any items for me; if I had possession of any classified documents or files; if I had ever downloaded files; if they had any information about my finances or money from the PRC or Taiwan; if they had ever seen an IBM 6150 computer tape cartridge—the kind I used to make my tapes.

Though we didn't know it then, all of this was evidence that the investigation of me had indeed shifted from "Wen Ho Lee, the Evil Spy" to "Wen Ho Lee, the Evil Downloader." Operation Sea Change was now the dominant play against me. Unknown to us, FBI Agent Messemer was spearheading a drive to check every locker and storage facility in New Mexico, in case I was storing secret, classified documents or tapes somewhere. Newspapers reported that more than 100 FBI agents and other personnel were on my case, spending more than $80,000 a day to investigate and watch me—more than my annual salary every day. With an investment like that, they *had* to find something to hang me with.

CHAPTER 9

It's hard to express just how deeply disturbed I was by the FBI sweep and grand jury probe of my family members. Throughout this ordeal, I felt that I would be able to withstand whatever indignities and humiliation they heaped on *me*. They had already taken away my job, my good name and reputation, my future. But I was almost 60, my children were grown, and I found courage in the truth: I had not given away any classified information, I didn't do anything to harm my country, I didn't do the terrible things I was accused of.

Now they were going after my family. Maybe they wanted Alberta to lose her job, and Chung to flunk out of medical school, to ruin their lives and put more pressure on me. After all the millions of taxpayers' dollars the government had already spent over the years to find something to charge me with, they still came up empty-handed, with not even a motive linking me to any wrongdoing for the PRC or any foreign power. This seemed to infuriate the politicians in Washington, who were in a feeding frenzy for a Chinese spy, and they were demanding my neck. Presidential candidate

Patrick Buchanan said I represented the worst penetration of the nuclear labs "since the Rosenbergs went to the electric chair in 1953." Senator Richard Shelby, the chairman of the Select Committee on Intelligence, said I committed "the worst breach that we've had in many, many years." Senator Frank Murkowski claimed I was responsible for "the greatest loss of nuclear military secrets in our nation's history." Though I had never given much thought to the political parties before, I was now very aware that these were Republicans trying to blame the Democrats because of me, and they were pressuring Clinton administration officials like Bill Richardson to take action. Senator John McCain, another presidential candidate, said, "What is incredibly disturbing is apparently the administration didn't take the charges seriously. Congress wasn't informed." Senator Trent Lott, the majority leader, warned, "I think Congress is going to have to toughen up in dealing with this administration, particularly when it comes to China."

Such strong words coming from big shots in Washington. Now it was time to persecute my family. I sat in White Rock, watching the FBI watch me, helpless to do anything to protect my loved ones. I'm sure this would be painful for anyone, and it was especially so for me because my family has always been the center and the foundation of my life—my extended family as well as my own wife and children. To say that we are close-knit would not adequately convey how close we really are.

Growing up in a rural village in central Taiwan, my family had almost nothing in worldly possessions. My parents and the 10 of us youngsters relied on one another for our survival. Home for us was a three-room adobe mud house. Our garden plot was less than half the size of my backyard in White Rock. We grew vegetables in our garden, and raised some chickens, ducks, geese, and pigs. We lived off what we grew, and there was nothing left over. My brothers and sisters and I caught fish and frogs every day for our dinner. I was good at catching fish with my bare hands. I didn't get my first shoes until I was a teenager. But I never felt poor—everybody around us was getting by just as we were.

My grandparents had come to Taiwan with their two young sons in 1905 from Fujian province on the coast of China. One of the boys would become my father. Back then, people were starving in Fujian, living from meal to meal. The garden island of Taiwan, a bit longer and wider than the state of New Jersey, was just 100 miles east of Fujian, across a narrow strait. The Fujianese knew of the rich fertile soil there, and even had a saying, "If you have one hoe, you can survive in Taiwan." My father was just a small boy when he and his family got into a boat crowded with a couple dozen people and crossed the Taiwan Strait. They found their way to Nantou, which was hardly even a village then. The land was wild and uncultivated, very primitive. My grandfather farmed and also hunted for wild boar in the hills. There were plenty of wild boar in those days, up in the mountains surrounding Nantou. Grandfather would make traps using a sharp hook rigged up to a metal chain and a spring, which was connected to a string stretched across the boar's path in the woods. When a boar crossed the string and set off the trigger, the needle would shoot into the boar—not killing it, but trapping it. Every few days my grandfather would check his traps. When he bagged a boar, he killed it with a long spear and carried it home on his back, walking several miles down the mountain to the village. After a few years, a wild boar got loose from his trap and attacked him, breaking his leg. It took him three days to get down from the mountain, and he died shortly afterward from tetanus.

My grandmother remarried. At the time, my father was only about ten years old, but he and his brother knew that their mother could not support them and the younger children she had had with my grandfather. So the two boys left the village to live as homeless squatters in the mountainous rainforest. They built a little adobe hut near a creek, in a small clearing on the mountain, and lived by hunting and fishing. I knew the spot when I was a boy, and it was one of my favorite places, set in a bamboo forest that flowed like the ocean whenever the wind blew. There are many monkeys in the forest, and the creek is full of perch, eel, small crab, and shrimp.

My father and uncle were able to live off the mountain, but they were penniless and not exactly great marriage prospects. Eventually, my father met my mother, who came from a family in the same small village. She was an only child, and her family consented to the marriage with my father with the understanding that one son would take on my mother's family name, so that their lineage would continue. I wrote out our family tree a few years ago, but the FBI took it when they searched my house.

When my mother and father were married in 1920, my father moved into her family home and began working their small plot of land. My mother was 16, and my father was 21. Over the next twenty-seven years, they had ten children, five boys and five girls. My eldest sibling, my brother Wenyee, was born in 1922. I, the seventh child and fourth son, was born in 1939. By then, the older children had moved out, but they still helped with the family. In our house there was one large bed, made of some boards covered with rice straw and a mat of woven rice straw. Six or seven of us would sleep on it together. When one of us turned, we all had to turn—that's how close we were.

We spent our days fishing, growing our crops, and foraging for food. We grew vegetables, rice, and sugar cane. Even our games revolved around food—digging up sweet potatoes from neighboring fields and cooking them in little ovens that we kids built out of dirt clods. After roasting them for an hour or so in a fire we fed with sticks and leaves, we'd have a delicious snack. Or we would follow the train cars loaded with sugar cane, and run alongside to grab a stalk. We peeled back the tough brown outer fibers and chewed on the sweet, delicious pulp. In the sugar cane fields, we hunted for beehives. We knocked them down with a stick—of course we got stung, but it was worth it. We'd eat the honey out of the hives, larvae and all—it was like candy. That was our fun—much better than the video games kids spend their time on today.

My mother wanted us to go to school and get an education. She never had a formal education, but she was very good at math and could do many complex computations in her head. She taught us how to do that. But up until I was seven or eight, I didn't know what school was. On my first day, my mother took me to the classroom, where there were about 40 or 50 other kids in the class. I was afraid, but my mother stood outside the classroom window the whole day, letting me know she was there, waiting for me. I watched her all day, and when school was over, she took me home. Then next day she told me I would be okay by myself. It was very special that my mother took me to school, because from the time that I was a small boy, my mother was sick with asthma. There were days when she lay down all day, unable to do anything. We couldn't afford to get medical treatment or pay for medicine. My mother tried to take her own life several times so that she wouldn't be a burden to our family— one of us kids had to be by her side constantly to watch her.

When I was born, the Japanese Army occupied Taiwan. Taiwanese people were second-class citizens. There was a school for the Japanese, and a separate school for the Taiwanese. The Taiwanese had to speak Japanese. My family says that I spoke Japanese when I was a little boy, but I don't remember any of it. They tell a story about Japanese soldiers who came to our home looking for rice one day. The soldiers asked me, "How many bowls of rice did you eat today?" The rice we grew was rationed and we would be punished, perhaps even killed, if we didn't give our extra rice to the Japanese. My family says I replied, "Only one bowl," to the soldiers. I don't remember this incident, but life was very harsh under the Japanese occupation. By the time I was five, Japan had lost World War II, and everyone was happy to see the Japanese leave and to win our freedom.

But the celebration didn't last long. Beginning in 1945, Chiang

Kaishek, head of the Kuomintang party which had been fighting the Communists for control of China, sent thousands of troops to Taiwan, to use our island as a base to fight the Communists. They were Chinese and we were ethnic Chinese, but the KMT soldiers treated the Taiwanese Chinese as the spoils of war, raping women and girls, stealing and looting, killing Taiwanese who resisted. On February 28, 1947, a day that we remember as "2-28," Chiang Kaishek's soldiers killed more than 20,000 Taiwanese, including all the doctors, teachers, and intellectuals. I was just a boy, but I remember that it was a big event. My oldest brother had many friends who were killed.

When Chiang Kaishek lost to Mao Zedong in 1949, the "temporary" KMT presence became permanent. The Chinese from mainland China were only 15 percent of the population, but they ruled by military force over the Taiwanese, who made up the 85 percent majority. We used to say that the Japanese occupation was harsh, but at least the trains ran on time and the country was clean. Under the Chinese KMT, the country was dirty, and nothing worked.

Today, Taiwan has a democratic government that developed after martial law finally ended in 1987, after forty years, but the politics was very corrupt when I was young. In those days, Taiwan was a military state, and my elementary school was regimented as well. Every day, we lined up like little soldiers, and the principal inspected us. The flag of the Republic of China was raised and the national anthem blared. Subjects like history or geography were boring, full of propaganda. Because of that, I didn't care much for them and instead focused on math, which I was good at. It was drummed into us that "Chiang Kaishek is the greatest man in the whole world; Mao Zedong is the worst man in the world and ruined China; the PRC is the worst country in the world." If anyone said otherwise, they would get into big trouble. Many people "disappeared" and were presumed to be killed by the government.

Growing up like this taught me to stay away from politics. In fact, my knowledge of the corrupt government in Taiwan is the reason why I contacted the scientist from Lawrence Livermore in 1982. I thought he might have gotten in trouble with the KMT government for giving a presentation there, and I wanted to know more because I was going to give a talk in Taiwan. Of course, I had no idea he was being investigated and wiretapped for possibly giving secrets to the PRC, the way I was accused. I thought he was in trouble with the Taiwan government.

My mother encouraged me to study hard so that I could have a better life. My father didn't care about education, and he wanted at least one of his sons to work with him on the family farm. So my third brother—Wentou, the father of William and Lori—volunteered to quit middle school to help. It was my eldest brother, Wenyee, who made it possible for us younger kids to get an education. He was a businessman by the time I was in elementary school, and he brought me to stay with him and his wife so that I could attend better schools in Taipei, the largest city in Taiwan. I attended Long Ang, a big elementary school there. When all the other kids were asleep during nap time, I went out to a big canal of crystal clear water at the front of the school to catch shrimp in my empty lunch pail. I ate them raw—they were delicious.

Each summer, I went back to my village in Nantou to stay with my family. I'd see my friends, help my parents and younger siblings, and spend hours fishing in the mountain streams. When my brother moved to another big city, Kaohsiung, I went with him. At school there, in the sixth grade, I had a wonderful teacher who gave me books of translated Western literature to read and encouraged me to think about my education and my future. He told me that I was good at math and one day I could become a scientist or engineer. I didn't even know what a scientist or engineer was, but I began to think about it.

My eldest brother saw that I was good in school, and he urged me to go to college. At one point, however, he had to move back to Taipei. He paid a neighbor to cook and look after me so that my education wouldn't be disrupted. Later, I moved in with an older sister who lived an hour from the school by train, so I commuted every day to school. Near my middle school, I found a place where I could catch fish in the mud, using my bare hands. The fish were small, like sardines, and I scooped them out of the mud carefully and washed them off. After filling my lunch pail with 20 or 30 fish, I took them home for dinner.

I started high school in Taipei, living with my second brother. But in 1955, when I was sixteen, my mother died. After years of suffering from asthma and feeling as though she was a burden to the family, my mother finally managed to commit suicide. When my sisters were out of the house, she hung herself from the wooden gate of our rice storage bin. One of my younger sisters found her and was so traumatized that she was never the same afterward.

Later that year, my appendix ruptured. I had emergency surgery and the anesthesia caused me to lose my memory for a time. It was a very hard year for my family and me. I then went to live with my eldest brother again, this time in the city of Keelung, and I resumed high school there. In high school, I became close friends with four other boys. All of us went on to get Ph.D.s in physics or engineering, and the four of us ended up in the United States. One of my friends was so poor that he would walk to the train station every day with a bag of coal to sell pieces to people. He'd make $1 to bring home to his family. His lunch pail only had plain rice. My sister-in-law would give me a little extra meat and vegetables to give to my friend. Compared to him, I was rich. But he became the number-one graduate in our high school, and got a scholarship to National Taiwan University, the top university in Taiwan.

I didn't make it to Taiwan National. In 1959, I went to the number-two school, National Cheng Kung University in Tainan. My eldest brother paid for my tuition. I loved literature and poetry, but I decided to major in physics, because that's what all my friends did. The fact that two Chinese American scientists—Chen Ning Yang at

Princeton and Tsung-Dao Lee at Columbia—won the Nobel Prize in physics in 1957 also motivated many Chinese students of my generation to go into the sciences. Later I switched to mechanical engineering when I realized that department was stronger. There I discovered fluid dynamics and hydrodynamics, and I found beauty in using mathematics to describe the motion of liquids and gases. I learned Lagrangian, Eulerian, and other numerical methods to describe the physics that takes place.

My father died while I was in college. In 1962, I was performing my obligatory military service near Nantou just before classes resumed in September. For young men in Taiwan, military service was mandatory, and in the summers I had to go into the equivalent of the ROTC. I went to visit my father, and spent the day with him. My father was a poor farmer all his life, but he was an honest man, so gentle and kind to me. He told me to come back the next day with my friends, and he would cook me a chicken. He went out in the yard and chased a chicken into a cage for our dinner the next day. When I came back the next morning, my father had suffered a stroke. He was still alive when I got to his bedside. I held his hand until his heart stopped beating. Later I went out to the yard, and I saw the chicken he had planned to cook. In spite of my sadness, I let it out of the cage and said, "You're a very lucky bird."

Before I did my compulsory military training, I was already aware of the corruption in Taiwan's Kuomintang government. Everybody in Taiwan knew it was dangerous to oppose the government. But in the military, I could see it firsthand. As a college student, I served as an officer, in charge of career soldiers who spent their days using military requisition sheet metal to make barbecue ovens, which they sold on the black market. The metal, supplies, and equipment were all government issue, mostly from the U.S. There was nothing I could do about it—I could see that these men and their families couldn't survive on the few dollars they were paid each month. The military was so corrupt and inefficient. My second eldest brother died while he was in the service, after contracting a simple, treatable illness, because his superiors wouldn't let him get some medication. My family was very angry with the military for my brother's senseless death.

These were some of the key events that shaped my early life and my relationship with my family. My parents and my elder siblings did everything they could to bring me up, to educate me, even though they had so little. Of course, I wanted to help them and my younger siblings when I was in a position to do so. When my third brother, Wentou, needed someone to take his son William to Taiwan in 1998, I could not refuse, even though my wife and children didn't want me to go, even though I might look bad at the lab—and even though this trip to Taiwan triggered DOE secretary Bill Richardson and counterintelligence chief Ed Curran and the FBI to launch their interrogations of me.

Given my experiences growing up in Taiwan, I have never been able to understand why educated Americans could so readily accept without question that I am a spy for the PRC, Taiwan, or any other country. Just because we are ethnic Chinese doesn't mean we are the same. America offered my family the opportunity for a better life, a life of freedom. All of my siblings who were able to move here have done so, building lives with their children and grandchildren, as Americans. Why would I want to join up with the PRC, when their scientists don't earn enough for a cup of coffee? I never doubted that the United States is the best place for my family—that is, until I was singled out as a traitor because I am Chinese American. And now they were after my family. I couldn't imagine anything much worse.

———

Such thoughts were in my mind when I faced my next ordeal the week following the sweep of my family: This time, it was a special "proffer" meeting with the government prosecutors. Mark Holscher

and Tina Hua flew to Albuquerque from LA, and Dan Bookin, a senior partner, arrived from the O'Melveny and Myers San Francisco
office on June 24, 1999—not even one week after the FBI hauled in
my relatives before a grand jury. It was the first time I met Dan, a
pleasant, businesslike man who was older than Mark. Like Mark and
Brian Sun, Dan had once been an assistant U.S. attorney. In fact, he
had worked with FBI director Louis Freeh in New York City on a big
organized crime case to clean up the Fulton Street fish market.

The purpose of the proffer meeting was to assess if the government was going to charge me with a crime, and it was an opportunity for my lawyers to show why they shouldn't. At the U.S.
attorney's office in downtown Albuquerque, adjacent to the Hyatt
Hotel, we met with the prosecutors in an interesting arrangement.
The prosecution team convened in one room and my lawyers were
in another room, while I sat in a separate room down the hall. John
Kelly, the U.S. attorney for New Mexico, was there along with another government prosecutor, Robert Gorence. So were three FBI
agents: David Kitchen, who headed the Albuquerque FBI office;
Robert Messemer, who had just interrogated my niece Lori in Minnesota; and another agent. The prosecutors posed questions for me
to my lawyers, who then came to me with each question after discussing it with the prosecutors and among themselves. I answered,
and they relayed the answer back. The prosecutors couldn't question me directly, and nothing I said was supposed to be used against
me. It was a kind of exploratory, "getting to know you" meeting, but
in reverse—we hoped they would decide not to see me again.

At this time, it was very clear that the government was aban-
doning its theory that I committed espionage and stole the W-88 secrets. Through my lawyers, they asked me again about my travel to
China, about my employment and my consulting work, but now
their focus was on my use of the LANL computer system. With
each question, my lawyers came into the room where I was sitting,
then went back to the other room to convey my answer.

The prosecutors asked about tapes of my files. There were no tapes anymore, because I had destroyed them. So I replied, "There are no tapes." That was a misstatement. I meant that there were no longer any tapes.

Mark and Dan gave them my answer, then came back. I knew there was a problem. "They say they have a record of your tapes, they say you made tapes. What about them?" I swallowed hard and apologized to Mark and Dan. I replied, "I did make tapes, but then I destroyed them. I meant that no tapes exist any longer."

For the first time in all my dealings with the FBI since this episode, I made a misstatement. I'm not perfect, and I would bet that anyone who had to go through as many interrogations as I have would make a mistake or two. I did much better than the government, which had lied about me so many times. After all the interrogations I had been through, this time—in the words of FBI Agent Robert Messemer—I made a "misstatement." The government already had the answer. I learned later that they were looking for information about the tapes when they questioned my family members in front of the grand jury.

My attorneys told the prosecutors that the tapes were destroyed. From that point on, the only thing the prosecutors wanted to know was what I had done with the tapes, but they offered no protections against prosecution, so my attorneys refused. As I expected, they made a big deal out of my "misstatement" about the tapes—leaking the incident to Congress and the media as another proof of my "deceptive nature" and therefore my guilt, even though what transpired in the proffer meeting was not supposed to be used against me.

U.S. Attorney Kelly said they would decide within a week whether they would file charges against me. Because my case was so infected by politics at every level, with Congressional Democrats and Republicans calling for my immediate indictment, Mark and Dan requested a meeting in Washington with Department of Justice officials and the prosecutors.

The political armies were amassing their forces against me. But at one Senate hearing, the Thompson-Lieberman governmental affairs committee, a high ranking DOJ official named Alan Kornblum was questioned for denying the FBI a search warrant of my office computer. Kornblum told senators that there wasn't probable cause to justify a search warrant. A witness at the hearing reported that Senator Domenici—my senator for New Mexico—replied, "That man doesn't deserve civil liberties." In another Senate hearing, Senator Murkowski referred to me repeatedly as "the spy Lee." He had to be reminded that I was the "suspect Lee." Another politician, Senator Robert Smith, couldn't even tell the difference between me and Bill Lann Lee, the highest-ranking Chinese American in the Department of Justice, the acting U.S. Attorney for Civil Rights. At a luncheon of the Federalist Society, he kept saying that the government needed to watch "Bill Lann Lee" more closely—clearly referring to me. Smith even claimed that the bombing of the Chinese embassy in Belgrade "was designed to distract the public's attention from the Bill Lann Lee matter."

Even the President of the United States made a public statement about my case. During his nationally televised press conference on the day after the proffer meeting on June 25, 1999, the president said that "Dr. Wen Ho Lee" had transferred data "into his personal computers." Even the president was wrong—I never downloaded my files to a personal computer. He must have confused me with former CIA director John Deutch, who transferred top secret files to his personal computer. During this press conference, President Clinton also said that my case was an example of "espionage."

With the intense political pressure to indict me hanging over us, Mark Holscher and Dan Bookin went to Washington the following week to discuss my case with a half dozen of the top DOJ attorneys. On July 1, 1999, they met with Jim Robinson, the head of the criminal division; John Kelly, who also made the trip from New Mexico; and a few others.

For the meeting, Mark wrote a 28-page paper about the possible prosecution against me for downloading files from the secure computer system to the unsecure system. In it, he outlined the factors that made my case unlikely for prosecution, had there been no political fervor to get me. Mark began his statement this way, addressed to the Department of Justice prosecutors:

> This case presents you with both the challenge and opportunity to stand up against unprecedented political pressure to use the criminal justice system to find a scapegoat for the scandalous lack of security at our nuclear laboratories. Based on rumors and leaks by federal officials, false stories about Wen Ho Lee have repeatedly appeared on national television and in every major newspaper. Dr. Lee has been branded a "spy" and accused of providing nuclear weapons secrets to the People's Republic of China. Unaware or unconcerned about the facts, Senators and Congressmen have publicly called for Dr. Lee's indictment. Now, even the President of the United States has misstated Dr. Lee's conduct on national television and cited him as an example of "espionage " by China. In the face of this relentless pressure, a decision by you not to charge Dr. Lee will no doubt be as hard a choice as any prosecutor has faced.
>
> Political considerations aside, the facts of this case clearly do not warrant criminal charges against Dr. Lee. There is no evidence that Dr. Lee disclosed or caused the disclosure of classified information to any unauthorized person. Nor is there any evidence that Dr. Lee acted with any intent to injure the United States. As a result, Dr. Lee did not violate any part of 18 U.S.C. § 793 [The Atomic Energy Act]. Not surprisingly, no person in history has ever been prosecuted under such circumstances . . .

If Dr. Lee were to be charged, the hallmarks of a selective prosecution could not be more clear: An investigation that began with accusations that Dr. Lee had given the plans for our nuclear bombs to the Chinese government has devolved into considering felony charges based on negligence, where there was no harm or intent to cause harm. No one has ever been prosecuted for violating 18 U.S.C. § 793 under such circumstances. There are, moreover, innumerable instances of negligent security practices in our nuclear laboratories and elsewhere in which the responsible parties have not even lost their jobs, let alone their freedom. (These other examples—which will be subjected to intense public scrutiny should this case go forward—include many instances in which classified information was actually disclosed.) Add to this the enormous political pressure for a scapegoat in the "Chinese nuclear spy scandal"; the statement by an administration official that race was considered in "targeting" Dr. Lee; and the statement of a senior FBI official that, if all else failed, Dr. Lee would be charged with "spitting on the sidewalk."

Two additional factors that should figure prominently in the exercise of your discretion to decline prosecution here are the illegal search of Dr. Lee's home and the illegal press leaks that have occurred in this case. The search warrant was facially overbroad and will taint any prosecution of Dr. Lee. . . . The repeated press leaks regarding Dr. Lee from the FBI and DOJ, which are illegal under the Privacy Act, destroyed Dr. Lee's reputation and caused him and his family immeasurable personal anguish. In exercising your discretion, you should consider that the overzealousness in this investigation already has caused Dr. Lee to suffer greatly, and will surely come back to haunt the government in any prosecution.

Mark's paper would prove prophetic—every hole he described in the government's case against me would indeed later haunt them.

Mark and Dan's presentation to the DOJ scored some points—
we later heard that there were some big conflicts within the DOJ on
whether to prosecute me. In all likelihood, their arguments kept me
from being indicted right after the first proffer meeting on June 24th.

But the outlook for me was far from rosy. Mark prepared for the
possibility that I might have to go to trial by finding local attorneys
in New Mexico who could also take up my case. He contacted a
prominent Albuquerque criminal defense firm, Freedman, Daniels,
Boyd, Hollander, Goldberg and Cline. He spoke with John Cline,
who had recently moved to New Mexico from Washington, D.C. It
was a serendipitous conversation, for John was very interested in my
case, and he had previously worked on the defense of Oliver North,
who had been accused of various offenses in the Iran-Contra affair.
That case also involved issues of classified information that might
be brought out at trial. John and his firm agreed to represent me as
local counsel if I was indicted, at a much reduced rate. I was fortunate to have such an experienced legal team come together, especially considering that I couldn't afford to pay even one of them.

————————

There was another gambit for my lawyers to consider. Months ago,
Brian Sun had been in conversation with producers from the television news program "60 Minutes" regarding one of his other clients.
"60 Minutes" wanted to interview me. For the longest time, Mark
wouldn't even consider it. He didn't want me to say anything to the
media, because whatever I said could be misinterpreted or used
against me by the government. He said it was too risky for anyone
facing criminal charges to expose themselves to tough, possibly con-
frontational questions, in front of a camera and millions of viewers.

But with the threat of criminal charges looming larger, Mark was
reconsidering the TV interview request. It seemed increasingly important to correct some of the highly publicized misperceptions about
me. Brian was in touch with a number of Chinese American groups

that were very disturbed about the way the spy allegations were re-verberating from Washington and across the country, implicating all those of Chinese heritage. The Committee of 100, made up of promi-nent Chinese Americans like architect I. M. Pei and cellist Yo-Yo Ma, had brought the issue before their annual conference, and its chair-man, Henry Tang, was talking with ABC News about the growing concerns. There were reports that racial profiling of Asian American scientists and engineers was taking place at the national laboratories and in defense industries. But Brian had also heard from many Chi-nese Americans and others who were reluctant to support me unless they could get a sense of the kind of person I am.

Mark and Brian discussed the possible conditions for me to ap-pear on "60 Minutes." To work out the media issues for the legal ef-fort, Brian brought on board Stacy Cohen, a seasoned public relations consultant who had worked with him on cases involving Chinese Americans accused of campaign finance violations. In July, most of the "60 Minutes" crew was on vacation. But Stacy had worked with producer Solly Granatstein before, and she reached out to him. "Wen Ho Lee's lawyers are interested in talking with you," she told him. Within a few days, Granatstein was on a plane to Los Angeles with "60 Minutes" correspondent Mike Wallace.

Wallace and Granatstein met with Mark and Brian over break-fast in late July 1999. Mark was still skeptical, but by the end of their meeting, they found a way for the interview to take place. Mike Wallace agreed that Mark could be in the interview room with me, off camera, to object to any questions that could present a prob-lem for me in a criminal trial, and that his objections would be edited out. In addition, Alberta and Chung also would be inter-viewed. With that in place, the "60 Minutes" team made arrange-ments to fly my kids and me to Washington, D.C.

The interview took place on July 28 at the Monarch Hotel in Washington. "60 Minutes" paid for the airplane and hotel for Al-berta and Chung, but I didn't want to accept any money from them, not even for my airline ticket. I didn't want to take anybody's money, so I paid my own way to fly on Southwest to Baltimore and to stay at a Days Inn.

The hotel room where the interview was to take place was crammed with lights, wires, and television equipment everywhere. I had never really watched "60 Minutes" on television—my children had to tell me that Mike Wallace is very famous. He was very courteous to me and my family, but there was constant friction between Mark and him. Mark interrupted many times as Wallace questioned me about my two trips to China, about my work in the X Division, about the handling of classified information.

At one point Mike Wallace turned to me and asked, "Would you tell your lawyer to stop being a prick?" I didn't understand, and I had to ask in reply, "Mr. Wallace, what is a prick?" Everyone started laughing, and Mark told me not to answer that question. Despite the tense moments and tough questions, Mike Wallace and the "60 Minutes" crew were fair, and I was grateful for that.

———

"60 Minutes" aired their interview with me on August 1, 1999. For their segment, they also spoke with Steven Schwartz, the executive editor of the *Bulletin of the Atomic Scientists* who had written articles about my case. And they talked to the man who fired me, DOE secretary Bill Richardson. It was nauseating to hear Richardson say he tried to protect my legal status and reputation as much as he could, but that I had violated DOE security policies—when so many other people committed security violations, too. Mike Wallace had to say to Richardson, "Oh, Mr. Secretary! You tried to protect his reputation? You ruined this man's life." It was so clear that Richardson had bowed to political pressure. Everyone in New Mexico knew that Richardson wanted to be nominated as the Democratic vice presidential candidate in the 2000 presidential race. Many believed that he wanted to enhance his national visibility through my case.

On the "60 Minutes" program, I said that I was innocent and hadn't committed any of the crimes of which I had been accused. I admitted that I had transferred files from the classified system to the unclassified system, but that I did it to protect my files. I stated that I never passed nuclear secrets to China and never intended to, that I gave the best years of my life to making America strong and to protecting the American people, and that I didn't understand why I was being called a traitor. When Mike Wallace asked me, "Why do you think they focused on you, Dr. Lee?" I answered, "My best explanation of this is . . . I'm Chinese. I was born in Taiwan. I think that's part of the reason. And the second reason, they want to find some scapegoat. They think I'm . . . perfect for them."

After I was released from jail, Mike Wallace ran a follow-up segment on "60 Minutes," with this comment from Ed Curran, the former FBI agent who headed the DOE's counterintelligence program, and the person who ordered the DOE polygraph test of me on December 23, 1998: "One of the worst things that happened in this whole affair was the press feeding frenzy about Wen Ho Lee, triggered mainly by the coverage in the *New York Times*. When Wen Ho Lee's name surfaced, it was devastating to our investigation because it further alerted him to our continuing scrutiny. Since Wen Ho Lee has not been proven guilty of anything and thus must be presumed innocent, the surfacing of his name has been devastating to his family and to his life."

Yes, it was devastating to my family. But I found Curran's words to be empty finger-pointing at the *New York Times*. While I have a particular disgust for the way that newspaper "reported" on me, the fact is that the leaked misinformation *had to come from somewhere*, and I wonder, What are people in the government, like Curran, doing about that, to find and punish the people responsible for *those* violations of national security and public trust?

CHAPTER 10

The "60 Minutes" program, combined with Mark's paper, probably kept me from being arrested sooner. Even before the TV program, a few Chinese American and Asian American groups had sent letters of concern to the media, politicians and the Department of Justice, criticizing statements that portrayed all Chinese Americans as potential spies for China. Most of their letters included some statement to the effect that "we make no comment as to Wen Ho Lee's guilt or innocence." Of course they didn't know me and I couldn't talk to any of them about my case, so they couldn't know about my innocence. I appreciated that they spoke up about my case.

I was familiar with one of the groups—the Overseas Chinese Physics Association, an organization of some 400 physicists, mostly Chinese American. Their organization was holding their regular conference, in conjunction with the American Physical Society, only 10 days after I was fired, on March 8, 1999. The OCPA council voted to speak out about the deteriorating work environment for Chinese American scientists as a result of government and media portrayals stemming from my case. They sent letters to the American Physical Society (APS), the world's largest physics society, and to the American Association for the Advancement of Science (AAAS), the world's largest general science organization, with 138,000 members. In response to the OCPA's letters, APS issued a general statement in June upholding scientific freedom, emphasizing national security, and speaking against wrongful characterization of immigrant scientists. Two weeks later, the AAAS board of directors passed a resolution denouncing as unjust and shameful the portrayal of any American scientists as disloyal, and any foreign visitors as suspect based on their ethnic origins.

The Overseas Chinese Physics Association had good reason to be alarmed. At least eight percent of America's scientists are Chinese American. Many were born here, but even more are like me, born overseas, arriving here as foreign students and staying, as naturalized American citizens. The national labs, defense industries, and security-related companies employ many Asian Americans, who make up a big portion of the top scientists and engineers in the U.S. Though their ranks include six Nobel laureates and numerous recipients of science and technology awards, a growing number reported workplace problems and stress. The chairman of the OCPA, Cheuk-Yin Wong, made this statement in a talk before the AAAS in August 1999:

> Chinese American scientists performing classified work in weapons labs and in defense subcontractors find their loyalty severely questioned. They have been subject to distressful jokes and innuendo. Equally awkward are instances when their fellow American colleagues avoided conversations on classified projects in their presence, as if their loyalty could not be trusted. In such a climate of distrust and suspicion, some Chinese Americans in classified work have requested transfers to unclassified projects. Some have opted for early retirement. Others stay on knowing very well that their upward mobility would be even more limited

now. Chinese Americans are concerned that in this atmosphere, project managers in weapons labs and defense subcontractors may have reservations about employing Chinese American scientists, about promoting Chinese Americans in leadership roles, and about putting them to head a major project. The working environment of these Chinese American scientists has deteriorated as a result. Their contribution to American science, technology, and national defense also may suffer as a consequence.

For those Chinese American scientists doing unclassified research in national laboratories and universities, the immediate impact is not as severe. Chinese American scientists are however concerned whether the negative media reports might affect the perception of science programming officers and proposal reviewers when they apply for research grants.

For those ethnic Chinese scientists who are not U.S. citizens (Chinese nationals) working in unclassified research in national laboratories, there are now greater restrictions on security matters and on funding of some areas of unclassified research. These restrictions apply to foreign nationals from sensitive countries, which include Chinese nationals. For example, in one of the unclassified areas of a national laboratory, nationals from sensitive countries performing unclassified work must be escorted by Americans when they walk outside their own building to go to the cafeteria or the library. In another national laboratory, several foreign nationals from sensitive countries have been denied access to their offices, postdoctoral fellows have not been renewed based on newly applied criteria, foreign nationals have been denied the opportunity to apply for laboratory positions for which they are qualified, and foreign national staff members are sometimes unsure about their sources of funding. In that weapons laboratory, a number of talented foreign national postdoctoral fellows, limited term staff, and permanent staff have already accepted positions elsewhere because of the uncertainty associated with the environment at the laboratory. A number of laboratory staff members who traditionally mentor postdoctoral fellows have decided not to recruit foreign nationals because of their uncertain future.

The concerns raised by the Overseas Chinese Physics Association were definitely being felt by the Chinese American scientists at LANL. Some people told me of incidents where conversations among scientists would awkwardly cease when a Chinese American walked in the room even though the person had the same Q clearance, or where schoolchildren would hurl snowballs and hurtful remarks at them. I heard reports that some of the other LANL physicists quit after I was fired, because they felt they might be next. It was well known among them from the news stories that the Kindred Spirit list of suspects included a number of other Chinese Americans, and no one wanted to be subjected to what was happening to me. Others transferred to jobs in unclassified areas, or left the weapons area completely.

The fear that other Asian American scientists and engineers could be targeted brought many together in special task forces against racial profiling. Commissioner Yvonne Lee, of the U.S. Commission on Civil Rights, led a special inquiry into possible racial profiling at the national laboratories. At LANL, a working group of Asian American employees came together to analyze the impact on employees. At Lawrence Livermore, a salary review revealed that Asian Americans were paid less than comparable non-Asian employees and that their promotional opportunities were unfairly limited— these findings prompted a class action lawsuit by Asian Americans at that lab. It was clear that, as a result of their handling of my case, the labs were going to suffer from the loss of a scientific talent pool.

After my appearance on the "60 Minutes" broadcast, more groups started to question whether my treatment in the media and in Washington was being driven by my Chinese ethnicity, and whether I was being made into a scapegoat. The Committee of 100 sent a letter to Attorney General Janet Reno, saying that my "high profile prosecution, with its attendant media circus atmosphere, could do incalculable harm" to the welfare of other Chinese Americans. Other Asian American groups noted that the way my race was used to question my loyalty was similar to the treatment of Japanese Americans who were rounded up during World War II.

Even though I had been forced to live like a hermit for several months, I followed the stories and news about my case. Alberta sent me articles written by other Chinese and Asian American people about the impact that my case was having on them. I appreciated that they spoke up, especially when many Chinese think that bringing attention to yourself is immodest and may also bring trouble. Before this happened to me, I would also have hesitated to get involved in someone else's problems, but now I began to realize that more people like me need to speak up.

Chinese language newspapers wrote many stories about me, with interviews of Chinese American leaders. The television program "Nightline" interviewed a number of Chinese Americans who had suffered repercussions in their jobs. There were letters to the editor and opinion articles. After all of their news coverage and the shrill, single-minded columns about me on their editorial pages, the *New York Times* saw fit to print only one opinion by a Chinese American—an attorney and former Marine Corps officer named Hoyt Zia. He wrote: "In the United States, there is something called due process. If the Government has evidence that Wen Ho Lee committed espionage, it should charge him and let the accusations be aired in a courtroom. If it doesn't, then it should put the matter to rest rather than allow innuendo and rumor not only to smear Mr. Lee but to call into question the loyalty of every Asian American."

Some of the articles were ugly in the way they talked about Chinese people. One of my local newspapers, the *Santa Fe New Mexican*, ran a very degrading editorial after the bombing of the Chinese embassy in Belgrade:

SO SORRY. WE'LL HIT RIGHT TARGET NEXT TIME. Dr.
Fu Manchu, that evil-genius character created by author Sax
Rohmer, has made fools of the CIA again. Imagine this scenario:
Sneaking into the NATO war room, the clever Chinese stole the
bomb-target map of Belgrade. In its place he left a fake map
showing the Chinese Embassy as the site of a Yugoslav arms-
procurement office. A U.S. stealth bomber blew up the target
with three bombs. . . .

Other American newspapers around the country thought this editorial was so amusing they reprinted it. I thought it was very sad—and
frightening, considering that if I had to go to trial, the editors and
readers of the *Santa Fe New Mexican* could be sitting on the jury,
judging me. Fu Manchu was a white man's racial fantasy of the evil
Chinese, and in the movies he was always portrayed by white actors,
never a real Chinese person. If these newspaper people thought it
was so funny to kill Chinese people, no wonder they didn't care what
they printed about me. A group called the Asian American Journalists Association sent out a notice to their colleagues in the news media, warning them to be mindful of such biased reports. Members of
the Los Alamos Chinese Cultural Association, to which I belonged
before all this, sent letters in protest to the Santa Fe paper. One,
written by our family friend, Tzehuey Peng, was published—and
then *she* received some hate calls.

At LANL, a security workshop trainer who delivered the annual
security lecture focused his talk almost entirely on the Chinese, and
said that the number of Chinese restaurants in Los Alamos—five—
proved that there was a lot of spying by Chinese going on. My
lawyers tried to get a copy of the tape, but the lab and the DOE refused to provide it.

The hiring of Chinese postdoctoral researchers, who are an important source of scientific talent in the world—including in the
U.S.—became an issue for the labs. Some officials even suggested
that no ethnic Chinese, including American citizens of Chinese de-

scent, should be permitted to do any classified work. At the Brookhaven National Laboratory in New York, scientists were required to wear special identifying badges, like the Nazis required of Jews, indicating country of origin. My daughter Alberta learned about this several months after my release and Judge Parker's apology. Perhaps even today, Chinese American employees somewhere are still wearing those badges.

Bill Richardson said on "60 Minutes" that he would never condone racial profiling, because he is Hispanic. He even created a special DOE task force to look into racial profiling and appointed a Chinese American, Jeremy Wu, as ombudsman over the entire DOE. But to me Bill Richardson's actions were a joke, because inside the labs he and the LANL management were blaming me for all the negative attention that the lab was getting—as though I had caused all the hysteria in Washington and the news leaks of their investigations.

———

A few days after my "60 Minutes" segment ran, another Congressional probe into my case released its report, this time from senators Fred Thompson and Joe Lieberman, for the Governmental Affairs Committee. Their hearings looked into mistakes that the different government agencies made in their years of investigation of me and the W-88. They described their findings as "a story of investigatory missteps, institutional and personal miscommunications, and—we believe—legal and policy misunderstandings and mistakes at all levels of government. The DOE, FBI and DOJ must all share the blame for our government's poor performance in handling this matter."

The Thompson/Lieberman committee report was very revealing, because it detailed the investigatory flow charts and "algorithms" that the government used to reach the conclusion that I was the prime espionage suspect. The report pointed to the problematic approach of focusing only on the W-88 warhead, when several other warheads were also mentioned in the PRC walk-in double agent's documents. The report said that the CIA concluded that China did not necessarily steal the information from the U.S., but could have come up with its own indigenous designs.

But the DOE investigators proceeded on the assumption that LANL was the source of the W-88 loss, and that the compromise occurred between 1984 and 1988. They reached this conclusion even though, as many other investigators and reports pointed out, the W-88 information was widely distributed. With this faulty set of assumptions, the DOE worked with the FBI to come up with a matrix of three lists: 1) individuals at LANL who had access to the W-88 design information; 2) individuals at LANL who had traveled to China between 1984 and 1988; and 3) individuals at LANL who had contact with visiting PRC delegations at LANL.

The Thompson/Lieberman report said that I stuck out on the suspicion matrix because I had been investigated before in connection to the Tiger Trap suspect at Lawrence Livermore lab—and because I had "*aggressively* sought involvement with a visiting Chinese scientific delegation, *insisting* upon acting as an interpreter for the group despite [my] inability to perform this function very effectively." [emphasis added] These statements all were untrue. I was *asked* to do these things by LANL officials. Like so many of these Congressional reports, this one gave new life to old lies and came up with a few new ones.

Nowhere did the report state that I had assisted the FBI with Tiger Trap at their bidding. This information had been made public months earlier. Instead, the investigators and these politicians viewed the service I performed for the FBI and my country's security to be evidence of my *disloyalty*. As in so many instances, the report just recycled many of the lies about me, even ones that had already been refuted, without noting that what they were repeating was wrong. I wonder, what can an American do when Congress lies about you?

But the Thompson/Lieberman report also revealed that the FBI and the DOE failed to investigate other suspects who appeared on their matrix—people who had similar travel and contact with PRC scientists, who had design knowledge of the W-88. The only way that the DOE, the Cox Commission, and other counterintelligence "experts" on China could justify singling me out was to use the unsubstantiated claim that China targets ethnic Chinese to extract bits of information from them. One of the people interviewed by this Congressional committee even pointed out that inside the DOJ, there were serious doubts about this matrix, since I was from Taiwan, not the PRC. But it didn't matter. I had to be "it," because I was Chinese.

————

One theme coming out of the various Congressional hearings was that the DOE, the FBI, and the DOJ could have proved I was really a spy, had they not botched the investigation. This was yet another way that the Republicans could blame the Democrats. In turn, government agencies like the DOE looked for somebody else to blame. I learned from news reports that Bill Richardson had appointed a few different internal reviews to determine how the lab let me "get away"—and who was at fault. The first review teams found that no wrong had been done by either the lab security officers or the FBI agents who concluded that I was not the spy they were looking for. In fact, they concluded that I was not a spy at all. But Richardson didn't like those results, so he kept appointing review teams until one came up with the answer he wanted. It was just as the FBI did, polygraphing and interrogating me until they could say that I failed a lie detector test.

On August 12, 1999, Richardson announced that he was going to discipline three LANL employees. He said "they failed to meet their responsibilities" in their investigation of me. Richardson didn't name the three employees, and said that he could not directly discipline them because LANL was managed by the University of California—though that fact hadn't stopped him from circumventing lab policy and summarily firing me on the national news. And, as in my case, the names of the three employees were leaked to the media.

Sig Hecker, the former director of LANL, was accused of not following through with a request from the DOE to limit my computer access. Terry Craig, one of the LANL counterintelligence officers, allegedly did not assist the FBI in searching my computer. Bob Vrooman, the former counterintelligence chief at LANL who had written letters critical of the Kindred Spirit investigation, was charged with failing to distribute an assessment of me—an assessment that didn't come out until after he retired—and for not informing LANL management that the FBI said it was okay to remove my security clearance. All three disputed the charges. I knew Bob and Terry, not well, but they seemed like nice guys. I felt bad for them, now they were in the same boat as me. Richardson was ruining their reputations, simply for his own political ambitions, so he could look good. They were scapegoats now, too.

But Bob Vrooman had already testified before several Congressional committees, and he was going to defend his name. Before he came to LANL, he had served in Vietnam and worked for the CIA as an operations officer. He issued a press release of his own, and said to the *Washington Post*: "I've had a distinguished career, and I'm not going to go down in history as the guy who screwed up this case, because I wasn't. This case was screwed up because there was nothing there."

Bob was the first high-ranking participant involved in my investigation to come out and say that my ethnicity played a role in how I became a prime espionage suspect. Bob's statement said, in part:

> I have worked on this case since June 23, 1995. I know that there is not one shred of evidence that the information that the Intelligence Community identified as having been stolen by the Chinese came from Wen Ho Lee, Los Alamos National Laboratory, the Department of Energy or from a DOE office. The in-

formation known to have been obtained by the Chinese was available in documentary form on many classified documents distributed to hundreds of locations throughout the U.S. government and contractor complex. No complete inventory of documents containing this data has been made or is possible, but as an example, one containing a rather detailed description of the W-88 had a distribution of 548 copies, of which only 180 are within the DOE complex. The rest of the addresses are in the Department of Defense, military services (including the National Guard), other government agencies, and contractors such as Lockheed Missile and Space Corporation. Please note that I am referring to 548 mailing addresses, not people.

Dr. Lee was identified by the Department of Energy's Office of Counterintelligence as the prime suspect based on an, at best, cursory investigation at only two facilities, Los Alamos and Lawrence Livermore National Laboratory. The details of this investigation are still classified, but it can be said at this time that Mr. Lee's ethnicity was a major factor. In spite of the lack of evidence that the loss occurred in the Department of Energy, the Secretary of Energy decided not to defend his Department. . . .

The criticism that the early investigation was marred because of a failure to look at Mr. Lee's computer files is not valid. There was never any discussion in the early FBI investigation about computer files. The facts are as follows. The FBI agent assigned to the Lee case was also working many other cases that were considered higher priority by his management. Mr. Craig, who worked for me, initiated discussions with the FBI case agent in an attempt to get him moving on the case. Mr. Craig suggested that the FBI look at Mr. Lee's e-mail. When this suggestion was not accepted, I intervened by talking to the case agent's supervisor. On February 14, 1997, he replaced the case agent with another agent. This agent worked the case more aggressively and we provided him with everything that he asked for.

It is important to note that Executive Order 12333 specifies that the FBI has responsibility for counterintelligence investigations within the United States. The Los Alamos National Laboratory Internal Security Office can only provide support to the FBI.

The Department of Energy Counterintelligence Program Code of Ethics states that "CI [counterintelligence] representatives will be judicious at all times, to ensure the reputations, character and dignity of individuals involved in any CI inquiry are protected." It further states "that by following the Code of Ethics, the CI professional will be assured that his/her motives and activities will be above reproach." By trying to protect Mr. Lee's identity, I have adhered to the DOE CI Code of Ethics. However, others in DOE have ignored the code as evidenced by the trial and conviction by rumor of Dr. Lee.

I have been an outspoken critic of the flawed investigation that identified Mr. Lee as the prime suspect in this case. I have expressed my views to representatives of three Congressional committees and the President's Foreign Intelligence Advisory Board. I do not agree with Mr. Trulock or with the Secretary of Energy that the information obtained by the Chinese came from the Department of Energy. I consider disciplinary action against me to be retaliation for opposing them on this issue.

Bob Vrooman's announcement was a big surprise to me, and it was a major revelation for my case. All along, my attorneys and I had maintained that I was being singled out and selectively prosecuted because I am Chinese American, but now a well-reputed counterintelligence official was making the same claim. It was national news, and now the whole country was hearing about it.

This news had a huge impact, especially for the Asian Americans who were watching my case closely. Except for a few individuals and groups, people had been very reluctant to say that my race and Chinese ethnicity had anything to do with the espionage accusations. Many were worried that I might really be a spy. But now, with so many reports poking holes in the spy theory, and with the statements from Bob Vrooman, more people began to speak out in support of me.

On August 18, 1999, after the "60 Minutes" broadcast, the Senate Governmental Affairs report, and Bob Vrooman's press statement, six national Asian American organizations sent a letter to Attorney General Janet Reno about possible racial profiling in the investigation of me. They asked Reno to ensure that race does not play a role in any other investigations and prosecutions involving security violations at the national laboratories. I was very surprised to see that the groups were not just Chinese, but also Indian Americans, Filipino Americans, and other Asian Americans. I had never really given much thought to the need for Asian people to come together in this country, but here were these groups sending letters about me. The groups all were in Washington, D.C.: the Asian Pacific American Labor Alliance, the India Abroad Center for Political Awareness, the National Asian Pacific American Bar Association, the National Federation of Filipino American Associations, the National Asian Pacific American Legal Consortium, and the Organization of Chinese Americans.

On October 6, 2000, because of my case, the Congressional Asian Pacific American Caucus, chaired by Congressman Robert Underwood, convened a hearing on possible racial profiling of Asian American employees at the national laboratories. One of the people giving testimony at the hearing was Kalima Wong, a geneticist and computer scientist from Lawrence Livermore National Laboratory and a fifth-generation Chinese Hawaiian American. Wong's statement discussed the climate inside the labs:

> . . . as a routine administrative matter, I had the authority as the primary signature over two others for official documentation required for DOE orders and inspections. The day after the Wen

Ho Lee story broke I lost that authority to act on my own and now had to have another person also sign with me. There was no warning, no explanation, and no apology to me. I was embarrassed and humiliated.

The whole Chinese spy allegation has set us back further. It seems now that there is license to do as was done to me because we Asians are potential spies. We face the aftermath of the incident daily. Implicating jokes about Chinese flowed liberally. ". . . You can thank the Chinese for all this tightened security . . . ," "All because of the Chinese spies . . . ," "Can't trust those Chinese."

Insensitive remarks abound, "Don't buy products made in Taiwan. . . ." "Our documents were stolen by the Chinese. . . ." "You Japs going to commit Kamikaze?" "Not only you look alike, you act alike . . . all of you." "Your kind don't deserve better." There is no apology, no letup. Why does it continue? Instead, there's a constant droning of more security measures resulting from the un-incriminated but insinuated Chinese spies—as if the only spies were Chinese/Asians.

With the growing criticism of the Kindred Spirit investigation, Notra Trulock, the DOE's chief of counterintelligence and the architect behind the case against me, resigned, only a few months after he received a $10,000 award from Bill Richardson for his handiwork. According to publications like the *National Review* and the *Washington Post*, Trulock himself was under investigation for security violations, because an article he wrote and distributed to the media allegedly contained classified information. During this period, other government officials also were cited for security violations—yet they were the ones accusing me of wrongdoing!

Bob Vrooman talked publicly about the failures of the Kindred Spirit investigation. He pointed out that the Kindred Spirit suspicion matrix discussed in the Thompson/Lieberman report turned up seventy LANL employees who fit the initial matrix criteria of traveling to China in the mid-1980s and having access to nuclear weapons technology. But the list was incomplete, according to Bob, because it didn't investigate the entire DOE complex or bother to look beyond DOE. They also missed a major class of travelers who visited the PRC weapons complex in Beijing. This flawed list of seventy names was whittled down to a short list of twelve names. This short list didn't include people who had exactly the same contacts and access as I did. Half of the twelve listed were Chinese Americans, including three Chinese American scientists who had no access to W-88 data and one who didn't even have a Q clearance.

Bob Vrooman also said the FBI didn't really think there was much to the Kindred Spirit investigation. Before December 1998, FBI officials refused to assign even one full-time agent to the case. The Albuquerque FBI agents had sent several memos to the FBI headquarters stating that they did not believe I was a spy. The dates of those memos were November 19, 1998, January 22, 1999, January 29, 1999, February 26, 1999—all dates occurring around my multiple interrogations and just before I was fired—and even as late as September 3, 1999. But after the leaks to the media and all the Congressional committees, more than sixty FBI agents with computer forensic and counterintelligence experience came to New Mexico, in addition to the fifty-member surveillance team that was watching me and my family around the clock.

All these Congressional hearings, revelations, grand jury dragnets, and meetings with prosecutors made me dizzy, taking me on a roller-coaster ride that wouldn't end. I still held on to the belief that once the truth was out, the 24-hour FBI surveillance would go away. The truth seemed to be dribbling its way out, and I dared to hope this would finally be over soon.

There was even some good news for our family. Chung had always wanted to be a medical doctor, but he didn't get into medical school right after graduating from college. This year, he applied without telling Sylvia and me, so we wouldn't be disappointed if nothing happened. He surprised us with the news that he was accepted by a school in the Midwest and would begin classes in September. Of course, we were very happy for him. I also felt some satisfaction in knowing that my children were grown up now and would be okay no matter what happened to me. We spent the rest of the summer and fall trying to be a normal family—we and the FBI.

But even as these various government reports showed the flaws in this massive, four-year project designed to prove that I was a spy for China, the FBI, the DOE, and the DOJ seemed more determined than ever to prove that I was guilty of something—anything. Though Operation Kindred Spirit had been thoroughly discredited, it was never officially repudiated or even criticized by the FBI or the DOJ.

Meanwhile, Operation Sea Change, the investigation of my computer downloads, was still virulent, with many of the same people who were involved in Kindred Spirit. There were continued rumblings that the DOJ might press for an indictment for gross negligence in the mishandling of classified information, under Title 18 of Federal Code, Section 793(f). That was the section that Mark wrote about in his paper to the DOJ. It would be a felony offense, punishable by up to ten years in prison. There had never been a federal prosecution under that statute, but the Department of Energy had to decide whether it was willing to risk declassifying and exposing some nuclear weapons information that my attorneys would seek to present to a jury in order to defend me. It was Bill Richardson's call to make.

By November 1999, we learned that Richardson had decided that he was willing to expose some of the nuclear weapons information I worked on and go forward with the prosecution of my case. In order to make the charges against me stick, they would have to show that the codes I downloaded were extremely valuable. I knew better than most at LANL how these nuclear bomb simulation codes functioned—and I would be able to show that some of the codes were garbage. Still, it wasn't clear if the New Mexico U.S. attorney, John Kelly, was actually going to indict me—and on what charges.

We knew there was the possibility of the gross negligence charge. Mark had already amassed a long list of other incidents of security violations that had never been prosecuted. Those reported incidents included:

> John Deutch, the former director of the CIA, who, according to numerous reports, was found to have 31 top secret CIA files on his unsecured home computer, which was used by all members of his household and was used to access the Internet.
>
> James R. Conrad, a defense contractor who, in 1983, transmitted classified information that included missile launch commands and wartime bomber routes over unsecured computer lines, as reported in the *Dallas Morning News*. He did not follow security procedures for the classified information on his computer.
>
> Kathleen Strang, an Arms Control and Disarmament Agency employee, who, according to the *Washington Post*, "improperly removed . . . [classified] documents from a storage vault at the State Department, repeatedly left them overnight in an open safe accessible to dozens of people without security clearances and then ignored several warnings from supervisors over a period of months." Her files included information on how the U.S. monitors nuclear tests and weapons development in other countries.
>
> CIA employee Fritz Ermath, who reportedly transferred secret and top secret files between his home computer and his work computer, resulting in a virus entering the CIA's classified network, according to the *Washington Post*.

A CIA agent who sold 25 CIA computers to the public without
    erasing or even checking for the top secret information on
    their hard drives.

A scientist at Los Alamos who backed up the "Green Book"
    from the classified system to the unclassified system in
    1998, apparently by accident. The Green Book is a secret
    assessment of the status, maintenance needs, and vulnera-
    bilities of some of the nation's most sophisticated
    weapons. He was fined and suspended, but wasn't fired.

A scientist who, while working for a defense contractor on top
    secret, national defense projects, stored hundreds of pages
    of top secret documents in his unsecured garage. He was
    investigated in the early 1990s.

None of these people was ever criminally prosecuted. Not a single one.

We also heard that John Kelly and Robert Gorence of the New
Mexico U.S. Attorney's Office were looking into a prosecution on
national security grounds for violating the Atomic Energy Act of
1954, for the intentional mishandling of classified information. On
the other hand, it seemed possible that they might pursue a lesser
charge of removing classified information "without authority and
with the intent to retain such documents or materials at an unauthorized location." This charge would be a misdemeanor punishable
by a $1,000 fine and up to a year in prison.

Once again, the DOJ started oozing information leaks like a bro-
ken sewer. Suddenly there were reports about missing computer
diskettes that I supposedly couldn't account for. These were lies—I
had never talked about computer diskettes. That was John Deutch,
who didn't know what happened to several of *his* diskettes, onto
which he had downloaded top secret files. Of course *he* wasn't facing
prosecution, and nobody was talking about jail time for his gross negligence and missing diskettes. In fact, he was still playing an active

role on prestigious federal commissions that were looking into national security issues. The government made these reports about me in the news, yet they refused to give my attorneys an inventory or details of the files that were supposedly in my possession. I wondered if the FBI was referring to diskettes seized from my house during their search. It seemed unlikely that anyone could itemize all the computer files, diskettes, tapes, CD-ROMs, Zip drives, and whatever else he or she might possess, but in any case, I was supposed to be able to account for everything that they were leaking to the media.

Mark had discussed the possibility that I might be indicted. If Mark couldn't be present when the FBI came to arrest me, John Cline would be there in Albuquerque to represent me. My lawyers and I went over the financial resources that I might be able to muster in the event that I would need to come up with money for bail. We had an inkling that I might be indicted soon, so I called Chung to warn him that if he learned of my indictment on the evening news, he shouldn't worry.

None of this discussion prepared me for my arrest on Friday, December 10, 1999. At around 12 noon, I got a phone call from John Cline, while I was chopping vegetables to cook for lunch. John was to speak at a lawyers' conference in Los Angeles, and had stopped by Mark Holscher's office to discuss my case. While he was at Mark's office, they received a call that FBI agents were on their way to Los Alamos to arrest me. They would be at my house in 15 minutes. John told me that Mark was on his way to the airport, to get to Albuquerque for my court appearance, and John would be on his way back as soon as he finished with his talk. John urged me to remain calm, to cooperate with the FBI, and to go quietly.

Finally, the stone that hung over my head for so long was falling. I didn't panic. I tried to stay calm and to prepare myself. Now I understood why several more reporters and TV satellites were gathering around my house today. The FBI and the Department of Justice had tipped them off. I later heard that Brian Sun and Stacy Cohen both had received calls from journalists around the same time that I was notified—the reporters had the full details of the charges and the indictment, which my lawyers and I hadn't even seen. The media knew all about it, but the FBI only gave me and my lawyers 15 minutes to prepare. That made me so angry. But then, why should I be surprised by this latest indignity in my trial-by-media? I could see this partnership between the FBI & Company and the media, who needed to sell papers and commercials by printing leaks and photographing my face as I was being hauled away to jail. Their interest in creating news was far more important than my right to justice.

There was no time for me to finish cooking lunch. But I was very hungry. I stopped chopping vegetables and told Sylvia she'd have to finish them. I quickly made myself a couple of turkey sandwiches. I ate one right away and wrapped the other for later. It was a good thing, because I wouldn't have a chance to eat again until late that night.

The first thing I needed to do was to tell my children. I got ahold of Alberta first. *The FBI is coming to arrest me. Don't be alarmed, but it's going to be on the news tonight. Don't worry, I'll be okay.*

Alberta started to cry. She tried to suppress her sobs, but her voice quavered. It was very hard for me to hear the fear and pain of my children. They were so worried for me. They were suffering, too. After I called Alberta, I couldn't bring myself to call Chung. I knew he was getting ready to take his final exams for his first semester in medical school. If I didn't tell him right now, he would at least have a few extra hours to study. Once he found out about my arrest, I knew he would be too upset to study.

Then I gathered up a few things—some pajamas, underwear, socks, a toothbrush and toothpaste, a bottle of water, and my sandwich. I put them in a brown paper grocery bag and waited with Sylvia. Though Sylvia was afraid, she tried to reassure me: "Remember, you managed to live through the cancer. We survived that and we'll survive this."

At about one o'clock, there was a knock on my door. More than a half dozen FBI agents were outside. They were all dressed up for the cameras, in their suits and ties. David Kitchen, the FBI agent in charge of the Albuquerque FBI office, came in and announced they were arresting me. I recognized agent Michael Lowe from a few other visits. Kitchen searched my body to make sure I wasn't carrying any weapons. I appreciated that he took me to a different room so that Sylvia would not have to watch this humiliation. Then we went outside, with TV cameras and photographers swarming all over.

They put me in one of the three or four FBI cars. Mike Lowe sat next to me. As we drove off to Albuquerque, I caught a glimpse of a few of my neighbors. Mary Norris was out there with her dog, watching the whole sordid event. As the FBI drove me away, she waved good-bye. I looked back at my home of 20 years, not knowing that it would be a long time before I'd see it again.

———

It was a long, anxious ride to FBI headquarters in Albuquerque. In the car, Lowe gave me a copy of the 45-page indictment. I read through the 59 counts, but their descriptions referred to the computer files in an unfamiliar manner that I didn't understand, "Code A, Code B," and so on. I asked Mike Lowe what they meant, and he said, "Don't talk, everything you say will be used against you." I spent the remainder of the drive in silence, without the faintest idea of what was in store for me.

At the FBI headquarters, I was fingerprinted, and many pictures were taken of me. The front, the side, the left, the right. When I went to the men's room, two FBI agents followed me in and watched. After all the pictures were taken, we went back outside to the car, headed for the courthouse. Many, many TV cameras were waiting outside for me. The FBI must have given them my whole itinerary for the day. They drove me the short distance to the new federal courthouse. We went in through the basement, driving into

a secured garage area, where a steel door shut behind the car. The
FBI turned me over to some U.S. marshals, who put handcuffs on
me and locked me in one of the basement jail cells. I was in
shock—I never expected to go through anything like this. My attorneys had talked about the possibility of an indictment for months,
but somehow I didn't realize that that meant I would be arrested,
fingerprinted, photographed, handcuffed, and jailed—the full criminal treatment. I sat in the cell with my hands secured by the cold,
heavy metal, waiting for the judge to call me into the courtroom.
That would be another new experience. I had never been in a courtroom before, not even for a traffic ticket.

At around 3:30 P.M. the marshals took me out of the cell to an
elevator, and then led me to a back entrance to the courtroom. Before I entered, they took the handcuffs off. This would soon become
a ritual for me—putting on and removing the shackles and chains.
Apparently, the Department of Justice didn't want reporters or the
public to see me in shackles.

The Rio Grande courtroom seemed vast that day. It would become familiar to me soon enough. I didn't see Mark, and learned
that his plane had been delayed. A petite woman with long, silver
hair came up to me and said, "I'm Nancy Hollander. I will be one of
your lawyers." Nancy was a partner in John's firm. Her mother was
a mathematician who had worked on the Manhattan Project. Another attorney from Freedman Boyd was with her—K. C. Maxwell,
who was young, and I thought she was Nancy's assistant. This was
the first time they were looking at my case. Except for pleading not
guilty, there was nothing much for Nancy to say to the balding, stern
federal magistrate, Judge Don Svet. He just recessed the court until Monday and ordered me to jail. I could see from the look on his
face that he wanted to put me in jail. The entire proceeding took
only about ten minutes.

Even if Nancy and K.C. had met me before, or if Mark had been
in court, there was little to say. This was the first time my lawyers and

I would officially hear the charges against me: 59 counts of violating the Atomic Energy Act and the Federal Espionage Act. Maximum penalty for 39 of the counts: life in prison. Counts 1 to 29 charged me with downloading 19 files to an unsecure area, and copying most of them to tapes with the intent to harm the U.S. or to aid a foreign nation. Maximum sentence for each count: life. Counts 30 to 39 were for acquiring 10 tapes with classified information, with the intent to harm the U.S. or to aid a foreign nation. Maximum sentence for each count: life. Counts 40 to 49 charged me with taking 10 tapes without authorization, with the intent to use the information against the U.S. or to aid a foreign nation. Maximum sentence: 10 years per count. Counts 50 to 59 charged that I had kept the 10 tapes, willfully failing to return them. Maximum sentence: 10 years per count. It was the legal equivalent of nuking me.

The indictment charged me with tampering, altering, concealing, and removing restricted data; receiving restricted data; unlawful gathering of national defense information; unlawful retention of national defense information. This is how they portrayed my downloading the files to the open, green computer system and then onto the portable tapes—about which I had already informed the prosecutors. But according to the indictment by the U.S. attorneys, my files and tapes were the equivalent of Armageddon. They said that the information I downloaded was so detailed and so sweeping that, *if it fell into the hands of a foreign government*, it could enable a foreign power to make a quantum leap in nuclear weapons technology. That "if" was what the whole prosecution of me was about. I knew my files had been kept safe and undisturbed ever since I made them in 1993 and 1994. They claimed that the very creation of these tapes by someone like me—a LANL nuclear scientist, an American citizen of Chinese descent—was a criminal act.

Even though I was not being charged with espionage, all the charges were wrapped up in the insinuation that I had acted in a nefarious, deceptive, and sinister manner—like a spy. The government told reporters that they so far had found no evidence that I gave the tapes to a foreign country, but were still investigating the possibility that I had passed them to China or Taiwan. One unnamed official even told the *Wall Street Journal* that espionage "is the only logical reason why that quantity of information [would] be downloaded." The leaks and the lies were starting their cycle all over again, as though the previous revelations of misstatements and misinformation had never happened.

U.S. attorney John Kelly had me arrested on a Friday, making certain that I would spend at least the weekend in jail. The earliest possible court date would be Monday, to hear the indictment and to argue for bail. After Judge Svet adjourned the court, I was taken back downstairs and locked in a cell. This time my hands and feet were shackled and chained to my waist. Nancy and K.C. told me to be strong, that they'd get to work on getting me out of jail. They gave me a sad look and said that I wouldn't be able to use the things I brought with me from home—that the jail would take everything away and give me prison-issue things. K.C. took my paper bag with my pajamas from me.

Mark soon came to my cell; his delayed flight had finally arrived. He told me how sorry he was for me to be in this situation, and he'd try to get me out on Monday. Of course, that was going to be hard, since Mark was the only one of my attorneys who had a security clearance, so he was the only one who could learn what was in Files 1–19 of the indictment. We talked for almost an hour. I think Mark was shocked, too. Mark issued a statement that I "was innocent and at no time did [I] criminally mishandle any classified material that was in [my] possession" and that I "did not provide the tapes to a third party."

The first day of my courtroom farce was over. I had just spent nine months as a virtual prisoner in my home. Now I would discover life as a prisoner behind bars.

PART
THREE

CHAPTER 11

The federal marshals took me away in handcuffs to the Santa Fe County Adult Correctional Facility. I don't know how many thousands of times I'd driven past it on I-25, not knowing it was there, just off the Cerrillos Road exit near the shopping outlets, on NM-14. The ride from the courthouse to the jail took one hour. I was in a transport van, just me and the guards. In my mind, so many questions and thoughts were swirling. What was going to happen next? Could the government find a way to kill me in prison? That's what Bill Richardson was trying to do. He killed my reputation first, and now he wanted to torture me into a confession. But I figured that if they didn't kill me, one day I would get out.

The December sun had long since set when we got to the jail. I could make out a large, modern brick complex that looked similar to a high school or other institution. The federal marshals drove down a long driveway before pulling into a garage area, and the steel doors clanged shut behind us. From the transport garage, I entered the booking area. A "welcome wagon" was there to "greet" me—the top wardens of the jail wanted to see the spy. First, there was a lot of paperwork to become an inmate. I gave my name and other information to a clerk, who gave me many papers to sign. My new surroundings included lots of thick Plexiglas imbedded in the white enamel-painted cinder-block walls—the same décor as the X Division, but the trim was painted in a turquoise blue. It was all very plain.

I was taken to a small cell with a window on the door. The guards watched as I changed from my street clothes into a red prison jumpsuit made of heavy denim material, stiff and not very comfortable. They put the shackles back on me and gave me a box for all my things. They let me keep two pieces of underwear. The clerk took everything else and made an inventory. The box was to be locked in a storage area where all the prisoners' personal possessions were kept.

It was almost nine o'clock and I was very hungry. I hadn't eaten anything since my quick turkey sandwich. My family didn't even know where I was—the judge didn't tell them or my lawyers where I would be imprisoned. I was allowed to make one phone call my first night in jail. I called my wife and told her I was in Santa Fe and that I would be okay. I told Sylvia that I didn't know how long I'd be in here. That was the only call I was allowed to make to my family for the entire month to come. My wife sounded frightened, and told me that my family members were all very anxious, not knowing where I was or what was happening to me. They remembered that the FBI had threatened execution, "like the Rosenbergs," and they were in a panic. It was terrible to make them worry so. They didn't deserve to go through the anxiety of not knowing. I knew it was deliberate, the FBI and U.S. attorney's way of putting pressure on them, to torture them too.

There was some discussion of whether to let me take a shower. Showers were only allowed Monday through Friday, and apparently I had arrived too late for shower time. I told them I couldn't sleep without a shower, especially if I couldn't wash up over the weekend. Finally they let me take one. They also decided to give me some food, even though it was after the food service time.

The guards put me in a cell next to the medical area, near the booking area. The cell door was heavy with two locks, each requiring its own key. A third lock was operated electronically by a central control guard who was contacted over an intercom. My door had a glass window where guards could watch me, 24 hours a day. A guard sat at a desk outside my cell door, facing directly into my cell. His job was to make notations about me every fifteen minutes, all day long. I was in a cell all by myself, but there were bunk beds for six prisoners. I picked a lower bunk, the one farthest away from the door, but it was still in full view of the guard. I had been given a plastic mattress roll—a pad about 1 inch thick. That thin plastic was to be my mattress on top of the metal bed. They also gave me two thin blankets.

The federal government had a contract with the Cornell corrections company, which ran the Santa Fe County jail. For each federal prisoner, Cornell received $65 per night for room and board. My cost to the taxpayers was $135 per night room and board. The jail was making money off me, so they gave me a "suite" that could sleep six. I had a toilet and a sink in the cell. There were no windows at all and, though I could turn the light off, the light from the hall and the face of the guard were ever present in the window of the heavy cell door.

I had no way of knowing if my treatment was typical or not, but I soon learned that I was a "special" prisoner. New inmates usually went into one of the big group lockups in the booking, where there are no beds, just a plastic pad and a blanket for each prisoner. With no place to sit, all you can do in the group lockup is lie down. Or scream and yell, which is exactly what some inmates did every night.

I didn't sleep at all for the first night. I was cold and hungry all the time. It was winter and all I had on was the denim jumpsuit, which offered no warmth at all. I didn't sleep on the second night, either. I think I slept an average of one hour a night the whole first week. In the nearby medical unit were inmates who were physically sick or mentally ill. They screamed and cried all day and all night.

Sometimes women prisoners would sing. I also could hear the angry inmates in the nearby booking lockup, cursing, shouting, angrily banging on their cell doors. The doors were metal, and the noise was loud. Between the crying, screaming, yelling, and pounding, I just couldn't sleep. I asked the medics for some sleeping pills, but they didn't have any. They gave me some Benadryl to make me drowsy, but it didn't help.

I felt that the government was torturing me now, that they were trying to break me down without coming right out and shooting me. I said to myself, They're trying to get me to cave in and confess to something that I didn't do, to get me to say, "Okay, you're right, I'm a big spy." I figured if I didn't confess, they'd want me to kill myself. But their dirty tricks only made me madder. My family knows how stubborn I can be. I wasn't going to let Bill Richardson and the government break my spirit. I kept telling myself, I will never give up, I will never surrender to their dirty tricks and lies.

Staying healthy was going to be a challenge. Not only couldn't I sleep, but the food was no good, and I couldn't eat much of it. At home, I ate fresh fruits and vegetables constantly as part of my own anti-cancer regimen. For more than ten years, I avoided red meat, and we tried to buy organically grown chicken. I ate the fresh fish that I caught. In jail, food was definitely going to be a problem—not only was the food bad, there wasn't enough. Each day, I got one small piece of fruit, a tiny apple or orange, or a small banana, about half the size of the ones I bought in the store. At home, I would eat at least five times that amount each day. I went into jail weighing 125 pounds. At the end of the first week, my weight had dropped to 118 pounds, and was steadily going down. A medical doctor came to the jail only once a week. If I got sick, there would be nothing I could do.

After a sleepless weekend, and feeling completely disoriented and unsure of my days ahead, I was brought back to court on Monday,

December 13. That was the day of my arraignment. Getting to the courthouse was an experience in itself. I was let out of my jail cell, then shackled at my wrists and ankles, which were then chained to my waist. In the booking area, the clerks processed me out, and the federal marshals took over, putting me in the transport van that was sitting in the enclosed garage area. One marshal carried a pistol, while the one riding shotgun carried an automatic rifle. There was a divider between us, but it didn't matter, because I couldn't move with my shackled hands and feet. As we pulled out of the detention facility complex, we were followed by another car that had a guy with a machine gun.

At the courthouse, I was again brought in through the basement and locked in one of the cells. My attorneys gave the guards a suit for me to change into. The proceedings were held in the same courtroom, again before the federal magistrate, Judge Don Svet. This time, the courtroom was very crowded. Sylvia and Alberta were there—Alberta took some time off from her job in North Carolina and flew home right after I called her about my arrest. I could tell that Alberta was upset by my appearance—I must have looked pretty bad after my horrible weekend.

There were many other friendly faces in the courtroom. I saw my neighbors Don and Jean Marshall; friends and former coworkers Bob and Kathy Clark, Bucky and Linda Kashiwa, Shao-ping Chen and his family, Chris Mechels, Chuck Montaño; our longtime family friend Cecilia Chang; the parents of some of my children's schoolmates, Phyllis Hedges, Ralph and Marilyn Stevens, and Carl Newton; my children's piano teacher, Rosalie Heller, and Alberta's fifth grade teacher, Jo Starling. I also saw many New Mexico people whom I didn't know, but would soon recognize as regular supporters—Alex Achmat, Bill Sullivan, Nance Crowe, Sei Tokuda, and Tatsuji Shiratori—there were so many I can't name them all. I was very grateful to see them there. I wish I could thank them all by name, but much of this is a blur now.

And so many reporters came to my courtroom hearings. I eventually began to recognize the regular ones, especially from the local offices of the *Albuquerque Tribune*, the Associated Press, Reuters, and the *Albuquerque Journal*. Though I will never be able to trust what I see in the news again, it did seem that most of the journalists worked hard and tried to be fair. I even noticed that the *New York Times* coverage of me had become more balanced after they assigned different reporters to my story.

The U.S. attorneys presented their indictment of me: that I had unlawfully collected and removed 19 sets of files containing secret and confidential restricted data related to atomic weapons research, design, construction, and testing, with the intent to harm the United States. They said I had downloaded the files onto an unsecure, open computer and onto portable computer tapes, seven of which were missing. The government said that 60 FBI agents who specialized in computer forensics conducted more than 1,000 interviews and searched more than 1 million computer files to come up with this indictment. U.S. attorney John Kelly told the media, "This case is being prosecuted because Wen Ho Lee has denied the United States its exclusive dominion and control over some of this nation's most sensitive nuclear secrets. Although Lee has not been charged with communicating classified information to a foreign power, the mishandling of classified information alleged in the indictment has, in the government's view, resulted in serious damage to important national interests."

Then the government presented two witnesses whose purpose was to show why the terrible Wen Ho Lee should stay in jail: Dr. Stephen Younger, the associate director of nuclear weapons programs at LANL, and Robert Messemer, the unpleasant FBI agent who interrogated my niece for several hours.

Steve Younger talked a lot about my codes and how extremely important and valuable they are. Prosecutor Gorence asked him if I could give the tapes to an unauthorized party, would I pose a risk to

U.S. national security? Younger replied, "These codes and their associated databases, and the input file, combined with someone that knew how to use them, could, in my opinion, in the wrong hands, change the global strategic balance. . . . They represent the gravest possible security risk to the United States, what the president and most other presidents have described as the supreme national interest of the United States, the supreme national interest."

All I could think when I heard that was, Wow, that's such a big lie. It's so big a lie that they must really want to keep me in jail forever. My coworkers from LANL who were in the room, other nuclear scientists who were familiar with the codes, were also shaking their heads in amazement.

Younger said a lot of other things—that it had not been my job to have access to most of the files I downloaded, and that nobody else at LANL downloaded classified information. He said it wasn't really necessary to have the user's manuals with the codes, because it was possible to "read the code like a book." He said he had read the code like a book himself.

When Younger said this, I knew he could not have looked at the codes. No one could read these codes like a book. Code physicists who have worked on these codes every day for years can't even figure out what some of the hundreds of thousands of lines of code were intended to do. I had kept the user's manuals to the codes locked up in my safe in the X Division. Without the user's manuals, it would be extremely difficult, if not impossible, to use these codes. But as a lab manager, Younger was extremely far removed from the work of bench scientists like me. Plenty of scientists in the courtroom that day were appalled by his misleading statements.

———

FBI agent Robert Messemer was the next witness. He said the quantity of data that I downloaded was 806 megabytes, equal to 806 reams of paper, more than 400,000 sheets. That would be a stack of paper 134 feet high, he said. He put on quite a show with those figures, trying to make my computer files seem gargantuan in scope, and lots of reporters used his examples. On the other hand, my 800 megabytes could almost fit onto a single CD-ROM disk, while so many home computer software applications—Microsoft Office, for example—far exceed that amount of memory. Why should it be so shocking that computer codes that simulate nuclear weapons explosions would take up at least as much memory as popular home computer software?

Messemer's job was to make me look like the most deceptive person alive. He said I had hidden the classification markings on three documents that were locked in my X Division office. This was one of the security infractions I was fired for—I doubted that I was the only scientist who did this. But except for me, no one had ever been fired for such a thing, let alone charged with 39 possible life sentences.

He also said I lied to the T Division scientist whose tape drive I used to make my tapes back in 1993: "Dr. Lee represented to the T [Division] employee that he wished to download a *resume*" onto the open system and the tape drive. According to Messemer, I was so deceitful that I tricked my colleague into showing me how to download onto a tape and even got his password, so that I could "meander" into his office when he wasn't there. I had never said "resume." I asked this colleague if I could use his computer to download files when he wasn't around since, obviously, if he was in his office, I would be in his way. There was nothing clandestine about it; I kept all the notes on how to download—which the FBI seized after their search of my house. The FBI also tried to shed suspicion on the fact that I wrote some of those notes in Chinese—my first language. The government introduced as evidence only one page of my notebook, a page with Chinese writing on it, not any of the pages that had only English on them.

Messemer said I used a similar ruse on another coworker after

I was reassigned to the T Division on December 23, 1998. I didn't have a tape drive in my new T Division office, and I wanted to delete any PARD or potentially classified files from my tapes. The fact that I asked to use his office when he wasn't there was again a sign of my deception, according to Messemer. Even the way the government described how I used a computer was made to sound surreptitious. "These were assembled, these files, very meticulously and very methodically," said Messemer. That's so ridiculous it's laughable—it's impossible to work with computer codes and not be meticulous and methodical. One sloppy mistake and nothing will work. "Yes, our computer forensics review indicated that Dr. Lee took a very methodical, meticulous approach to the assembly of all these files. And, moreover, he did so in the evening hours, not during regular business hours, and he did so on weekends, which we also viewed as being somewhat secretive."

Finally, Messemer said that I had sent letters out in 1993 and 1994 seeking employment at seven overseas institutes, after I received a RIF notice that I might be laid off. Two each to Singapore and Taiwan; one each to Switzerland, Germany, and Hong Kong.

Mark Holscher asked Messemer if they had any evidence or document that I intended to harm the United States, which the 39 life-sentence counts against me charged, but Judge Svet didn't allow the question. "I'm not going to change my ruling. Move on to something else," he ordered. Jean Marshall, my neighbor, also was called to testify on my character and that I was not a flight risk, but Svet's mind was clearly made up from the moment he walked into the courtroom.

Prosecutor Gorence summarized the government position:

> Your Honor, . . . Dr. Lee has never provided a statement in any way about the whereabouts of these tapes. You have heard what these tapes represent, and the information downloaded on an open computer system and remained there for five years, about as serious qualitatively, information that this country possesses [sic].

And to restate what Dr. Younger said, the unauthorized pos-
sessor of those seven tapes walks around with the information
that would yield a complete nuclear thermonuclear bomb design capability. . . . The information in the hands of someone not
authorized to possess it, combined with Dr. Lee's cognitive ability to assist in the utilization of that information, could render a
change in the global strategic balance of power. . . .

I cannot contemplate a more serious risk to U.S. national
security than to have a person like Dr. Lee walking around with
access to that type of information. . . . I assert to the court that
the risk of his liberty pending trial is so enormous . . . the "community" in this case is 270 million persons that face a degree of
peril by virtue of what he did, and information that remains unaccounted for today, if he's walking around. And I'm not saying
he took it someplace, but the risk of him doing that is so extraordinary and so extreme that he poses a danger to the community in the way I broadly defined it. And I believe he is a flight
risk as well, with foreign ties, family, job prospects abroad, and
would ask that you order detention prior to trial.

Not surprisingly, Svet sent me back to jail. Though I knew nothing of
the criminal process and had no way of judging if I might get released,
I hoped that we could show how wrong the government was in making such a big deal out of what ordinarily would have been treated as
an administrative matter. But I could see that Svet's mind was set and
I knew I had no chance. The day had been an elaborate show, but the
outcome was predetermined. Mark and John told me they would appeal the order of detention, and we might have better luck in front of
another judge. On the way back to jail, I kept thinking how the government said I would jeopardize the safety of 270 million Americans
if I was released on bail. How could I be so much more dangerous today than I was four days ago, before I was imprisoned?

———

Among the many serious problems that the indictment triggered, one of the most critical was the situation with my lawyers. My pro bono arrangement with O'Melveny and Myers, Mark Holscher's firm, was for pre-indictment representation. It would no longer apply, once I was indicted. Mark told me that the management committee in his firm would need to have a serious meeting, because the legal costs of a trial would be more than $1 million, perhaps a lot more in a national security case like mine. Some of his managing partners wanted him to say that I was "innocent." That question always required asking in reply, "innocent of what?," because I had been accused of so many things, including espionage. Others wanted Mark to tell the committee that he would win my case, when in fact the odds were stacked against me. There were other issues too, because his law firm had other cases where they represented the University of California and the Department of Energy. But Mark told me that Dan Bookin, whom I had met at the June 24 proffer meeting, stood up and said that this is the best thing a lawyer can do, to help somebody who is in trouble. Mark Wood, the head of the firm's litigation department, said that O'Melveny and Myers has a tradition of representing people who need lawyers. After they spoke, the management committee unanimously agreed to let Mark and other attorneys at the firm represent me.

I was very happy to learn that O'Melveny and Myers decided to continue with my case pro bono. Mark would add my case on top of his other work. I trusted Mark, and I liked him. There were many times when I would ask him, "I can never pay you, why are you doing this?" He would answer, "That's a good question," and we would both laugh. Mark would say I could pay him by taking him fishing and cooking him dinner. I still owe him the payment.

But there were some things Mark's firm couldn't do. One of the continuing problems in my case was the constant flow of leaks that poured out of the government: private information about me, my family, my finances, my employment history—everything about me.

O'Melveny and Myers couldn't sue the government, because of conflicts they had with other cases where they had represented the DOE. Brian Sun's law firm, O'Neill, Lysaght, and Sun, agreed to take on the lawsuit. Brian had already represented several members of my family pro bono, and he was responsible for being the liaison with community and professional groups that might support my case. He had also brought in a consultant, Stacy Cohen, to handle crisis management and manage the publicity surrounding me. Brian's firm was much smaller than Mark's, so the pro bono work took a bigger bite. I didn't know Brian as well as Mark, but I was also very grateful to him and his team, especially when they worked all day and night after my arrest to quickly assemble my privacy lawsuit.

The week after I was arrested, Brian and two other attorneys in his firm, Luan Phan and Heather Hersh, flew to Washington, D.C., to meet with some other lawyers, Tom Green and Mark Hopson, who were partners at a large law firm, Sidley and Austin. After working day and night, they filed a lawsuit against the Department of Energy, the FBI, the Department of Justice, and other unnamed parties on Monday, December 20, 1999—only ten days after my arrest and one day before my birthday. It was a nice birthday present to be able to show the government that I wasn't going to roll over and stop fighting just because they arrested me—and that we wouldn't put up with their constant leaks over these many months. Mark had written numerous letters to various federal agencies for violating my privacy rights, but they hadn't stopped. My privacy lawsuit cited many of the leak incidents, and ended with:

> As a direct and proximate cause of Defendant's intentional and willful violations of the Privacy Act, Plaintiffs have suffered an "adverse effect" . . . in the form of direct and indirect injury to Plaintiffs' reputations, extreme public embarrassment, humiliation, anxiety, ridicule, emotional distress, mental anguish, physical pain and suffering, trauma, past, present and future loss of

income, and damage to career progression and professional reputation. Plaintiffs also have been subjected to substantial harm,
embarrassment, inconvenience, and unfairness as a result of the
Privacy Act violations committed by Defendants.

Brian and the other lawyers from his firm announced the filing of
the lawsuit with a press conference in Washington, D.C. Alberta
and Chung were there to speak for me, because I couldn't speak for
myself. It was hard to see my children forced to go out and fight my
battle. I knew from the days when Chung was president of his class
in high school that he did not care for public speaking, and Alberta
had never done anything like this before. Up until now, my lawyers
didn't want any of us to speak to the media. But now, with the
daunting challenge of fighting 39 life sentences, we had to do something to stop the lies from becoming accepted as truth. I didn't really want my children to be the messengers—I wanted Chung to
concentrate on his medical studies, and I was worried for Alberta's
health and safety. But my children wanted to speak up, and Stacy
Cohen and the lawyers tried to prepare them to face reporters from
all the major print and national broadcast news outlets. I heard later
that a reporter asked my kids if they thought I was being used as a
scapegoat. Alberta checked with the lawyers to see if she could answer and then replied decisively, "Absolutely."

There was also Freedman, Daniels, Boyd, Hollander and Cline,
the law firm in Albuquerque that would take on much of my defense. I had only met John Cline once, in the early fall, but now I
was getting to know him, Nancy Hollander, and other members of
his firm very quickly. As my incarceration stretched into days and
weeks, it was John and Nancy who visited me on a regular basis,
taking the long drive through the desert from Albuquerque to the
Santa Fe detention facility. In those first several weeks, there wasn't
even much about my case we could talk about, since neither John
nor Nancy had been granted a security clearance to talk about clas-

sified information. And even if they had been Q-cleared, the jail was
not a secure facility where we could talk about the nuclear weapons
codes that were at the core of my case.

I realized that it would be up to me to explain my codes to my
attorneys and to teach them the physics and math and computing
behind all of the charges in the indictment. In my solitary confinement, I tried to prepare lists of books, references, and topics that
John and Nancy could refer to for background, in between our visits. In addition to the attorneys, there was Barbara Bond, John's assistant; Ann Delpha, a paralegal with their firm; and Larry Trujillo,
an investigator who volunteered to help in my case. They were researching nuclear weapons—to discover, for example, how much of
what I was accused of "stealing" was already in the open literature
and available on the Internet.

The Freedman, Daniels, Boyd, Hollander and Cline law firm
was beginning to spend significant time on my case. My arrangement with the firm was not pro bono. John and Nancy agreed to put
a cap on their daily fees, so that they charged me for only 8 hours
per lawyer even if they each worked 16 hours on my case on a given
day. The firm knew that I didn't have anywhere near the money
needed to pay for their legal fees, and they agreed to be paid
through money that could be raised by a legal defense fund that had
yet to be set up. I didn't know how so much money was going to be
raised from strangers—I had never heard of such a thing. Mark and
Brian said it had been done before. If the defense fund got donations, John's firm would be paid. But if not enough money was
raised, the firm agreed to continue working on my case pro bono.

With the prospect of mounting legal bills, the fund-raising to
pay for my expenses began almost immediately. Brian and Mark
engaged a certified public accountant to begin keeping track of any
donations made to the Wen Ho Lee Legal Defense Fund, which
they set up. They also wanted to make sure that contributors understood that the donations were not tax deductible. My family
friend Cecilia Chang, a New Mexico businesswoman who had

owned a chain of successful computer stores, started a website to disseminate information about my case and to begin raising money. Cecilia's husband, Dan, was also a Taiwanese American scientist who had worked at Sandia National Laboratory in Albuquerque, and they had two children close in age to Chung and Alberta. When the Changs visited the Los Alamos area, sometimes they stayed overnight at my house.

Cecilia and Dan had moved to the San Francisco area, and Cecilia started speaking out on television and making contact with local Asian American groups to have a fund-raising event on my birthday, December 21. They organized a party in only a few days. Alberta flew all the way from North Carolina to speak at the fund-raising party—and that night they managed to raise $20,000 toward my legal fees. I was very surprised and appreciative when I learned about it. At least we could begin to pay my attorneys something.

Other groups and individuals were also very concerned by the indictment and my imprisonment. In New Mexico, a support group formed almost immediately, initially led by Alex Achmat, a retired hotel executive, Phyllis Hedges, a Los Alamos attorney, and William Sullivan, a scientist at Sandia National Laboratories. In New Mexico, Asian Americans aren't very numerous, but the local Chinese American organizations and the Japanese American Citizens League signed up as supporters early on. Many of the local supporters came from all over the state to attend hearings at the courthouse, to picket outside, to send petitions around, and to let the New Mexico media know that there were plenty of people who disagreed with the government.

Elsewhere around the country, Asian American groups were protesting. Even though I was in jail, Alberta tried to keep me informed about what was going on. In San Francisco, Mabel Teng, a member of the city's board of supervisors, called a press conference to protest my imprisonment, and attorney Victor Hwang, from a San Francisco civil rights group called the Asian Law Caucus, talked about racial profiling. I had never heard about racial profiling before, but I learned that it referred to the way Middle Eastern Americans are targeted at airports on suspicion of being terrorists, and how drivers who are African American and Hispanic American are singled out by police for supposed traffic violations. And now, how Chinese American scientists are accused of being spies.

On a national level, 14 Asian American groups signed a joint statement about my treatment. I was very surprised to see that so many groups were concerned about what was happening to me. Their letter said, in part:

> We are deeply disturbed about the Justice Department's manner in investigating and prosecuting Dr. Wen Ho Lee, a Chinese American scientist formerly employed at Los Alamos National Laboratory in New Mexico, and the negative effects of this case upon the Asian Pacific American community in the United States. Our concerns are the following:
>
> First, the government's investigation that led to Dr. Lee's indictment was flawed by negative ethnic stereotypes and fueled by anti-Chinese hysteria.
>
> Second, Dr. Lee has been unfairly singled out in an unusual, if not unprecedented, criminal prosecution for conduct when it appears non–Chinese American government employees who have mishandled classified information have not been similarly charged.
>
> Third, there is an apparent lack of due process and abuse of discretion in the government's decision to oppose Dr. Lee's release on bail during the pretrial phase of this case.
>
> Fourth, there is persistent and misleading media coverage which continues to portray this case as one of "Chinese espionage," involving an alleged "Chinese spy" when, by its selection of charges in the indictment, the government has not charged that Dr. Lee disclosed U.S. classified information to any other person, much less to anyone connected to China.

Robert Vrooman, former security chief at the Los Alamos

National Laboratory and a central figure in the Lee investigation, has publicly acknowledged that Dr. Lee was selected as the target of the investigation because of his ethnicity. We condemn racial profiling in such government investigations. . . .

Today, there are more than 150,000 Chinese American engineers and scientists working in industry, government and academia, including some 15,000 in the defense sector. Chinese American scientists have won five Nobel prizes in physics and one in chemistry for the United States. Asian Pacific American scientists and engineers now form the backbone of American high technology, accounting for perhaps one-third of all technical personnel in Silicon Valley alone, and have made our nation stronger, healthier and richer. And yet, because of the manner in which the government has handled Dr. Lee's case, they are all at risk for being targeted as well.

We therefore urge the government and media to remember the invaluable contributions made by Chinese Americans and other Asian Pacific Americans. The use or tacit approval of racial profiling in government or in private sector defense-related employment will surely deter some of the very best and brightest engineers and scientists from serving our nation and helping to protect its future. It would be the ultimate, bitter irony for America if, due to Dr. Lee's case and the current anti-Chinese hysteria in some quarters, our national security were to be damaged by the loss of these dedicated professionals to public service and to our own defense industries. We, the undersigned organizations, are pledged to ensure that all Americans (without regard to race, color or national origin) will have the full right to serve this country to the best of their abilities.

[Signed by:]
Asian American Legal Defense and Education Fund
Asian American Manufacturers Association
Asian Pacific American Legal Center

Association of Chinese-American Engineers and Scientists of
New Mexico

Chinese American Citizens Alliance

Chinese Americans United for Self Empowerment

Chinese-American Engineers and Scientists Association of
Southern California

Committee of 100

Japanese American Citizens League

National Asian Pacific American Bar Association

National Asian Pacific American Legal Consortium

New Mexico Chinese American Action Committee

Organization of Chinese Americans

Overseas Chinese Physics Association

My lawyers filed a motion to revoke Judge Svet's order to keep me in jail, and a hearing was set for December 27, 1999. I would have to stay in jail until then—for my birthday, for the Christmas holidays. It was hard to believe that a year ago at Christmas, I was trying to help the DOE and the FBI with their polygraph interrogation of me. It seemed so long ago now, once upon a time when I thought I would be treated fairly, equally. When I was so naïve.

The same week that Svet sent me back to jail, I had my first visitors—Alberta and Sylvia came to see me at the jail on a Thursday afternoon, between 1 and 2 P.M. That was my assigned time, when I would be taken to a special cubicle, separated by Plexiglas with a small, built-in microphone. Other inmates had visitors in a large area, but my visits were secluded because of my solitary confinement treatment and to allow the two FBI agents to monitor every word we said. Unlike other inmates, I was allowed only members of my immediate family as visitors.

I could see the shock on my wife's and daughter's faces to see me in a red jumpsuit, looking thin and exhausted. Every time I wanted to speak, I had to reach up in front of my face to push the microphone button. My hands were shackled and chained to my waist, as were my ankles, so this was an awkward maneuver that accentuated my restraints. Alberta could hardly bear to see me this way, but she tried not to cry in front of me.

There was another problem with our visits. At home, my family only spoke Chinese to each other, but we were forbidden to speak in Chinese. So our conversation at the jail was awkward, superficial, and painful. Naturally, we didn't want to say anything important, or to show our feelings in front of the two FBI agents.

Alberta told me she was taking a month off from work to stay in White Rock with Sylvia, to try to get more support for my case and to work on raising money for my legal defense. Chung wouldn't be able to come until the following week, when his final exams were finished. I didn't even want to know how his exam week went because I knew my indictment and all the uncertainty of my being in jail, the privacy suit, and the legal bills, would make it impossible for him to concentrate. In the meantime, my attorneys seemed confident that their motion had a good chance of succeeding.

On Monday, December 27, 1999, I returned to the Rio Grande courtroom in Albuquerque for the motion hearing. Again, I changed out of my jumpsuit in the basement jail cell, and my shackles and chains were removed before I entered the courtroom. People later told me how haggard and thin I looked—Alberta said I seemed so much smaller—but I was very glad to see my family in the courtroom, and so many friends, neighbors, and supporters. I gave a small wave "Hi" to Alberta and Chung—which caused Robert Gorence, one of the prosecutors, to come over to the defense table to scold me and my attorneys. "You better control your client—no communicating with anybody," he barked at us. I suppose he was being cautious, in case my innocent wave to my children was really a sneaky, insidious spy signal. He told the federal marshals to take appropriate action against me and my kids if it happened again. It was an especially cruel and unnecessary act that has been hard to forget.

This motion hearing lasted three days, with Judge James Parker presiding—the same judge who would ultimately apologize to me. The judge who was supposed to preside over my case, John Conway, was out of the country for a cruise that would ring in the new millennium. Even with the change in judges, the prosecution's approach followed pretty much the same themes as the December 13 hearing—to portray my downloading as the worst and most devious crime that was ever committed against national security. This time, they brought a lot more witnesses. In addition to Steve Younger, they brought Richard Krajcik, my former boss in the X Division, whom I went to for advice and support during my FBI interrogations.

I expected more intelligent testimony about the codes and my work from Dick Krajcik, but he made some incredible claims. First, he said that these codes are "the crown jewels of the nuclear weapons programs." That was unbelievable. There are commercial software programs available that do a much better job than Code B, one of the codes dealing with the primary stage of a nuclear bomb. I worked with Code B on a regular basis—it is well known to be an old, problematic code full of garbage and even indecipherable bugs. I had often suggested that we completely scrap Code B and write a new code from scratch, or buy the commercial code. I don't suppose my opinion made me popular with management in the X Division, and I wondered if that's why Krajcik and Younger were giving such a distorted description of my work. I had seen it happen many times before at LANL—if you fell out of favor at the lab, then LANL management would paint you as completely bad. That's what the lab did to a former coworker in the X Division who was one of the best code physicists at Los Alamos.

Krajcik made many other statements that were simply inaccurate: for example, that I had no work-related need to access an entire code, that I only needed the specific hydrodynamics subroutine that I worked on. According to him, since I didn't *need* these codes for legitimate purposes, my files must have been created for evil purposes, what Krajcik called "Dr. Lee's private collection," my "chilling collection of codes and files." As a code physicist who had to test the hydrodynamics code I was writing, of course I would need to test my subroutines with the entire code. How else could I see if it ran properly?

During Gorence's questioning of Krajcik, he said on several occasions that I had "taken" and "stolen" the codes from LANL, that the files were "stolen by Dr. Lee." Finally Mark had to stand up and object. The witnesses all acknowledged that there was no evidence that anyone unauthorized had accessed my files on the open, green system at any point during the five or six years that the files sat there.

Prosecutors Kelly and Gorence also called as witnesses two coworkers from X Division who used to be friends of mine, John Romero and Charlie Neal. They were helping the FBI comb through my office and files. John was the person who recognized from my notes that the files were on the open, green system. John and I both worked for many years together on Code A, the code that could be used for the secondary and primary stages. John was at least able to explain that the codes I had were very much related to my work and that I used them. He told the court that I had "played an active role in the birth of the code" from the time of its inception in 1979. I was glad that came out, because the lab officials, Richardson, and the FBI had all along presented me as someone who had no business touching these codes, when in fact I contributed to their creation and functioning. But the prosecutors also used John, like Dick Krajcik and Steve Younger, to say that he could conceive of no purpose to move my code to the green computer system. John Romero said at one point, "It's just not conceivable to me that someone would take our code and move it into an open computer. . . . It's just nothing we could even fathom doing because we all know that it's a nuclear design code."

Hearing this from John, I thought, okay, that's your opinion, maybe you never lost years of work the way I did. There were other computer experts who worked at LANL and knew the computer systems inside out and who knew about the instability of the computers from 1993 to 1994, when I did my downloads, like scientist Chris Mechels, who had worked for LANL and the CRAY computer company. Chris was not afraid to speak up and was quoted in the news making this point, as well as noting the lax computer security at the time that allowed scientists like me and others to find our own solutions to problems.

As I listened to the prosecutors claim with such indignation that it was *inconceivable* that I would download nuclear secrets to an unsecure computer system, even with three levels of passwords, I wondered if anyone ever applied the same standard to John Deutch, the former CIA director. I tried to imagine a scenario where the government might say this: "Your Honor, it is *inconceivable* that John Deutch would download the details of the CIA's national security apparatus onto diskettes and his unsecure home computers that were used by several members of his household and connected to the Internet. . . . It's just nothing we could *even fathom* doing, because we all know that these are our national security secrets. And so therefore, John Deutch, you must go to jail for the rest of your life and sit in solitary confinement, because it is possible that bad people could have obtained those secrets." But no, none of the politicians accused him, because they said he was merely violating security rules in order to work at home. I, on the other hand, intended to harm 270 million Americans.

It was strange to see my old friends get up and testify against me, to make me seem sneaky and deceptive. I knew that other coworkers and friends were also being asked by the FBI to say things about me. It didn't feel very good, but I tried not to judge them; I didn't want to judge them the way I was being judged. Some people, like John Romero and Charlie Neal, were flown out to Washington, D.C., to meet with big shots, even at the White House, I heard. I think it must have been hard for them to have to make choices about their jobs and careers when the whole government is saying their friend and coworker is an enemy. I had made the decision to help the FBI as well, to talk to the Lawrence Livermore scientist. That's when I thought the FBI had something to do with justice. So I didn't feel it was for me to judge them.

———

Another new witness called by the prosecutors was Dr. Paul Robinson, the director of Sandia National Laboratories. Robinson used to be at LANL, as associate director for national security, but had left in 1985. People at the lab say he left after he was passed over for the director position. But Robinson had friends in high places, and Senator Domenici nominated him to be ambassador to the Nuclear Test Ban Talks between the USSR and the U.S. in 1987. When he returned, he was appointed president of Sandia National Labs, in Albuquerque, which are responsible for the non-nuclear portions of nuclear weapons, such as the electronics and the engineering. I couldn't figure out why Gorence had Robinson testify, since he wasn't even at LANL during the period under question. But his role as a witness was to show how I put the entire national security at risk. Here's one exchange:

> GORENCE: . . . What is the risk to U.S. national security that Judge Parker should evaluate if Dr. Lee either has access and control over them, or could direct someone to do something with these tapes? What are we talking about here?
>
> ROBINSON: These tapes could truly change the world's strategic balance. The previous worst case I am aware of classified information being stolen also happened at Los Alamos [sic] Klaus Fuchs taking a design, that if detonated, could demonstrably kill 100,000 people in a city, in a dense city, if detonated.

These would allow the design of weapons that would kill several million people if a single weapon were detonated in a city. In that sense, it raises the level of danger and concern. This is information which must truly be protected, should be protected.

GORENCE: But if we don't know where these tapes are . . . what would you quantify, given your experience and your knowledge of what they can produce, is the level of the bet or risk that Judge Parker is taking in putting Dr. Lee out at liberty where he could talk to someone and communicate this information or their whereabouts? . . . What are we dealing with here in terms of a bet?

ROBINSON: I have got to say that this Court, I believe, faces a you-bet-your-country decision.

A "you-bet-your-country decision"? So now Judge Parker had to bet: My country versus me. It was obvious what his decision would have to be.

————

For their last witness the prosecution once again called FBI agent Messemer. He repeated many of the statements and lies he presented to Judge Svet on December 13—including the falsehood that I said I wanted to "download a resume"; that I withheld names of people I met in China from my trip reports; that I had assisted the PRC by talking about Lagrangian methods with some scientists; that I had received three letters from PRC scientists. He told Judge Parker all these things to show how deceptive I was. My attorneys had offered every possible form of monitoring me at home, with my neighbors Jean and Don Marshall offering to be "custodians" over me. Judge Parker asked Messemer several questions to see how an extremely restrictive at-home bail situation could work, with visits only allowed by my children and in the presence of an FBI agent and the Marshalls. Messemer said the FBI would have to have agents who could speak three Chinese dialects monitoring me around the clock, and even then I might pass something through to my children.

"It could be as innocuous . . . something like, 'How is the weather today?'" Messemer told Judge Parker. "It could be as simple as, 'Uncle Wen says hello,' that is the message that is given to the right party who understands now that they are to do something with those tapes. You see why we are concerned, even messages of appearing to be nothing but good will and gestures of good will have to be taken with a grain of salt, if you will, and have to be examined and reevaluated to see whether there is something that is insidious."

Messemer dared to say that it was more important to keep me locked up *now*, compared to *before* my arrest, because *now* I might try to get revenge on the United States for locking me up. Not even Franz Kafka came up with this bizarre logic.

The judge tried very hard to see if there was some combination of conditions that could be imposed on my release, even subjecting Sylvia, who had been charged with no crime, to have her communications monitored. But everything my attorneys agreed to, everything the judge suggested, was countered by another prosecution theory. They even suggested that enemy foreign agents from some as yet unspecified countries would swoop into White Rock with planes or black helicopters and some ninjas would snatch me away. Of course ninjas were Japanese, not Chinese, but the prosecution theories had become so far-fetched that it didn't seem to matter. No, I wasn't charged with espionage, but everything about the hearing was cloaked in the assumption that I might commit a treasonous, capital offense, aided and abetted by black helicopters from China in the night. For all his trying to figure out a bail release, when it came time to make the "you-bet-your-country" decision, Judge Parker sent me back to jail. This time it would be for an indefinite period.

———

We were all terribly let down by the judge's decision, and the cumulative events of the three days. It was Richard Myers' birthday, and he was especially disappointed. Richard was the husky attorney from Mark's firm who I at first suspected to be an FBI agent or federal marshal.

Among the supporters and friends from Los Alamos who came to court, some felt that we were outgunned by the full resources of the federal government. When both sides went into closed-door sessions with the judge, there were nearly a dozen prosecutors— and only Mark for my defense. Mark was the only member of the defense team who could go in because he had a Q clearance; my other attorneys were still waiting to be cleared. The government's side of the courtroom was packed with expert witnesses; we didn't have any experts yet. It was not a very happy moment when I said good-bye to my attorneys. I had not even been allowed to offer a good-bye to my family—Gorence had made such a big deal of my greeting to my kids that the federal marshals whisked me away.

On my ride back to the Santa Fe jail, once more in my shackles, chains, and red prison jumpsuit, I felt crushed under the weight of the huge show I had just witnessed—the allegations, accusations, lies, and misrepresentations. I was up against a behemoth, this giant government. I was but one man—how could I possibly win? I began to face the possibility that I could be in jail forever. That's clearly what the government wanted.

I wondered, Is this real or is it a dream? I was reminded of K, the character in Franz Kafka's book *The Trial*. The charges against him were never clear, nor was there any apparent way for him to counter the ambiguous charges made by unspecified accusers in an incomprehensible court system. The actual charges against me were steeped in thick secrecy, in the name of "national security." I had somehow entered this insane, topsy-turvy world. Of course I knew it was real, but it made no sense. If I violated some lab security rules, okay, so fire me. But 39 life sentences?

The global strategic balance. 270 million American lives. The crown jewels of national security. Black helicopters. Uncle Wen says hello. You bet your country. Kelly and Gorence painted such an exaggerated, malevolent interpretation of what I had done. It was a work of pure science fiction, with me cast as Fu Manchu. The truth of all this was hidden behind the heavy veil of national security. How could we tell the truth of my case?

CHAPTER 12

I spent the turn of the century in solitary confinement, in my windowless cell, amid the cries and moans of the medical ward. In jail, New Year's Eve ranks below Christmas Eve, when steak is served for dinner, the only special meal service out of the whole year. Though my hunger was constant, I didn't want to eat red meat and possibly increase my risk of cancer, so I didn't touch the steak, and missed out on the annual special meal. However, the New Year was useful to the FBI, which used the millennium change as another excuse for keeping me in jail. The FBI said that the international terrorist threat and the chaos resulting from the collapse of worldwide electronic systems on New Year's Day would keep them too busy to monitor me. After those fears fizzled out, I was still left shivering in my cold jail cell, in the dead of the New Mexico winter.

The year 1999 had been twelve months of hell, and prospects for 2000 seemed equally grim, if not worse. My lawyers call this period the "Dark Days," when nothing seemed to go right for us. I was stuck in jail under extraordinary conditions—and from my lawyers' viewpoint, there was the possibility that I might go crazy or give up because of the way I was treated. It was also much harder for us to communicate with one another while I was in jail. My lawyers were frustrated because they had to wait for their security clearances to come through before they could even analyze the substance of the indictment. They also had to wait for the federal bureaucracy to create a secure room where they could review classified documents with me and prepare their law briefs for my case. That was moving very slowly and creating a big delay for my defense, which really couldn't begin in earnest without the secure room. And without our own sets of documents, it was impossible to counter the government's accusations from the December detention hearings. Some people—friends and supporters—were even questioning whether my attorneys were up to the job of defending me, especially when the government was so effective at prosecuting me in the media.

The DOJ kept telling the court and the news media that all I needed to do was to cooperate with them and tell them what happened to the tapes—that it was my fault that I had to stay in jail. Many reporters seemed to accept the government's argument. Even Vernon Loeb, the reporter for the *Washington Post* who had challenged many of the *New York Times* reports, said in a Washington-post.com exchange on January 5, 2000:

> Whatever you think about Wen Ho Lee's probable guilt or innocence, the fact remains that he committed an egregious security violation at Los Alamos and downloaded a vast store of nuclear secrets onto tapes for which he cannot now account. If he were to come up with the tapes, or give U.S. authorities a convincing description of how he destroyed them and where, say, they could find the melted plastic residue, I feel his solitary confinement would quickly end. The hardball is all geared to finding the tapes, which have U.S. authorities extremely worried. If Lee actually did give them to, say, Taiwan, it truly could change the

global strategic balance and have enormous consequences for
Taiwan, China and the U.S. . . . Having watched Wen Ho Lee
sit poker-faced in court for three days last week, I kind of think
he may never talk, other than to say he destroyed the tapes. But
if he [is] of a mind to talk, no bail and solitary confinement
should be something of an inducement.

But "cooperating" with the prosecution wasn't that simple. I had already talked with the FBI more than 20 times without an attorney,
and so the constant statements that I refused to cooperate were really
unfair and untrue. In letters to the government written during the
previous year, Mark Holscher had offered several times to have me
take a polygraph test conducted by a mutually agreed upon test-
giver—not the FBI, which had proven itself too willing to "reinter-
pret" the test results. The government never took us up. Gorence
wanted to interrogate me again without offering me any protection in
return. In response to Mark's offer of a new lie detector test, Gorence
faxed a letter dated January 5, 2000, which included these points:

To address the government and Judge Parker's concerns, Dr. Lee
would have to answer a number of questions, orally, in person,
to special agents of the Federal Bureau of Investigation. We
would expect Dr. Lee to answer the following areas of inquiry:

1. Do the tapes presently exist?
2. Where are the tapes today?
3. Do any copies of the tapes exist?
4. From the time of the creation of the tapes, were the tapes or
    their contents shared or provided to any other person
    through any means whatever?
5. Were all the tapes destroyed?
6. Where were the tapes located form [sic] the date of cre-
    ation until the date they were destroyed?

7. How were the tapes destroyed?

8. When were the tapes destroyed?

9. By whom were the tapes destroyed?

10. Where were the tapes destroyed?

11. Did anyone assist you in the destruction of the tapes?

12. Was any other person present when the tapes were destroyed?

13. Was the information on the tapes ever transferred to any other medium, such as another electronic medium or paper?

I was willing to answer these questions with a polygrapher, but Gorence also insisted:

> It is the government's view that complete and candid answers to all of the above questions are *a prerequisite for the government to even begin to reconsider its position with respect to Dr. Lee's pretrial detention.* [emphasis added] If and when Dr. Lee answers these questions, the government would undertake to corroborate or refute, through further investigation, the statements made by Dr. Lee. The government may want to ask additional questions based on its investigation, and it may ask Dr. Lee to submit to a polygraph with reference to one or more of the questions set forth above. Only then and only after the government is confident that it has received a truthful statement from Dr. Lee would it be prepared to reevaluate its position concerning pretrial detention.

My attorneys advised that, since the government offered no assurance that they would ever consider letting me out of jail, it would be unwise to do their bidding. Even people involved in a minor traffic incident are warned to say nothing until their legal rights are protected, and here, with the threat of a capital offense, the prosecutors offered no legal protection in exchange. So we refused Gorence's "offer."

Refusing meant I would stay in solitary confinement, with the pressure intended to induce me to talk.

During that first week of January, John Kelly, the U.S. Attorney of New Mexico, announced that he was resigning from office—and therefore would be stepping down from this case. He planned to run as a Democratic candidate for the U.S. Congress. Kelly had been one of the strongest proponents of prosecuting me; he was at the White House meeting where the decision was made to indict me, and he argued inside the Department of Justice to have me arrested, even in the face of opposition from other DOJ officials. When I heard he had resigned, I felt he was an ambitious politician who had been planning for months to run for office—and my head would be a useful political trophy for him. I could bring him national attention, thanks to all the lies and distortions coming from his office. I'm glad it all ultimately backfired against him. But at the time it wasn't clear how his resignation might affect my case. I wondered if it would delay my trial even further. The longer the trial was delayed, the longer my imprisonment.

Amid all this uncertainty, there was one bright spot in the news. During the December hearings, the government introduced as an exhibit the results of the disputed polygraph test that the DOE's contractor, Wackenhut, had given me on December 23, 1998. That was the test I was told I had passed, only to find that the FBI changed the result and told the media and Congress I had failed— and that my supposed failure meant that I was a spy. This new exhibit of the polygraph results proved that I had indeed passed—just as I had been told initially. The FBI version of my polygraph results had been contrived. A CBS reporter, Sharyl Attkisson, investigated the results and made this TV report for CBS News:

Lee was asked four espionage-related questions:

"Have you ever committed espionage against the United States?" Lee's response: "No."

"Have you ever provided any classified weapons data to any unauthorized person?" Lee's response: "No."

"Have you had any contact with anyone to commit espionage against the United States?" Lee's response: "No."

"Have you ever had personal contact with anyone you know who has committed espionage against the United States?" Lee's response: "No."

The polygrapher concluded that Lee was not deceptive. Two other polygraphers in the DOE's Albuquerque test center, including the manager, reviewed the charts and concurred: Lee wasn't lying.

The polygraph results were so convincing and unequivocal that sources say the deputy director of the Los Alamos lab issued an apology to Lee, and work began to get him reinstated in the X Division. Furthermore, sources confirm to CBS News that the local Albuquerque FBI office sent a memo to headquarters in Washington saying it appeared that Lee was not their spy.

But key decision-makers in Washington remained unconvinced.

Several weeks after the polygraph, the DOE decided to assign it the unusual designation of "incomplete." Officials in Washington also ordered a halt to Lee's reinstatement to the X Division.

When FBI headquarters in Washington finally obtained the DOE polygraph results, yet another interpretation was offered: that Lee had failed the polygraph.

The FBI then did its own testing of Lee, and again claimed that he failed. Yet sources say the FBI didn't interrogate Lee at this time, or even tell him he had failed the polygraph—an odd deviation from procedure for agents who are taught to immediately question anyone who is deceptive in a polygraph. . . .

CBS News spoke to Richard Keifer, the current chairman of the American Polygraph Association, who's a former FBI agent and used to run the FBI's polygraph program. . . . We asked Keifer to look at Lee's polygraph scores. He said the scores are "crystal clear." In fact, Keifer says, in all his years as a polygrapher, he had never been able to score anyone so high on the non-deceptive scale. He was at a loss to find any explanation for how the FBI could deem the polygraph scores as "failing."

My attorneys also obtained from the government a transcript of the March 7, 1999, interrogation by Carol Covert and John Hudenko—the time they told me that unless I confessed to giving nuclear secrets to China, I might be executed, like the Rosenbergs. When the transcript was made public, it generated a wave of outrage because it exposed yet another side of the FBI's ugliness. We had to find other documents and information that could disprove the many lies the FBI was using against me. But the government could hide everything by invoking the magic words "national security," keeping everything classified and secret—the way they had classified my downloaded files as Secret and Confidential *after* I was fired. Breaking through the secrecy would be a big legal challenge.

One of the first of many motions my attorneys filed was to challenge the constitutionality of the Classified Information Procedures Act (CIPA), which forced defendants like me to reveal—pretrial—any classified information that we might want to use in my defense. The attorneys argued that CIPA is unconstitutional. CIPA was supposed to protect the government, not the accused, by making it more difficult to expose classified information in court. In order to obtain information that would be critical to my defense—like the files I was accused of mishandling—my lawyers would have to give the prosecution lists of all classified documents we might want to use. The government can argue about each requested document, and the judge would have to rule. Even if the judge agrees that we should be allowed to see a particular classified document, the prosecutors can still try to provide a substitute document. CIPA would force us to reveal our defense case to the prosecution before trial, which my attorneys, and others before them, argued was unconstitutional. My attorneys didn't expect to win their argument, but they said it had to be done. Not surprisingly, Judge Conway denied that motion.

In these dark days, my attorneys also filed an appeal of Judge Parker's order to deny me bail. On February 29, 2000, our appeal was denied, as my attorneys expected. The U.S. Court of Appeals for the 10ᵗʰ Circuit said that the government had established "clear and convincing evidence that there were no conditions or 'combination of conditions of release that will reasonably assure the safety of any other person and the community and the nation.'" In other words, I was too dangerous, and the only way to protect 270 million Americans from the sinister evil I might inflict was to incarcerate me.

———

I think my spirits were at their lowest point during this time. For my first month in detention, I wasn't allowed out of my cell except once a day, Monday through Friday, to walk 15 feet down the hall from my cell to take a shower. On weekends, I couldn't even do that. I had no idea whether it was night or day; I didn't see the sun or moon for more than a month, except for those few days in December for my detention hearings. A light stayed on in my cell at all times, even when I tried to sleep. One hour per week, I could see my family during their visiting hour—with two FBI agents standing right by us, listening to every word. Once, when Alberta was telling me about something new in her job, the FBI agents made her stop, just because she was talking about computers. I also was allowed out of my cell when my lawyers visited, once or twice a week, to meet with them. Otherwise I stayed in my cell for 24 hours, as there was no outdoor exercise time for me during that first month. No books, no newspapers, no television, no radio, no paper, no pens, no hot water, no contact with anyone except under very restrictive conditions.

The prosecutors invoked something called "special administrative measures," or SAMs, to set the rules of my confinement. To be imprisoned under SAMs, I was very special—I had joined the ranks of an elite group of fewer than a dozen of the most dangerous federal prisoners—all of whom, unlike me, had been convicted of crimes. At least, this is what we were told. I never learned of any other prisoner being treated this way. The SAMs spelled out, on more than fifteen pages, how I was to be treated. I was required to sign the order. Thus, with the full knowledge and personal approval of Attorney General Janet Reno, prosecutor Robert Gorence, who became the acting U.S. attorney after Kelly resigned, mandated the following jail conditions:

> Solitary confinement, no contact with anyone else except as
>> defined, so that I would be unable to communicate any
>> classified information;
> No written or recorded communications with anyone;
> No attorney phone calls allowed to be patched through to a
>> third party;
> Only attorneys permitted to visit;
> Severe restrictions on the use of translators;
> Correspondence to me requiring translation could only be
>> done by a court-approved translator;
> If any of the monitored phone calls violate these stringent
>> rules, all family phone calls would be terminated;
> All mail correspondence to and from me would first be
>> screened, analyzed, and photocopied by the government.

There was the added provision that in case of a conflict between the jail rules and the SAMs, the more severe rule of the two would prevail. This was sick and disgusting. All of this to make the government and politicians look good, like they had finally put the Chinese spy away.

After that one phone call the first night, I wasn't allowed to make any more calls for the next few weeks. The jail officials took their orders from the FBI—they wouldn't allow me to do anything without FBI authorization first. Even though the FBI arrested me, they hadn't worked out the details of my imprisonment. So I wasn't permitted to do anything that regular inmates could do until the U.S. attorney and the FBI handed down their edicts.

I thought I was being treated like every prisoner—shackled and chained, with a 24-hour personal watch guard jotting down my every move, whether I was awake or asleep, when I showered, when I used the toilet. The guards, at least, got a break from the routine; they changed shifts every eight hours. For me, there was no letup in this degrading treatment. Janet Reno, the government, and even some Asian Americans and other folks have said that everything must have been okay in jail because I didn't complain. But especially during my first month in jail, I didn't even know that I *could* complain. Nancy Hollander made many requests on my behalf—to allow my family to speak Chinese to one another; to get my family's visiting time changed to Saturday so it would be easier for my children to travel to see me; to get more fruit for me; to allow me to have a radio; to arrange for exercise time. Each request was a struggle in itself. Nancy's persistence made it possible for me to survive in jail. It also helped that many people wrote letters to Janet Reno and other government officials about my jail conditions. Nancy told a reporter that she was shocked by my conditions: "I've had murder clients, drug clients, clients accused of taking millions of dollars from the federal government, you name it, but I've never had a client treated like Wen Ho Lee."

Not knowing my rights as an American to be free from "cruel or unusual" punishment, I accepted my treatment without question. I didn't know to complain that I was constantly cold, shivering most of the time because all I had was the red jumpsuit, undershorts, and two thin blankets. My beard grew scruffy and my fingernails became long because I didn't have razor or nail clippers. I asked the warden if he could help me. He eventually gave me some rusty, used nail clippers. When I asked him if there was some additional clothing I could have because of the cold jail temperature, he brought in an old, beat-up pair of sweatpants—I can't imagine where he found these discarded items to give to me. I tore the sweatpants so that I could put my arms through the pant legs and wear it like a jacket. It wasn't until I was later moved next to another prisoner's cell that I learned I could simply buy what I needed from the jail commissary. The FBI must have instructed Warden Romero and the guards not to give me any information or anything that would improve my dismal conditions. They wanted me to be as miserable as possible.

————

My primary concern was to keep my mind and body healthy. I was accustomed to hiking at least three miles each day, up and down the New Mexico mountains and canyons. For my first month, I was locked in a 6- by 15-foot cell for 24 hours a day, and later I was moved into a smaller one. I tried to exercise for two hours every day, one hour in the morning and one hour in the afternoon. Since I didn't have a watch, I had to guess at the time. My workout routine included jogging around the tiny space, jumping up and down while holding onto the bed frame, doing jumping jacks, bending and stretching, and other exercises I devised.

For my mental health, I knew I had to keep my mind occupied. I tried not to dwell on the lies and the many problems of my defense. I spent time working on my case, trying to remember anything that would be useful to my lawyers. I asked for paper and was given a few sheets at a time. With my pencil, I made notes to discuss with John and Nancy during one of their visits once or twice a week. I resolved to write a math textbook. I asked for books from the jail library, but there was no way of knowing what the jail would send me. Gradually, I received books from outside—but I was only allowed to have books that were mailed directly from the publisher, with the covers torn off, not from individuals. I don't know what happened to the books that so many kind people sent to me themselves; perhaps the jailers kept them.

Food presented a bigger challenge. Both the quantity and quality of the food was low. I couldn't measure how much weight I was losing, but I could see that my skin was hanging loose, all wrinkled and baggy, especially on my hands and neck. I had never seen this before. I didn't get out into the fresh air and sunlight, so I knew I was lacking in Vitamin D. At home, I never ate red meat—only chicken, fish and turkey. In jail, we got scrambled eggs, sausage and toast for breakfast. I'd eat the eggs and toast, not the sausage. Lunch and dinner usually contained white bread with a thin slice of meat, or a hot dog. Maybe we got a chicken leg, once a week. The bologna we received had an unnatural fluorescent red color. I had never eaten processed meats like salami or bologna before, and I couldn't bring myself to eat them now, even though I was constantly hungry. I ate like a vegetarian in jail, except that there were no real vegetables or salad, and only a small piece of fruit a day. The vegetable was usually canned string beans or canned corn. If they served any salad, it was smaller in quantity than what airlines serve as salad. I was hungry all the time, and I wondered if I would get sick from these conditions.

After a few weeks, I was finally allowed to make one 15-minute call per week, but only to a member of my immediate family. In addition, I had to make an appointment with a jail official ahead of time so that she could dial the phone number for me. The calls could be made only on Tuesday between 3 and 4 P.M., or Thursday between 9 and 10 A.M. If the jail official wasn't available during that time slot, I couldn't make the call, and I had to wait until the next allotted time. Other inmates could make calls at any time. Before I could actually talk on the phone, the official had to read two pages of instructions on what we were allowed to say and what was for-

bidden. No conversation in Chinese, only English. No tape record-
ings were allowed, even though the FBI was monitoring and recording the calls. After all that, the 15-minute call ended up being only
five minutes. Of course, it was a collect call. I made one call to
Chung, and it ended up costing him $60. He was living on a stu-
dent's budget, so I didn't call him anymore. During my nine months
in jail, I called my wife and Alberta only three or four times.

———

In mid-January 2000, after a month of being shut in that dark cell,
the jail officials moved me to Pod A, the maximum-security part of
the detention facility. Pod A had other prisoners in solitary confinement. It was one of four pods, each with 12 cells, six on the upper
level, six on the lower level. The cells were locked. Also, the small
common area in front of the cells was locked and separated by a
Plexiglas and steel wall from another locked common area that was
also monitored by a guard. I no longer had my own personal guard
standing watch and making notes every time I scratched myself.
Two guards were on duty watching the pod at all times.

Each cell in the pod had a bunk bed. My cell was smaller than
my previous "suite," which had three bunk beds, but at least I had a
small slit of a window, high on the wall, where I might peek out at
the Santa Fe desert. Pod A housed the worst criminals and had no
TV, no radio, no hot water, and no newspapers. We were all kept in
our own cells, but people talked and shouted at each other through
the doors and the air vents. Before, when I was in total seclusion, I
had no sense of how my treatment compared to anyone else's. Prisoners in the other pods had hot water, TV, newspapers. They
weren't shackled and chained.

Even in Pod A, they treated me differently. I was not allowed to
make phone calls, and when I was let out of my cell, the guards
put my shackles and chains on in the innermost common area. The
other inmates in Pod A would shout from their peepholes, "Hey, Wen

Ho Lee!" and strange questions or stupid comments. I never bothered to answer back. Some of them were very scary-looking—I had never seen people who looked like that before. Most were quite young, maybe 21 or 22 years old. I felt bad for them, especially because most of them had had little education. Being in solitary confinement was very difficult for them because they had nothing to do. At least I could work on my math book and write my notes.

My neighbor in Pod A was a young guy, about 30 years old, named Byron Chubbuck. He was a celebrity of sorts in Albuquerque. People called him "Robin the Hood" because he robbed banks and told the tellers he was giving the money to poor children. Byron and I talked through the air vents. Byron was quite smart. He had dropped out of high school but got his GED and took college courses, and had the equivalent of a BA in chemistry. He wrote poetry. If he had been my child, he probably would have gone to medical school. But he was from a poor family; he didn't have a chance to have an education, and he got hooked on drugs. Eighty percent of the other prisoners were in for drugs. Drunk driving, too. There were some murderers, rapists, and other violent people, but most were there because of substance abuse. These young guys must have started taking drugs when they were just kids and didn't know better, and then they ended up in jail. Byron said that the government sells drugs to poor people, and that the police often frame people by planting drugs on them. I don't know if that is true, but in jail it was obvious to me that drugs are screwing up our country.

Byron told me about the commissary. He told me I could use the commissary checklist to buy all kinds of things—toothpaste, shampoo, and other sundries. A razor and a new nail clipper. Sweatshirts, sweatpants, socks, and underwear. When I learned about the commissary, I was both happy and disgusted. Finally I could wear something more comfortable than the red jumpsuit—but there had been no need for me to shiver for so many weeks. I had come into the prison with $25, and Alberta had sent me a couple hundred dollars—plenty for me to get what I needed. I also discovered I could buy tuna fish from the commissary, packed in a foil bag, not a can. I could eat some protein, at last. I lived on the tuna for about a month, but then the commissary discontinued selling it. I resorted to buying crackers to supplement my diet. I even bought ramen noodles, which I had to "cook" with warm tap water, since I was not allowed to have hot water.

When I had leftovers, like the bologna or salami sandwich or things I couldn't eat from my meal tray, I asked the guard, Can you give this to whoever wants it? Those big, young guys were even hungrier than I was. But shortly after I arrived in Pod A, someone tried to poison me. Nancy Hollander had written to the warden, asking for certain things to improve my conditions, including more food because I was losing so much weight. On February 5, 2000, in response to Nancy's letter, I received two trays for breakfast. One was from the regular cart, and a special tray had my name on it. I only wanted to eat one breakfast, so the guard gave the tray with my name on it to my neighbor Byron Chubbuck. Within an hour, he became violently ill, with severe vomiting and diarrhea—he had to get help from the medical ward. We theorized that someone tampered with the food tray that was meant for me, maybe a government agent who was posing as an inmate, or an inmate who was working with the government. I never discovered what happened, but after this incident, I never touched the food on any tray that had my name on it, unless it had some food I could wash carefully, like a salad or fruit. I was afraid that next time the poisoning would be lethal.

One day, a prisoner in Pod A committed suicide. He was in jail for killing his girlfriend, and he hung himself. Like the other prisoners, he was a young guy. I felt that's what Bill Richardson and the government wanted me to do. Then they could brag that they got rid of the Chinese spy. Alberta worried about this. On one of the days before I was arrested, Alberta was home and we talked about the possibility that the government might put me in prison. She said,

"Dad, if you go to prison, you must promise me you won't kill your-self." Of course I wouldn't kill myself, but now that I was in jail, I knew exactly how to do it. In jail you can kill yourself two ways. Every week the jail gives you a plastic bag for garbage. If you cut the bag, you can make it very strong, like a rope. Then you can hang yourself from the bunk bed. Or you can use the sheet. The sheets are so thin, they can easily be tied into a rope. That's how the guy hung himself.

Sometimes the other inmates would organize a protest by clog-ging the toilets. They did this by flushing the toilets continuously and making the water overflow into their rooms. If they blocked the space between the door and the floor, they could get the water to rise in their rooms up to a foot deep. If two or three inmates on the upper level did it and unblocked their doors at the same time, hun-dreds of gallons of water could come rushing out, pouring down the steps, flooding the first floor. This happened at least 20 or 30 times during my incarceration. The first time it happened, I didn't know what was going on. The water ran into my room—about 5 inches deep of sewage. I used a paper cup to bail the water, then wiped it up myself. Later I knew how to tell when the flooding was going to happen, because I could hear the toilets flushing. I used a towel and plastic bags to block the door and keep the water out.

The inmates who did the flooding would get punished. They would have to sit in darkness. The guards would take their mat-tresses away and even make them take their clothes off, and they'd have to sleep on the cold metal beds.

Sitting alone in solitary confinement with a light bulb burning continuously, all night long, I sometimes felt like I must have made a mistake and should not have come to America in 1964 for my Ph.D. Maybe I came on the wrong plane. Maybe I came to the wrong place at the wrong time. I must have done something terrible to have ended up like this. But it's all past now. I cannot change what has been done. As I sat in jail, I had to conclude that no matter how smart you are, no matter how hard you work, a Chinese person, an Asian person like me, will never be accepted. We always will be foreigners. Bill Richardson said my treatment, my incarceration, had nothing to do with racial profiling. What a liar—it had everything to do with discrimination.

It was a hard time, a difficult time. I knew I had only two choices—to kill myself or to fight for my life. I knew that right away. I thought I might have to stay in jail my whole life. But when I read the indictment, I knew I would have to get out some time, because the indictment was all lies, exaggerations and fabrications. So I thought this farce would have to end eventually—I just didn't know when.

During my wife's first visit to the jail, she told me she tried to pretend I was in a coma and she didn't know if I would one day wake up. One of our neighbors, a Korean American woman, had been in a coma for a long time before she died. She told Chung and Alberta to think of me that way. Of course I wasn't in a coma—I was alive and fully conscious, but their interaction with me, through prison Plexiglas and the constant FBI presence, must have felt as constrained as my neighbor's children's communications with their comatose mother. It was Sylvia's way of coping with the situation. I understood that. My way of coping was to try to comfort myself, so that I wouldn't feel constant distress or anger.

———

Sometime in January 2000, John Cline got his Q clearance approved. Nancy Hollander's came a few weeks later. At last my Albuquerque attorneys could begin to learn what was behind the charges, what Files 1–19 and Codes A–I were about. John began spending several hours a day at a special government office in Albuquerque where he could read classified information about nuclear weapons codes, about Los Alamos and the work that I did. Soon K. C. Maxwell at Freedman Daniels and Richard Myers of O'Melveny and Myers got their security clearances too, as well as Barbara Bond and Ann Delpha. I also had my Q clearance restored so that I could discuss classified matters with my lawyers. A room at LANL was made available to my lawyers, and I was even brought to LANL from jail on a few occasions to work on my case. The defense team was making progress.

Each step forward was so important to us in these dark days, especially when the legal motions seemed to be going nowhere. For one thing, Nancy Hollander's letters to the jail had led to some small improvements in my incarceration. In February, I was allowed to have a small radio to listen to, which I tuned to a classical music station. Music was so much a part of my daily life. I was very happy to have it restored. The radio station also helped me keep time during the day, in the absence of a clock. I made a chart on a piece of cardboard, keeping a daily musical diary listing the time and the name of each composition that aired, along with the composer. I started receiving a little more fruit in the evening, an extra orange or two at the end of the day. I was also getting to go outside, in the enclosed exercise courtyard, Monday through Friday. During that one hour of exercise, my wrists and ankles were shackled and chained to my waist. A guard watched me as I gingerly kicked a soccer ball around the high-walled courtyard, taking small, mincing steps so that I wouldn't trip on my chains. I had to be careful, because if I fell down, I wouldn't be able to break my fall, with my hands in manacles. But at least I could breathe some fresh air during my one hour out of my small jail cell.

Even more encouraging were the protests being raised by various scientific groups about my incarceration. I learned from my attorneys and my family that the American Physical Society, the American Academy for the Advancement of Science, and the Committee of Concerned Scientists sent letters to Janet Reno and the Department of Justice, voicing their concerns over the denial of bail, conditions of detention, and the appearance of racial bias.

Joseph L. Birman, chairman of the Committee on Human Rights of Scientists of the New York Academy of Sciences, wrote this letter to Reno on March 14, 2000, which said in part:

> For more than 20 years, this Committee has been deeply concerned about governmental treatment and repression of scientists throughout the world. Among the cases in which we have intervened were those of Professors Andrei Sakharov, Fang Li Zhe, Benjamin Levich, and recently Alexandr Nikitin, to name just a few. Often the scientists named in these cases were accused by their governments of violation of secrecy, treason, and other high crimes. Our Committee has always paid close attention to the conditions under which these and other individuals were held during their detention, as well as related matters such as denial of bail, access to counsel, and openness and fairness of trial.
>
> We earnestly call to your attention that Dr. Lee's treatment during his detention has had a seriously chilling effect on the scientific community, especially because of the suspicion that his ethnic background has played some role in this treatment and in the unproven public allegations made about his possible motives for the acts of which he is accused. . . .
>
> In addition, reliable reports reach us that the recruiting and retention of top scientific staff at our major national laboratories, including weapon laboratories, have been damaged by this affair. We urge that you look into the treatment of Dr. Lee and see to it that the physical and psychological conditions of Dr. Lee's detention conform to the highest international standards for the humane treatment of people in detention awaiting trial. Continuation of the harsh treatment of Dr. Lee will expose us to ridicule when we criticize such treatment in other countries around the world.

Hearing that other scientists cared about what was happening to me gave me something positive to think about in jail. I was surprised that other people were speaking out, too. Labor unions like the International Longshore and Warehouse Union and such church groups as the Episcopal Church's International and National Concerns Committee—even local committees of political parties—were passing resolutions urging fair and humane treatment from the government.

I also learned from Alberta that Asian American college professors and administrators were urging Asian scientists and engineers to boycott the national labs. I thought this was a very interesting idea. The boycott was initiated by Professor Ling-chi Wang, chair of ethnic studies at the University of California at Berkeley, and a group called Asian Pacific Americans in Higher Education. On March 11, 2000, APAHE's membership adopted this resolution:

> . . . Be it therefore resolved, that the Asian Pacific Americans in Higher Education (APAHE) strongly condemns the mistreatment of Dr. Wen Ho Lee by the University of California, the U.S. Department of Energy, and the U.S. Department of Justice and the practice of racial profiling and discrimination in the national laboratories against Asian American scientists and engineers;
>
> Be it further resolved, that the APAHE sends a letter to U.S. Attorney General Janet Reno, demanding that (1) all charges of "mishandling classified data" against Dr. Wen Ho Lee be dropped; (2) he be released immediately and unconditionally, pending completion of the FBI investigation of all lab employees and former CIA director John Deutch who had similarly mishandled classified data; (3) he be reinstated to his job at the Los Alamos National Laboratory with back pay; (4) a public apology be made to Dr. Lee and his family by Secretary Bill Richardson of the U.S. Department of Energy and Dr. Richard Atkinson, president of the University of California; and (5) the illegal practice of racial profiling of and discrimination against Asian Americans in the labs be terminated immediately;

Be it further resolved, that as long as Dr. Wen Ho Lee continues to be unfairly and unjustly prosecuted and persecuted,
the *APAHE calls upon all Asian American scientists and engineers
not to apply for jobs at the national labs operated under contracts
with the U.S. Department of Energy as the most effective protest
against the mistreatment of Dr. Wen Ho Lee and against the use of
racial profiling and discrimination in these facilities*; and

Be it further resolved, that the APAHE calls upon all institutions of higher education to hold campus forums on the Wen
Ho Lee case and to assess and evaluate their attitude toward
and treatment of Asian Americans in their respective campuses,
making sure that racial profiling is not in use and Asian Americans are accorded equal and fair treatment in all aspects of
campus life . . ." [emphasis added]

On May 26, 2000, a second national organization of scholars and
educators, the Association for Asian American Studies, called for
Asian American scientists to boycott federal laboratories by not ap-
plying for jobs with them. Alberta told me the boycott was contro-
versial and that many Asian American scientists inside the national
labs were opposed to the idea, on the argument that the labs could
only change if Asian Americans were there to improve them. I saw
it another way. All my life I had encouraged the young people in my
family, including my own children, to pursue the sciences. But now
I would never recommend that path to another Chinese or Asian kid
again, especially when they might be treated unfairly or even get put
in jail as a scapegoat, the way that I was.

For all the venom spewing out of Christopher Cox and other
Washington politicians about the "questionable" loyalty of Chinese
American scientists, the fact remained that America's scientific talent depended on Chinese Americans and Asian Americans. Even
without an official boycott, not a single Chinese American submitted an application to work as a postdoctoral scientist at Los Alamos

that year—which had a very serious impact on the lab. Those boy-
cotts definitely caught the attention of politicians who never considered that Chinese or Asian Americans might make a positive
contribution to national security.

Letters from concerned citizens did not, however, change the
tenor of the debate in Washington, which was more focused on why
I wasn't locked up much sooner. In March 2000, Senator Arlen
Specter issued the lengthy "Report on the Investigation of Espionage Allegations Against Dr. Wen Ho Lee," which repeated every
FBI leak, lie, and exaggeration about me, without acknowledging
that many of those statements had been proven wrong. Specter
filled his report with the same kinds of irresponsible comments that
others had circulated, and added his own new ones—for example,
"Information that could change the global strategic balance was left
exposed on an unclassified computer system where *even an unso-
phisticated hacker* could gain access to it." [emphasis added] This
and so many other comments like it were simply not true. I had seen
more than my share of politicians who were too willing to distort information for their own benefit.

My biggest surprise in these months was to see my daughter Alberta blossom into an articulate crusader who crisscrossed the
country to talk about my case. After Alberta's first speech in December 1999, she was very much in demand, as requests from various organizations, professional and student groups, came pouring
in. Nobody had heard my side of what happened, which my lawyers
had instructed me not to talk about, and now I couldn't speak to
anyone even if I wanted to. Alberta became the spokesperson for
our family, and I was so amazed that my sheltered daughter turned
into a strong young woman who could talk to groups of strangers
and appear on TV. As a father, I didn't like how much flying she had
to do, and I worried that she could be jeopardizing her health and
her job by traveling around the country, taking two or three trips a
week in addition to her full-time job. Alberta had the added pres-

sure of being the only member of our family who was employed. Before all this happened to me, I would be the one to help Chung through medical school. Now, if he needed financial help, he had to turn to Alberta. Fortunately, Alberta's employers were very understanding; they even let her transfer to San Francisco so that she could be closer to home and to the base of community support for my case. She was intent on speaking out, and there was nothing I could do to stop her.

From the letters I received in jail, I was learning how effective Alberta was. Here's a note I received from someone in Los Angeles:

Dear Mr. Lee, We heard and met with your daughter, Alberta Lee. She has been very eloquent in sharing with us what you have been going through and how hard it has been. With every news article that comes out, we become more convinced of your innocence and unfair treatment. Please stay strong, we are all behind you.

A student who heard Alberta speak wrote this:

Dear Dr. Lee, You may think a "thank you" card strange but here is the reasoning. In your fight against discrimination you help out thousands of Asian Americans now and in the *future*. So I thank you and please have the knowledge that people (including me) are rooting for you. Good luck and be strong!

Not all the letters I received were friendly. One person from Buffalo, New York, wrote:

Get out of this country, you worthless piece of shit—and take your children with you. None of you traitor chinks are welcome in the USA.

Or this one:

> Once a Chinese, always a Chinese, and that goes for your children, too. They are Chinese just like you. There is no place in America for them to hide the fact that their parents are Chinese spys [*sic*] who have betrayed the USA. Your whole family is hated. You need to go back to China. We don't want your people.

And one note, with a crude Star of David drawn on the envelope, had a picture of a big crucifix inside with the message, "You f__ed [*sic*] the Chinese at our expense. We will get you back!"

Threats like these made me worry for my family, especially for Alberta, who was becoming so prominent and exposed to strangers by speaking up. I didn't worry so much about Chung. After all, he was a male, and his medical school world was more controlled, with far fewer variables. But I also thought that the FBI might try to do something to my family, to plant some false information, or even worse. My neighbor in Pod A, Byron Chubbuck, told me such things happened all the time. To me, it was plausible, given all the lies the FBI had already told. My family turned these poisonous letters over to my lawyers, in case anything did happen. Knowing that some people wanted to hurt my family made me very angry at Bill Richardson, the FBI, John Kelly, the DOJ, and all the politicians and people who didn't care what lies they told, who they destroyed, as long as they could help themselves.

But most of the letters I received were like this one, from a family in Albuquerque:

> Dear Dr. Lee! You do not know us—but we want you to know you and your family have our sincere support! We have no doubt about the true injustice you have received and we are deeply concerned about the USA's commitment to its founding fathers'

Declaration of Independence. Actually, we are ashamed of what has developed. Hang in there—our prayers are with you and your family!

Postcards and letters from Alberta were especially precious to me. She wrote to me almost every day and made a point of sending a note or postcard from the different locations where she was speaking. Doing this reminded her of the times I sent postcards to her and Chung every day when I traveled on LANL business. She always included some details about the events she was attending, like this rally she attended in Sacramento, California, on April 27, 2000:

Dear Father,

I am in Sacramento right now. I just spoke representing you as a victim of racial profiling. The main theme of the rally was for passing a resolution for policemen and other law enforcement officers to log statistics about the ethnicities of people they pull over. This is because there are a large number of people who are pulled over because they are black or Latino. I spoke for about 5 minutes in front of a crowd of about 700 people. It was by far the largest crowd I've spoken to and I was very nervous. Afterward, a lot of people came up to me and said they were touched. Also, a Latino man spoke about his experiences as a migrant farm worker being threatened by the police for his official work permits. A black woman spoke about working as a policeman, and when she wasn't in uniform, her coworkers would pull her over or stop her.

This just shows how much injustice is happening to people of color. It also shows how everybody is waking up to racism, and to the amazing injustices. I want you to know that there are a lot of supporters. About eight people from a retirement home came out to see me, as did some other Chinese Americans in the community.

Dad, we are fighting for you! I love you and am very proud
of you. Alberta.

I was so very proud of my daughter—and I was learning a lot from
her. Alberta was on national television, in newspapers and magazines—the *New York Times* even ran a big story about her, by James
Sterngold. As a parent, I was a little worried about Alberta's visibility, but the articles greatly brightened my life in jail. I felt so lucky
to have children who had grown up to be such fine adults. Many of
my supporters in Los Alamos, New Mexico, and elsewhere were
classmates of Alberta and Chung, their friends, and their former
teachers. I heard that there was even a protest rally through White
Rock that was organized by Jo Starling, Alberta's fifth-grade teacher,
who also lived nearby, and attorney Phyllis Hedges, whose daughter
went to school with my kids.

Later, some people told me they thought of Alberta as a mod-
ern-day Mulan, the Chinese girl in the fairy tale who became a war-
rior to save her father. I don't know about that, but I could see that
Alberta was intent on fighting for my freedom. In these dark days,
my greatest source of comfort came from my family and our friends,
including the many kind people who I had not met but were so willing to express their concerns on my behalf.

CHAPTER 13

In March 2000, my attorneys made an important discovery: The files I downloaded were classified as PARD—Protect as Restricted Data—not Secret or Confidential, as the indictment charged. The files were classified as PARD in 1993 and 1994 when I downloaded them, and were not changed to Secret and Confidential until April 1999—a month after the files were discovered, more than a month after I was fired. In the LANL hierarchy of files, "Unclassified" was the lowest level, "PARD" was next, then "Confidential," "Secret," and "Top Secret." As I've mentioned, PARD was a special category that allowed scientists to use huge files like computer codes without having to lock the stacks and stacks of computer printouts in vaults the way Confidential and Secret materials were supposed to be. Such computer codes were known to contain mostly, if not all, unclassified data. This finding was very significant and would be the first of several breakthroughs in my defense, as we tried to pry out critical evidence that was hidden by the government's ability to keep "secret" information away from us.

The handling of PARD documents was less stringent than Confidential or Secret files. PARD data could be left out on a scientist's desk in the secure area overnight. In fact, in the X Division, other code physicists would sometimes stack piles of PARD printouts in the hallways, to be used as door stops and to keep their offices from getting too cluttered. It was well known that this took place with printouts containing the same type of data that I was accused of downloading. Though the PARD category was used mostly in reference to hard copy, or paper, documents, the less secure handling requirements had clear implications for my electronic files.

I thought that this big discovery would force the government to end its prosecution. After all, if the indictment was proven to be wrong and my files were not Secret or Confidential, as it charged, how could they continue to prosecute me? But my attorneys said no, the system doesn't work that way and I wouldn't be released soon. I didn't understand how the charges could stick when the indictment made a serious mistake, like saying two plus two equals five. But the prosecutors claimed that this was only a technical detail, a point that would have to be taken up at trial. So I learned that according to our system of criminal "justice," people can still be kept in jail indefinitely, even when the charges have been proven wrong.

———

There were several legal issues that my attorneys were hotly pursuing, now that they had their security clearances. They could finally begin sifting through the mountains of classified government information necessary to review for my case, even as we waited for the secure room to be built. Since Judge Conway had denied our motion asserting that CIPA, the Classified Information Protection Act, was unconstitutional, the legal team had to begin drawing up a list of the classified documents we might need. Of course they didn't know what classified scientific documents might help our case, so I worked hard to remember what papers might be useful. The science of my case was going to be a core issue of my defense. How valuable were these computer files? As the scientist who worked with these codes on a daily basis, I knew that these codes had serious defects that made them of questionable value. The U.S. government, on the other hand, claimed that these "crown jewels" were so valuable that 270 million Americans could be wiped out, and the huge importance of this merited the 39 life sentences they were seeking for me.

My case was like a black box—the government said the box contained diamonds, and I said the box held sand. But the government controlled the access to the box. CIPA was the legal key for us to open the box and look inside. John Cline was to present our argument to Judge Conway, and he would have to persuade the judge that the documents we sought were important enough to override any of the prosecution's national security claims. John's first challenge was to understand the science, so that he could fashion our CIPA key.

The selective prosecution by the government was another big legal issue. Mark was preparing the arguments to show how the government was singling me out for prosecution when they had never treated anyone else in this way for mishandling classified information. This was a difficult legal issue to pursue, and the biggest barrier was to obtain the documents we needed to get from the government—documents that we knew existed but we would have to convince the judge to make available to us. Mark and Richard Myers were steadily accumulating the numerous examples of other security violations and how they had—or had not—been punished, including what John Deutch did, and many others like him. Selective prosecution was considered to be a difficult legal argument to win. But in my case, it seemed clear that if I had not been of Chinese heritage, I would not be sitting in jail.

With her expertise on illegal searches and seizures, Nancy Hollander was also preparing a motion to suppress the ten boxes of material that the FBI took from my home on April 10, 1999. The search warrant that the FBI used to gain access to my home was overbroad and not specific in its search request, in that they looked for any items with a Chinese character or a telephone number on it, or any computer-related items. Because their search was too broad, the FBI took many personal things, including photos of Milan, Italy, an address book belonging to Alberta, correspondence between me and a college professor from 1971 to 1972, a manila envelope addressed to Alberta containing several personal letters, and my 1969 doctoral thesis. The search warrant also did not have a particular legal document attached to it, as it was supposed to have. If the items the FBI seized from my house were disqualified, that would also include my notebook identifying the files that I downloaded. Disallowing that evidence could have a big impact on the government's case against me.

Then, of course, there was the issue of what country I was supposedly aiding with the intent to harm the United States by violating the Atomic Energy Act. The most serious accusation against me, 42 USC § 2275, receiving restricted data, states in part:

> Whoever, *with intent to injure the United States or with intent to secure an advantage to any foreign nation*, acquires, or attempts or conspires to acquire any document, writing, sketch, photograph, plan, model, instrument, appliance, note, or information involving or incorporating Restricted Data shall, upon conviction thereof, be punished by imprisonment for life, or by imprisonment for any term of years or a fine of not more than $100,000 or both." [emphasis added]

The prosecutors had not shown any motive or intent on my part. My lawyers knew they didn't have any motive to attribute to me. They also hadn't named any other foreign nation that I was supposed to be trying to secure an advantage with. Mark was preparing a motion called a Bill of Particulars to force the government to name the countries it would claim I was seeking to assist.

All these legal issues had to be hammered out before my case ever got to trial, while I waited in pretrial imprisonment. In addition to all these motions on the criminal charges, there was the Privacy Act lawsuit that Brian Sun and his firm were preparing. The judge in that case had put the lawsuit on hold, pending the criminal case. But there were so many variables and legal issues in my lawsuit I was trying my best to get a legal education so that I could understand them. I had to teach my lawyers about physics and at the same time become their law student. I found that the concepts were not too complex, but the language was very difficult. When I read the briefs, I had to sit with a dictionary and ask my law "professors" what the words meant.

We had one more bit of news about the prosecution. Ever since John Kelly resigned from his post as U.S. attorney, his spot had been vacant, with Robert Gorence acting in his place. In March there was the surprise appointment of Norman Bay, a Chinese American federal prosecutor, a Harvard Law School graduate who had grown up in New Mexico. I didn't care one way or another about what happened to Gorence, even though he had scolded me for waving to my family and was so nasty in the way he kept saying that I "stole" the computer files I used for my work. But I thought it was obvious that they appointed a Chinese American to prosecute me as window dressing against public suspicions of racial scapegoating and selective prosecution. I heard that in the 1950s, the government appointed a Jewish judge and a Jewish prosecutor to the Rosenbergs' case in order to avoid any appearance of anti-Semitism, at a time when few Jews held such high government positions. I had nothing against Bay, but I thought it was interesting how some Chinese Americans were getting appointed to various DOE, DOJ, and LANL high-level jobs and task forces *after* my case and the accusations of racism surfaced. None of this could hide the fact that the emperor had no clothes on.

————

On April 15, 2000, the day we had been waiting for finally arrived: The special "vault-type room" was ready for use, a full four months after my arrest. At last my lawyers would be permitted to work on the classified parts of my case at a secure room in the courthouse where I could go and meet with them about my defense—where classified documents could be used and stored. The federal General Services Administration had to obtain special funding to remodel a couple of conference rooms at the courthouse so that no electronic signals would be able to penetrate or escape from the specially enclosed facility. I was told that it cost $85,000 to prepare and outfit this special room. John had worked closely with the DOJ to get the vault-type room completed—he knew what needed to be done because of his experience with the Iran-Contra case, which also involved lot of classified information. If he hadn't had that experience, then who knows how much longer it might have taken.

My life as a prisoner changed dramatically with the opening of this room. Now I could leave the jail four days a week to work on my own defense, to interact with other human beings—and, most important, to eat some decent food, fresh fruit, and vegetables. My whole routine changed, and I had a purpose. From Monday to Thursday, I woke up at 6:00 or 6:30 A.M., ate my breakfast, and, by about 7:00 or so, would be waiting in the booking area, to be checked out by two federal marshals—one driver, one riding shotgun. We made the hour drive to the Albuquerque courthouse, and I waited in the lockup until someone from my legal team arrived to accompany me to the vault-type room. Usually that person was Barbara Bond, and later, Ann Delpha, after she got her Q clearance. I was permitted to be in the vault-type room without a guard as long as I was accompanied by a member of the legal team. At about 4 P.M., I would be escorted back to the courthouse basement by the federal marshals, to await transport back to my cell in Pod A at the Santa Fe detention facility.

Though I was allowed in the vault-type room, I was still monitored. To get into the room, which was on the third floor of the courthouse, you needed a key card for the first door; there were two outside combination locks, and inside there was a code alarm. A federal marshal sat outside the room at all times, where he could monitor the room on closed-circuit screens fed by two video monitors. All cell phones and communication devices were left with the marshal, who sat outside the room whenever I was inside. While I was free to be with my legal defense team without the immediate presence of guards, my leg shackles stayed on.

My first day at the vault-type room was like Christmas. Nancy, John, and Barbara were there. Nancy had stocked the room with lots of food in its refrigerator. It had a microwave and a water cooler too. Nancy told me, "We're going to take good care of you, Wen Ho." As K.C. later commented, "You have a lot of moms to watch out for you here." Barbara and Ann were always asking me if I wanted them to buy me something different to eat. On that first day, I met Barbara—she was so friendly and nice, she made me feel comfortable right away. But right after Barbara was introduced to me, she left the room. I later found out she left because she began to cry at the sight of me and she didn't want me to know. Barbara said I looked so thin, white, and sickly, so unlike earlier photos she had seen, and the shackles and chains that distorted my movement horrified her. She has a very soft heart.

No sunlight was allowed through the windows high up near the 25-foot ceilings—they had to be shuttered at all times, in case China sent some ninjas with black helicopters to grab me. But I didn't care about that. Now I could eat oranges and bananas, and turkey sandwiches with salad greens and good, fresh bread, not the spongy white bread the jail served. There was hot water in the vault-type room, which I didn't have in jail, so I could finally have a cup of tea. Sylvia gave my lawyers tins of my favorite tea to keep at the room—the tea that comes from Nantou, Taiwan, my hometown. Alberta sent fruit from Harry and David, so we were always stocked with beautiful fruit in season, like flats of sweet Bing cherries and juicy strawberries. I ate nonstop when I was there, to try to gain back some of the weight I had lost and to rid myself of my prison pallor, a symptom of vitamin deficiency. At first the jail warden said that I couldn't bring back any food with me to the jail, but after Nancy sent them another letter about my weight loss and the jail foods I couldn't eat, they let me bring back a turkey sandwich and some fruit.

I referred to the vault-type room as "my office." My "job" was to provide my defense team with the science behind the legal issues of my case. I didn't know about the law, but I could explain the testimony of Younger and Robinson and Krajcik and the other witnesses. I needed to teach everything I knew to my lawyers, especially John Cline, who, when he argued the CIPA motion on classified information, would need to describe Files 1 through 19, nuclear physics, computational methods, weapons codes, computer security, and so on. I needed to help my lawyers understand the "crown jewels," the LANL systems and processes. Even before the vault-type room was open, John had been studying nuclear physics on his own for a few months. Now that we could actually talk at the room, he came there with a list of questions for me. What are Lagrangian methods? How do they differ from Eulerian methods? What are the advantages of Lagrangian or Eulerian methods? What is mesh tangling? What is a shockwave? Are such things used in nuclear weapons codes? What are the different components of nuclear weapons simulations codes, as referred to in the indictment? What are the source codes, the data decks, the input decks . . . etc. Of course, there were many questions that I can't discuss here, because they are classified. I liked to joke that John was my pupil—he said I was a good teacher, but he was a very good pupil. He didn't have a math or physics background, but he was able to master the science because of his logical mind and good memory.

In order to make the CIPA case, to open up the black box and show that the so-called crown jewels were actually sand, there were two particular scientific points for me to teach my attorneys. First, the codes I worked with were not the crown jewels, and, second, much of the information about the bomb and the codes were readily available in the open literature, on the Internet, and in public libraries.

The science of nuclear weapons begins with the basic principles of physics, Newton's Second Law that states Force equals Mass times Acceleration. F=MA is one of the universal principles behind every collision, like the apple falling from a tree onto the young Isaac Newton, or the collisions among neutrons, the subatomic particles that are released in a nuclear reaction. In a light-water nuclear reactor, the neutrons in the uranium fuel collide, causing the atoms to split or fission. This releases heat. The heat from the uranium core acts like an oven. Water surrounds the core, and a primary cooling system transfers the heat to a secondary loop of water. The heat from this secondary loop drives the turbines that generate electricity.

In my early years as a nuclear scientist, I wrote computer codes that described the hydrodynamics of nuclear reactors. My codes on nuclear reactor safety were well known. In fact, once the Taiwan government asked me for a copy of an unclassified paper I wrote on reactor safety, which I sent to them. The FBI and Senator Arlen Specter, in his March 8, 2000, hearing, however, wrongly made it sound as though I had sent nuclear weapons secrets to Taiwan— something that they would continue to insinuate.

A nuclear bomb uses similar principles of physics, but of course the application is different. In an atomic bomb, the uranium or plutonium fissions, generating tremendous heat, but there is no water coolant as there is in a nuclear reactor. Instead, the heat energy is released in a massive explosion, sending a shock wave blast that kills people, and then emits radiation, which destroys the eyes and burns the body, among other harmful effects. Atomic bombs, like the 20 kiloton "Fat Man" bomb dropped on Nagasaki, are limited in size because plutonium 239 is so unstable that it will start a chain reaction spontaneously when more than a certain quantity is combined. I can't say how much here, but it is a small-enough quantity that it restricts an atomic bomb's usefulness as a weapon. However, the plutonium atomic explosion can be used as the primary stage of a hydrogen bomb, to be the "match" to light the hydrogen secondary stage. The hydrodynamics of the primary can be simulated on a computer through Code B, one of the codes I worked on for several years.

I taught my attorneys about the computer codes and the physics equations I used to model or simulate these events. Newton's Second Law supplied the basic principle, but my equations were not that simple. The force component in a bomb involves a high explosion, radiation, temperature, massive sound waves, gravitational forces. Mass also has variables related to the particular element used—for example, uranium, plutonium, beryllium, or the heavy forms of hydrogen, deuterium and tritium. The number of variables to account for are more numerous in an atomic bomb than in a nuclear reactor, and greater still in a hydrogen bomb.

We discussed the discoveries in nuclear weapons science and the evolution of the hydrogen bomb. It has a big advantage over the atomic bomb, because you can make it bigger or smaller by adjusting the hydrogen fuel. The deuterium and tritium are stable, so you can put as many atoms as you want to make a really big bomb. The Russians produced a 20-megaton hydrogen bomb, and the U.S. detonated one about that size, too—that's 1,000 times more explosive power than the Fat Man bomb that devastated more than two square miles of Nagasaki and caused approximately 45,000 immediate deaths.

The code used to simulate the secondary was referred to as Code A in the indictment. Code A is more complex than Code B. In addition to the variables used in the primary, the code for the secondary bomb must include equations for radiation, neutrons, charged particles, hydrodynamics. Each of these has additional variables that describe position, angle of rotation, time, speed, and so on. With so many variables for each factor, it is impossible to "solve" the equation, so you have to make assumptions and approximations.

Numerical methods like Lagrangian and Eulerian computations are used to approximate what happens in physical problems with many variables. With these computational methods, you apply a mesh or a grid to create cells or zones that you can track over time to show what happens in that zone. For example, if you draw a mesh on a tennis ball as it hits a wall, you'll create lots of small cells. Moment by moment, the variables in those tennis ball cells change—the pressure, density, energy, velocity and so forth.

Ever since the time I told the FBI that some Chinese scientists may have asked me about Lagrangian methods, the FBI and members of Congress have used this to say I solved some problems for China using Lagrangian methods. That is such nonsense, like saying a discussion about algebra is the same as giving them secrets.

My point is this: Everything I just described is very well-known, very public, with much written on these topics in the open literature. The physics has been around for a hundred years—the secret of the bomb became public when it exploded in Japan. There are no secrets related to the science, and the codes I worked on modeled the science. I suppose there are production and manufacturing secrets as to how particular bombs are made, but I had nothing to do with those processes. The W-88's dimensions, which the government tried to pin on me, more likely came from Sandia National Laboratories or a defense contractor, not from a code physicist like me. The FBI, the DOJ, and the politicians make it sound as if I had downloaded nuclear design codes and given them away—Stephen Younger, the associate lab director at LANL, even called the codes "a Ph.D. course in nuclear weapons design." This was false. Actually the codes modeled the physics of nuclear reactions—you could not use them to "design" a nuclear weapon without a great deal more information.

My attorneys, particularly John, became well versed in these subjects, in their minutiae. John was prepared to discuss the nature and contents of the source codes that I wrote and the other codes I used and maintained; the data files, which contained information on the properties of materials in a nuclear weapon; the "equation of state" files, which describe how materials respond in different conditions of temperature and so on; opacity files, which focus on the response of materials to radiation; data tables, which contain nuclear test data; input decks, which provide the design geometries, approximations, and "fudge factors" that help make the codes work. He also knew about the users' manuals to these codes, and how the codes I downloaded were not functional without the users' manuals, which I kept locked in my safe in the X Division. Robert Gorence and Steve Younger seemed to think the manuals were unnecessary, but John would be able to show otherwise when he presented our CIPA motion.

We also went over why I say Code B is a garbage code. The prosecution's LANL experts and the FBI portrayed "legacy codes" like Code B as the most precious strings of code in the world, when actually many are worthless, antiquated junk. I showed my attorneys a code that is available on the commercial market that is far superior to Code B, which can be used to simulate nuclear explosions as well as other situations. Any company or country can buy this code. I can't name it here, but this code is distributed around the world and several countries use it. I had made this point many times at LANL, to my coworkers in the X Division, that we should throw Code B out when even commercial codes can do a better job. Many other code physicists agree with me, but to create a better code would require weapons designers to do some work to convert their input decks of bomb geometries and fudge factors to the new code.

Barbara Bond, with the assistance of Ann Delpha and Larry Trujillo, did exhaustive research to locate what is available in the open literature about nuclear weapons. I could remember many of the references to research papers as well, which Barbara located and added to our collection of evidence. I would evaluate her finds, and my attorneys studied them. Much of what Barbara found simply underscored the availability of this nuclear weapons information—like the 1979 article, "The H-Bomb Secret," that appeared in *The Progressive* magazine and described the hydrogen bomb in detail, or the Princeton University college student who wrote a senior thesis on how to build a bomb, or the TV program about a 15-year-old who built an exact replica of a nuclear bomb out of papier-mâché. Or the *Swords of Armaggeddon*, an exhaustive seven-volume collection of nuclear weapons information by Chuck Hansen that exists on CD-ROM.

In fact, the "crown jewels" are largely the crown junk. This is the biggest nuclear weapons secret that LANL and the government have to hide. The cornerstone of nuclear deterrence is to scare the rest of the world into thinking that our weapons are bigger, stronger, faster, and far more destructive than theirs. And while this is true, the science of nuclear weapons hasn't progressed much since the end of the Cold War and the Nuclear Test Ban Treaty of 1992.

As a scientist, I find this situation to be very sad. The only way for a scientist to make discoveries in physics is to experiment. Without testing and experimentation, there are no advances in nuclear weapons. At LANL and the other nuclear weapons labs, scientists spend their time figuring out what to do with rusty, old nuclear bombs, the 70,000 aging nuclear bombs that America has produced since 1945. Nuclear bombs are made out of metals—uranium and plutonium are metals. The metal rusts, just like a car. We don't even know how the old bombs will work. This is what nuclear weapons scientists spend their time on now—"stockpile stewardship." Fixing old bombs and digging up old test data. Like eating leftovers for dinner, it's better than nothing.

That's why I devoted as much time as I could to finding new and commercial applications with my science. To work only on old bombs and old science is demoralizing.

It was critical to my defense that we bring the science behind my codes into the courtroom, to open the "black box" and expose the crown jewels. The CIPA motion was so important to my defense for this reason. First we would have to convince the court that the information was relevant to my defense—information that could be found in the open literature, in classified government documents and in my head. Once we crossed that big hurdle, we would have to argue over the specific manner in which Files 1–19 would be presented at trial. As my attorneys learned their physics lessons well, I felt greatly encouraged.

————

My lawyers and I worked very closely for the next several months, locked together in the vault-type room, and we got to know each other well. Going to "my office" four days a week lifted my spirits tremendously. I no longer felt helpless, because I could work on my own defense. Plus, I like talking with people and being sociable, which solitary confinement denied me. The lawyers and legal assistants working on my case were all such decent and good people. I truly enjoyed being around them. Nancy Hollander was always watching for my welfare, asking me about my treatment in jail. It is not my nature to complain, but she would somehow find out what was going on. For example, coming to the room was a great relief, but it also meant that I lost my daily hour of exercise. When Nancy found out, she got the prison officials to let me exercise after I returned to the jail in the late afternoon.

Mark Holscher came to work at the vault-type room every few weeks. I'd say, I'm sorry, I can't pay for your airfare and hotel. But Mark always joked, Don't worry, I'm single, I can eat at McDonald's, and when you get out you can send me a fish once each week. I told him fine, I'll send you a fish, but I don't know if it will be any good when you get it. We made lots of jokes. I observed that Mark exercised a lot and was very careful about what he ate. I never saw him eat beef or pork; sometimes he just ate salad, and he drank green tea. Because Mark was single, lots of ladies paid attention to him in the court. But during this time, he got engaged to be married. After I got out of jail, I met his fiancée. She is a very nice person, and Sylvia and I went to Los Angeles for their wedding. I had lots of advice for Mark about marriage and how his freedom soon would be over. He always listened to what I had to say. One thing about Mark, I think he must be a good poker player. He told me, don't show the government your trump card. We have to keep that card until the government is ready to talk with us, and he was right.

The pace of work at the room was set by John Cline, with his disciplined yet relaxed work style. He always dressed casually, except when he had to see the judge. John moved to Albuquerque from Washington, D.C., but he is not a stuffy guy, as I imagined Washington people to be. John is very smart, with a sharp memory, but he does not eat very well. Every day I made myself a turkey sandwich, with some lettuce and salad dressing. I would heat the sandwich in the microwave. It tasted very good, and before I returned to jail each afternoon, I would make myself another one to eat for dinner. I also made the same kind of sandwich for John and the other legal team people, but after a couple times I noticed they didn't want to eat this sandwich. I guess they didn't like it. Instead, John would eat pretzels and potato chips, lots of junk food. I would say, John, that's not good for you. He always replied, I know, but I like it. We talked like this a lot.

I spent most of the time in the room with K. C. Maxwell, Barbara Bond, and Ann Delpha. At least one of them was with me at all times, since I was not allowed to be alone in the "office."

When the lawyers had to write their briefs, the room would be full of people and very busy. In addition to working on the research and teaching my attorneys, I also tried to make myself useful by making photocopies for Barbara and Ann, things like that. The court forbade me to touch the computers, but I could do other things.

I enjoyed talking with my "office mates." K.C.'s job, as a young lawyer, was to read through all the transcripts and legal documents, searching for items useful to my defense. She found the details of FBI agent Messemer's lies. She's a good lawyer, but I gave her lists of books and classical literature to read—I told her that she has to know other things besides law. Barbara has four kids, so we talked a lot about raising kids and what's good for their education. I liked to talk to Barbara about my kids, and I encouraged her to have music lessons for her kids because the process of learning to play music helps children's brains to develop. I could tell that Barbara is very good with her kids by the way she was always checking with me to see how I am. Even if I said I was okay, she would still check up on me. Ann, too. Ann was going to school as well as working at the law firm, so I tried to help her with her mathematics. I taught her what logarithms are and how to use them. Barbara and Ann bought the food for the vault-type room, and constantly asked me if I wanted anything special. I always said no, because I was happy with what they bought. I knew I could survive jail now.

Besides the legal team, I got to know the federal marshals quite well. It took three of them to make the trips between the Albuquerque courthouse and the Santa Fe jail. Then, when I was in the vault-type room, one had to sit outside and monitor me all day. There were only twelve marshals, so this was a big drain on them. They told me that when my case happened, it screwed up the whole federal district of New Mexico. I had many good conversations with the different marshals during the hours we spent driving together. We talked about music, literature, nuclear power reactors, their families and educational backgrounds. Most were very nice people who treated me well, even though I was such a burden for them. One of the marshals, Arthur, told me I was the most interesting prisoner he had ever transported. One day I asked him who he picked up the day before, and he told me—a murderer.

It is easier for me to try to forget the painful aspects of my daily life as a prisoner. I try to think about the positive things, like the nice people I met, and the good times I had working closely with the legal team in my office. But at the time it was very different, not knowing what this huge government behemoth had in store for me. Not knowing when, or if, I would ever be free again.

————

Sometimes when the marshals drove me into the federal courthouse, there were demonstrators standing on the busy street corner with banners and placards that read "Free Wen Ho Lee!" I learned from Alberta, Sylvia, and my legal team that there were many dedicated supporters in Albuquerque who were rallying support for me with petitions, by talking to newspapers, and by speaking out on the radio and TV. This was different from my supporters' network at Los Alamos, where many were my friends, neighbors, and former coworkers. I had never actually met any of the Albuquerque supporters before, and they didn't know me. But I got to know some of their names from the news—like Alex Achmat, Bill Sullivan, Nance Crowe and Merrillee Dolan in Albuquerque. Alex Achmat, who started the Albuquerque support committee, was a member of the Green Party and a retired hotel executive, and he was often quoted in the news speaking knowledgeably about my case. So was Bill Sullivan, a scientist at Sandia National Laboratories, which Paul Robinson headed. I admired that he would stick his neck out for me when his big boss had testified that my codes were a "you-bet-your-country" issue. At LANL, there was also a group of employees who were involved in organizing a labor association at the lab—Citizens for Los Alamos Employee Rights (CLER) and United Professional and Technical Employees (UPTE). Chuck Montaño and former LANL employee Chris Mechels from CLER were speaking up for me, and I thought that was very brave of them.

Sei Tokuda, Tatsuji Shiratori, and others from the New Mexico chapter of the Japanese American Citizens League also were supporting me. Their group was trying to get a historical marker in

Santa Fe to commemorate the site where 4,555 Americans of Japanese descent were imprisoned during World War II on suspicion of being disloyal Americans—not far from where I was being jailed on suspicion of being a disloyal Chinese American. Some things hadn't changed much in 60 years. I learned in the news that even today some people oppose the historic marker; they still believe those *American* Japanese were the enemy, even though none of those Japanese Americans was ever found to be disloyal. Their experience made me wonder if people 60 years from now would still want me to be locked up.

After the vault-type room was opened, the rest of April and much of May and June were spent doing the legal research and discovery to prepare several motions in anticipation of going to trial—CIPA, selective prosecution, the improper search warrant, finding out what countries I was supposed to be aiding. But in the meantime, there were some important developments. In the beginning of May, the DOJ removed Robert Gorence from his position as lead prosecutor in my case. The former U.S. attorney John Kelly had previously resigned to run for office, but no official reason was given for Gorence's demotion. News reports gave a reason that I don't wish to repeat. The important thing is, the prosecution now had no one at the helm. Within a month, the DOJ appointed a new attorney to lead the case—George Stamboulidis, from Brooklyn, New York. Stamboulidis was an experienced federal prosecutor, but he had no experience in a national security or nuclear secrets case.

Then came the Cerro Grande fire that burned 48,000 acres of Bandelier National Monument, destroyed more than 200 homes in Los Alamos, forced the evacuation of Los Alamos and White Rock, threatened the plutonium storage area of LANL—and led to the discovery that some portable hard drives were missing from the vault in the X Division. The evacuation required securing the lab's most sensitive information—when lab workers checked on the hard drives, they were gone and unaccounted for. I was in shackles and chains, so I couldn't have stolen the hard drives, though if I had been home, I might have been blamed for that, too. The missing hard drives also brought attention to the fact that in all my years in the X Division, I rarely went into the vault where the Top Secret information and blueprints for the bombs were kept, even though I had full access to the vaults. Mark pointed this fact out many times, but of course the politicians in Washington didn't care about any "non-deceptive" behavior on my part.

The missing hard drives contained far more data, in quantity and sensitivity, than my downloaded files. They described how to disarm the full range of the American nuclear arsenal, and included intelligence information, some of it regarding the Russian nuclear weapons program. I was fired from LANL for not following security procedures. Yet several high-ranking LANL officials had violated LANL security procedures by not reporting the hard drives as missing for three weeks, plenty of time for unfriendly governments to steal those secrets. Stephen Younger, who said my files would change "the global strategic balance," was disciplined in connection to the missing hard drives. Of course no one was locked up in jail for this huge security violation, and the managers in charge were given a week off with pay to recover from the "stress" of the investigation. The handling of this security failure stood in sharp contrast to my case, a point that was noted by the news media.

I felt sorry for the families that lost their homes, but I couldn't help thinking that this fire contained a message for LANL, about the lab's hypocrisy and double standards. After several weeks and a great deal of media attention, the hard drives mysteriously reappeared, behind a copy machine. The FBI made a big show of trying to catch the scientists who took and then returned them. Sixty-plus FBI agents moved into the X Division, polygraphing and interrogating many people. I heard that a number of scientists at the lab became more sympathetic to my case, now that they had had a taste of the FBI's bullying tactics. One X Division scientist was reportedly disciplined after he gave a "Heil Hitler" salute to an FBI agent in the hallway. But eventually the FBI closed their investigation, empty-handed, with no explanation of what had happened to the missing hard drives. That surprised me a little. Lack of facts didn't stop them in my case.

On June 2, 2000, there was another announcement: Judge John Conway recused himself from presiding over my case. His stated reason was that he wanted to lighten his case load because he was planning to retire soon. There may have been another reason. I do not wish to speculate about that. But his withdrawal came suddenly, another abrupt change in the courtroom. How this would affect my case remained to be seen.

In the vault-type room, Barbara Bond sometimes asked me if I was depressed or worried. I sometimes wondered about the people who stood in judgment of me. My answer was always the same: At least I know one thing, I know that I am innocent.

CHAPTER 14

Another judge was assigned to my case—Judge James Parker, the judge who had ruled in my December detention hearing to send me to jail. I wasn't sure if this was a positive change, but around the courthouse, the general feeling was that Judge Parker might be more independent in his rulings than Conway, who was known to be close to FBI director Louis Freeh and to Gorence. Judge Parker moved quickly to set up several dates to hear my attorneys' motions, beginning within a few weeks, at the end of June. A trial date was set for November 6, 2000, only five months away. I worried there might be too little time to get ready for trial since my attorneys only just recently had gotten to look at the classified documents, whereas the government had been developing their case for years. At the same time, any delay meant more long months in jail.

Throughout June, the legal team was busy researching and writing several legal pleadings. On June 26, 2000, we had the first hearing before Judge Parker. It dealt with two major issues. First was our motion to get the government to say what country or countries I was supposedly trying to assist, and second was our effort to suppress the "evidence" that the FBI took as a result of the improper search warrant used at my home.

These marked the beginning of a flurry of many important courtroom hearings that could significantly affect the outcome of my trial. In the cavernous Rio Grande courtroom, I sat at the big table on the judge's left with my lawyers and our legal team. Seated on the other side were the people who wanted to put me in jail for the rest of my life. On court days I changed out of the gray prison sweat clothes I had bought from the commissary into my dark suit, shirt, tie, and shoes that Barbara Bond brought to the federal marshals. It became my routine, to change clothes in the basement jail cell and to be brought up in shackles and chains, which were removed when I was in public view.

I watched each argument, each witness, like I was watching a play, wondering, Okay, what is that guy going to say now? I wasn't the only one watching. With each open hearing, the court was packed with my family, friends, supporters, and many journalists. Mark and Nancy presented their arguments about the search warrant, how it was poorly prepared and improperly worded, and how Americans are protected against "fishing expeditions" by police and FBI in our homes. At this court hearing, Mark also pressed for the names of the countries the FBI thought I might help, in a Bill of Particulars. The government prosecutor, George Stamboulidis, tried to offer the strange rationale that it was not necessary for the government to specify what country I was aiding, though at some point they would have to convince the judge and a jury why and how I intended to harm my country, the United States. Mark pointed out to the court that in order to prepare my defense, we needed to know what country or countries in the world we might need to research, obtain expert witnesses on, even visit. If I wasn't sure about the legal terminology being used, Mark or John would explain it to me, or

someone else on the legal team would, later on, in the vault-type
room. When I had something to tell my attorneys, I tugged on one
of their sleeves to whisper, "He's wrong," or "That's not correct."

Judge Parker listened patiently to the arguments. Often he
asked his own questions. For this hearing, as with most, he didn't
make a decision right away. At the end of each hearing, my shackles
and chains went back on, I was taken to the locked cell in the courthouse basement, and I took off my suit and put on my jail-issue
sweat clothes.

Judge Parker gave his ruling a few days later—we won on getting the countries named, but we lost the motion on the search warrant seizures.

————

On July 5, just after Independence Day, prosecutor Stamboulidis released the names of the countries in the following brief statement:

> The defendant was interested in seeking employment abroad.
> In 1993, at or about the time of the first offenses charged, the
> defendant addressed letters seeking employment in Australia,
> France, Germany, Hong Kong, Singapore, Switzerland, and Tai-
> wan. In addition, testimony at the December 29, 1999, deten-
> tion hearing also established that the defendant made contact
> with representatives of the People's Republic of China's Insti-
> tute of Applied Physics and Computational Mathematics,
> which has been involved in the design and computational simu-
> lation of nuclear weapons.

The government's list was a big revelation. My attorneys expected to
see the PRC and maybe Taiwan, but Australia, Switzerland, France,
and Germany? Hong Kong and Singapore had no nuclear programs.
Of the countries on this list, only France and the PRC had nuclear

weapons . . . but France? The government's case against the "Worst Spy Since the Rosenbergs" had turned into a job search. It was now evident to everyone that the prosecution had no case, no argument against me. News reporters ridiculed the list. One article quoted intelligence expert Tom Powers as saying, "This doesn't strike me as a motivation for espionage at all, and if they were arguing that, I would take it as a sign they are totally lacking in any evidence of espionage. I'd read it as them just throwing their hands in the air."

Los Angeles Times columnist Robert Scheer was even more blunt. In his article titled "Spy Case Is Evaporating, but Not the Bad Smell," Scheer wrote:

> Lee's apparent crime was only, according to the government, that "the defendant was interested in seeking employment abroad." And why shouldn't he, given that the Los Alamos lab was threatening massive layoffs as a consequence of the end of the Cold War? Catch 22, no? . . .
>
> What we are left with is not the hunt for the "crown jewels" of U.S. nuclear secrets, the "jewels" that were so often the subject of lurid headlines about Lee in respectable newspapers, led by the *New York Times*. Rather, what we have here is the willingness of government bureaucrats—who hounded this man for five years and came up with nothing substantive—to cynically destroy Lee in order to save face. . . .
>
> This cruel game has gone on long enough. At the very least Lee should be permitted to post bail and meet freely with his attorneys to prepare his case. But the right thing to do would be for the Clinton administration, the China hawks in Congress and their supplicants in the mass media to admit that they were part of something very ugly. It is time, in other words, to make amends to the man that they so cavalierly tarred and feathered with such paltry evidence.

I agreed with Scheer's analysis of why the government put me in jail and how they were now stuck in a cesspool of their own making. But I wondered how the government could find a face-saving solution to their problem—which was also my problem. I did not believe the government would just give up, after they had hyped "the deceptive and evil Wen Ho Lee" for so long and so loud. This play— this fairy tale of the Emperor's New Clothes—was still going to continue, with my life and my freedom at stake.

———

The next courtroom battle was on July 12, 2000, in a closed hearing to argue over our CIPA motion about classified information we intended to disclose at trial—in particular, Files 1–19, the "crown jewels" that I had downloaded and was accused of "stealing." The closed hearings were held in the Rio Grande courtroom. Sometimes the closed hearings were held in a small conference room just behind the courtroom. The small room was more difficult for me, because about 15 or 20 of us would cram into this small room, and I would be very close to Messemer, Krajcik, and people who were telling terrible lies about me.

As John argued our CIPA motion, it was clear that the government did not want us to be able to present Files 1–19 in court. They wanted everyone to believe their words that "these are the crown jewels and Wen Ho Lee should spend the rest of his life in jail." But in this hearing, John Cline gave the most elegant, technical discussion about my downloaded files and why they were not the crown jewels. He spoke for more than an hour about Lagrangian and Eulerian methods, mesh tangling, the science behind my codes, and the work I did on them. He presented what is in the open, public literature and why these files were relevant for us to show that I did not harm 270 million Americans.

I was sitting next to Mark Holscher and Richard Myers as John presented his argument to the judge. Mark leaned over to me and said, "He's doing a great job." I replied, "John sounds like he has a graduate degree in physics, everything he says is one hundred percent correct." The prosecutors were completely lost. The judge asked Stamboulidis for a response, but all the prosecutor could say was he didn't know, he needed to talk with the experts first. Judge Parker, who has a bachelor's degree in chemical engineering, accepted my attorneys' CIPA argument and ordered that Files 1–19 were relevant to my defense in several respects. The decision didn't mean that we would be able to present the information at trial—yet—because the government still had the opportunity to show that other documents could be substituted for Files 1–19. But without a doubt, Judge Parker's order—that the prosecution find a way to describe to a jury the nuclear secrets they accused me of stealing—was a huge victory. We had crossed a big hurdle in the CIPA issue.

———

I didn't want to feel too hopeful, but the legal tide seemed to be turning in our favor. The prosecution's countries list and Judge Parker's CIPA ruling gave us a momentum and confidence that were quite different from the dark days when the government held all the cards. Mark continued to press for internal government documents that would show how I was selectively prosecuted for something that many others had done because I am of Chinese heritage. Messemer had already testified that no person had ever been prosecuted under the Atomic Energy Act—except me. What Mark did have was a growing list of numerous examples of national security infractions that were never criminally prosecuted, many of which were never even punished as infractions. He found statements by senior intelligence officials admitting to a government practice of racial profiling. Even the search warrant used to search my house recounted the FBI's position "that PRC intelligence operations virtually always target overseas ethnic Chinese."

Two respected counterintelligence officials also emerged.

Robert Vrooman and Charles Washington both gave sworn statements declaring their belief that I was singled out for investigation as an espionage suspect because of my ethnicity. Vrooman, the former chief counterintelligence officer at LANL from 1987 to 1998, refuted FBI agent Messemer's account of how I came to be the only person investigated in Kindred Spirit, with this:

> Agent Messemer's statement that the individuals selected for investigation were chosen because they fit a "matrix" based on access to W-88 information and travel to the PRC is false. Dozens of individuals who share those characteristics were not chosen for investigation. As I explained in my prior declaration, it is my firm belief that the actual reason Dr. Lee was selected for investigation was because he made a call to another person who was under investigation in spite of the fact that he assisted the FBI in this case. It is my opinion that the failure to look at the rest of the population is because Lee is ethnic Chinese.
>
> [The] contention that the Chinese target ethnically Chinese individuals to the exclusion of others, therefore making it rational to focus investigations on such individuals was not borne out by our experience at Los Alamos, which was the critical context for this investigation. It was our experience that Chinese intelligence officials contacted everyone from the laboratories with a nuclear weapons background who visited China for information, regardless of their ethnicity. I am unaware of any empirical data that would support any inference that an American citizen born in Taiwan would be more likely than any other American citizen.

Charles E. Washington was the former acting director of counterintelligence at the Energy Department and a decorated Vietnam veteran with extensive military intelligence experience. I never met

Washington, but his declaration to the court was very revealing and significant. His sworn statement included these points:

> While I do not know the specifics of these alleged infractions, based upon my experience at the Department of Energy, I know that there were instances where DOE employees compromised classified or other sensitive information, where computers were improperly used, and where files were inappropriately marked, but criminal investigations were not opened.
>
> I have concluded that if Dr. Lee had not been initially targeted based on his race (Taiwanese-Chinese), with the resulting wide press disclosures that he had purportedly [words deleted] and the politicizing of the situation, he may very well have been treated administratively like others who had allegedly mishandled classified information.
>
> In the counterintelligence training I have received and in my counterintelligence experience, I am unaware of any empirical data that would support a claim that Chinese Americans are more likely to commit espionage than other Americans. Further, I know of no analysis whatsoever that has been done as to whether American citizens born in Taiwan would be more likely to commit espionage for the People's Republic of China.
>
> I am aware of Department of Energy employees who were not imprisoned or prosecuted for committing offenses that are much more serious than the "security infractions" alleged to have been committed by Dr. Lee. I am personally aware of a DOE employee who committed a most egregious case of espionage that cost our nation billions of dollars and drastically impacted our national defense. That DOE employee was not prosecuted.
>
> I was informed of the government's claim that no other individuals have committed similar offenses to Dr. Lee and avoided prosecution. Although I do not currently have access to Depart-

ment of Energy and FBI files regarding investigations of other DOE employees, I am certain that DOE files contain information that would prove that this claim is false. There is a big difference between a security infraction and espionage; security infractions are less serious. Security infractions within DOE are not unusual, and as long as one is in good favor, security infractions generally do not result in harsh discipline, much less criminal prosecution and pre-trial confinement. Many security infractions involving classified information simply result in a form being completed that indicates the violator was verbally counseled, even though these counselings frequently did not occur. I do not believe that prior to the AI involving Dr. Lee, that other DOE employees who were in good favor underwent this type of extreme scrutiny and criminal prosecution, when they committed security infractions.

The counterintelligence expertise of Bob Vrooman and Charles Washington cast serious new questions on the Kindred Spirit investigation—and clearly pointed to the issues of selective prosecution and racial profiling raised by my attorneys. I felt very grateful to both men—Washington didn't even know me. Their full statements also included references to Notra Trulock and how his investigation came to focus on me. After their affidavits were unsealed by the court, their statements were widely reported in the news media and on many Internet sites. Notra Trulock filed lawsuits against Vrooman, Washington, and Bill Richardson, as well as against Cecilia Chang, the owner of *www.Wenholee.org*, for including a link from her website to *www.fas.org*, the website of the Federation of American Scientists, which posted Vrooman's and Washington's affidavits. Trulock is also suing *me*. I found this to be another bizarre twist in this whole surrealistic tale, considering that I was sitting in jail because of his actions and statements about me. Trulock obtained the legal support of a group called Judicial Watch, which made its initial claim to fame by suing President Clinton. I'm fortunate that Brian Sun's firm and Sidley and Austin in Washington, D.C., are representing me against Trulock's lawsuit, and I'm sorry that some of the people who came to my defense are also being harassed. Luckily, the DOE is representing Bob Vrooman and Charles Washington, and Cecilia Chang was able to obtain pro bono legal counsel. For me, it is just a continuation of the legal harassment I have been subjected to for years now. It all makes me wonder if it will ever end.

―――――

Besides these discovery motions, my legal team was still trying to get me out of jail on bond. I had been in solitary confinement for "pretrial detention" for more than seven months. At the July 12 hearing, Mark told Judge Parker that he intended to seek my release on bail again. The judge ordered the prosecutors and my legal team to work with a federal mediator to see if some terms of agreement could be reached for a pretrial release on bail. Mark prepared a devastating critique of the government's rationale for keeping me imprisoned pending trial. He summarized how the government persuaded Judge Parker to imprison me using three principal arguments: 1) that the data I had downloaded was so sensitive that the life of every American was endangered if the judge let me out on bail; 2) that I might somehow communicate this "you-bet-your-country" information to the PRC or some other hostile foreign power; and 3) that I had demonstrated the most insidiously secretive and deceptive conduct. Based on those three issues, I had been locked up, pretrial, under conditions more severe than convicted criminals, far longer than the Supreme Court had ruled for other cases, far beyond the recommended limit of ninety days for pretrial detention, and beyond the "speedy trial" that Americans are supposed to receive.

Mark exposed that FBI agent Messemer had given false testimony when he said that I told my colleague that I wanted to "download a resume." Mark documented that on several separate occasions, my colleague told Messemer that I had said I was downloading some *files*, not my resume. The grand jury testimony was very clear. When asked, "Did he tell you—did Mr. Lee tell you what information he wanted to download onto this tape that you're referring to?" the scientist answered, "No. Just that he wanted to download some files." His grand jury testimony referred repeatedly to the "files" and the "data" that he understood I was downloading. On at least three other separate conversations, my colleague discussed with Messemer how he did not know the content of my "downloaded files"—conversations that Messemer wrote up in FBI reports. Yet Messemer stated under oath in two separate hearings that I wanted to use the computer "in order to download a resume"—a fabricated deception on my part that he described in court as "nefarious."

As far as aiding the PRC or a hostile power, Mark and John showed that the prosecution voided their own argument that I intended to harm the U.S. when they revealed the list of "hostile" countries I might be working with—Australia, France, Germany, Hong Kong, Singapore, Switzerland, and Taiwan. And regarding the claim that I downloaded the "crown jewels," Mark was able to obtain statements from two of the country's most highly respected nuclear physicists, Harold Agnew, who came to Los Alamos during the Manhattan Project days, and Walter Goad, who had been at the lab since the 1950s. Harold Agnew had already written a letter to the *Wall Street Journal* that was critical of the nuclear hysteria in Washington. Through a serendipitous contact, Mark was able to meet with Dr. Agnew, and obtain a statement that included the following:

I am familiar with all aspects of U.S. nuclear weapons design and manufacture. When I was director of Los Alamos, I, along with many other scientists, oversaw the basis for the design of the W-88, which is a modern U.S. nuclear warhead.

I disagree with the statement that if the People's Republic of China (PRC) or some other nuclear power obtained the codes at issue here, it "would change the global strategic balance" and would jeopardize the security of American citizens.

If the People's Republic of China had already obtained these codes, or were to obtain these codes, it would have little or no effect whatsoever on today's nuclear balance. In reaching my firm conclusion, I am not expressing any opinion on the guilt or innocence of Dr. Lee, nor would I condone the passing of nuclear codes or any classified information by a United States individual to a foreign power, or the mishandling of such codes.

To fully understand why the codes for the United States nuclear stockpile would be of very limited use to the People's Republic of China or any other foreign country with a nuclear arsenal, one must understand that the PRC and the former Soviet Union have developed their own codes for the design of nuclear weapons. These nuclear weapons were tested by the PRC and the former Soviet Union from 1949 until 1996, using various techniques. The Soviet Union and the PRC developed codes tailored specifically for the materials, weapons designs, delivery vehicles and manufacturing capabilities that these nuclear powers possess. Thus, today the PRC possesses a nuclear capability based on tested nuclear weapons and its own existing codes. As I concluded in my letter to the *Wall St. Journal*, in my opinion, "no nation would ever stockpile any device based on another nation's computer codes." Nor would they place any weapon in their stockpile without a nuclear test.

In addition, it is unlikely that the codes in question would be used by any nuclear power. It appears that most, if not all, of the codes presently being refined and developed at Los Alamos Laboratory were modified after all of the current U.S. nuclear systems had entered our nation's stockpile. It is highly likely that most, if not all, of the revised and updated codes in question were never used in their present state to design an existing nuclear weapon that has been tested and stockpiled. Thus, the PRC or other foreign power should not assume that these codes were the exact codes used for existing nuclear weapons that have been tested.

No one, especially not the FBI and the DOJ, expected to be challenged by some of the nation's top nuclear scientists. Walter Goad was another very distinguished nuclear scientist, a Fellow Emeritus of LANL's Theoretical Division who had achieved many scientific honors. I didn't know Walter Goad, but our times at the lab overlapped and I recall seeing him on a few occasions. The legal team met Dr. Goad through Dr. Ed Gerjuoy, a physicist and lawyer from Pittsburgh who assisted us as a liaison to the scientific community. Dr. Goad's statement in a declaration to the court in my defense was moving and equally significant. It included:

Development of nuclear weapons is the work of many hands. Science, engineering, fabrication and testing are all necessary, and in all these efforts creating workable concepts is the key to success. At the core of the work is a team of theoretical physicists who must find workable concepts for the basic design of the weapon itself. They have to understand and analyze all the physical mechanisms and material behaviors involved in the explosion of the weapon, and with feedback from all the other groups involved, come up with the detailed design. I was a member of this core theoretical team at Los Alamos, contributing to every aspect of its work. . . .

I have studied the indictment of Dr. Wen Ho Lee, and the transcript of his detention hearing before Judge Parker. I have also studied the testimony of Dr. Stephen Younger before Magistrate Judge Svet.

Dr. Younger before Magistrate Judge Svet, and then Dr. Paul Robinson before Judge Parker, testified in apocalyptic terms of danger to the U.S. strategic position posed by the computer codes and data copied onto tapes by Dr. Wen Ho Lee. My experience and expertise tells me that these assertions are exaggerations, grossly misleading in their import. . . . [T]he scientific knowledge and computational expertise required for nuclear weapons design is now widely dispersed. Therefore any nation with a substantial scientific establishment is capable of designing nuclear weapons on its own. Only a group already deeply engaged in the design of nuclear weapons could profit from the Lee tapes (if they still exist). At most, the U.S. codes and data could augment, not revolutionize, their efforts. Furthermore, changes in the world strategic balance require not just scientific expertise and information, but the commitment of extensive technical and industrial resources to the practical development, production, and deployment of weapons and weapons carriers. . . .

Summing up, Drs. Younger and Robinson assert that in foreign hands the Lee tapes could reorder the world strategic balance, that their possible existence poses a danger equivalent to "betting the country" or leaving the "crown jewels" open to theft. From the perspective of my experience and expertise, these assertions represent unbridled exaggeration. The result is not a measured judgment of risk, but incitement of apprehension, even paranoia, that can override fairness and justice.

Unhappily, our history has seen other examples in which exaggerations of danger have overridden the traditional American values of fairness and justice—most memorably to people of my generation, in the era of Senator Joseph McCarthy. These currents of fear are always deeply troubling and damaging, and in this case are doing specific and incalculable damage to the very military-scientific establishment that is ostensibly being protected.

It is hard to overstate the impact that these various revelations had in Judge Parker's court and in the court of public opinion. The absurd list of countries, the declarations of Vrooman and Washington, Agnew and Goad, were blowing up the very core of the government's case. I was still in solitary confinement, shackled and chained—and the worst case since the Rosenbergs amounted to this? To counter the mounting negative press, big guns like Janet Reno were telling reporters that I was no naïve, bumbling scientist—that I had committed my evil deeds in a calculating and conniving manner.

I have never claimed to be a perfect human being. But the government was wrong to keep portraying me as the worst guy in the world. Even now, the government issued a new legal brief rehashing old information—that I tried to use my badge swipe card to enter the X Division 16 times on Christmas Eve, and that I "admitted" in 1998 that I may have assisted a PRC scientist with a math problem.

Regardless of the government's tricks, I learned from Alberta and my lawyers that public dismay was growing in many quarters over the excesses of the DOJ and the FBI. The Federation of American Scientists, which was created by the first nuclear weapons scientists of the Manhattan Project, sent a letter to Judge Parker on behalf of its 2,500 members, asking for my release on bond. The FAS had consistently monitored my case over these many months, and Steven Aftergood, its senior research analyst, was especially effective at presenting science and reason in contrast to the exaggerated nuclear claims that surrounded my case. In their letter to Judge Parker, Henry Kelly, the FAS president, wrote, "Incredibly, Dr. Lee has now served over seven months under extraordinarily harsh prison conditions, although he has been convicted of no crime. This is hard to reconcile with our understanding of American justice. It seems more like the Red Queen's policy in *Alice in Wonderland*: 'sentence first—verdict afterwards.' We believe that the continued incarceration of Dr. Lee is indecent. We hope you will find that it is also contrary to law."

More than 1,400 scientists from around the world signed a petition protesting the "cruel and degrading" treatment I was subjected to. The petition was circulated by the New York Academy of Sciences, the Committee of Concerned Scientists, the American Association for the Advancement of Science, and the American Physical Society. When Joseph L. Birman, chairman of the New York Academy of Sciences' Human Rights Committee, sent the petition to Janet Reno, he also said, "The actions taken against Dr. Lee run contrary to our understanding of the American ideal of justice. How can we approach other countries to improve their human rights records unless our own country adheres to the highest standards?"

The Society of Professional Scientists and Engineers, an independent union of Lawrence Livermore National Laboratory employees, passed a resolution to send a letter to Janet Reno, stating that the charges "do not justify the harshness of his pretrial confinement. . . . we are not aware of other cases, in which a person who committed security violations received similar treatment." In Los Alamos, the Congregation of the Unitarian Church, made up mostly of LANL present and former families, voted by a 97 percent majority to call upon the U.S. government to immediately institute humane treatment and to seek a pretrial release for me under conditions that respect my human dignity. LANL physicist Carl Newton, who with Phyllis Hedges headed the local efforts on my case, introduced the resolution. Alberta went to the meeting of the Unitarian congregation with Carl, whose daughter was a high-school classmate of Alberta and Chung.

Even Amnesty International, the international human rights group, made a statement about my case, saying that my treatment in jail, particularly the use of shackles and chains, violated international human rights law and should be immediately discontinued. Amnesty International cited this international rule:

Rule 33 of the United Nations (UN) Standard Minimum Rules for the Treatment of Prisoners provides that restraints should be used only when strictly necessary as a precaution against escape during transfer, on medical grounds on the direction of the medical officer, or to prevent damage or injury. The rules also state that restraints should never be applied as punishment and that "chains or irons shall not be used as restraints." The rules also provide that every prisoner (including pre-trial detainees) should have at least one hour of suitable exercise in the open air daily. Amnesty International believes that the overall conditions under which Dr. Lee is detained contravene international standards, which require that all persons deprived of their liberty be treated humanely and with respect for their inherent dignity. Amnesty International is urging the Justice Department to urgently review Dr. Lee's conditions of confinement and ensure that he is being treated in accordance with international standards.

These expressions of support gave our legal team a big boost, and gave me encouragement. We talked about the letters and support activities in the vault-type room. Through my attorneys and Alberta, I learned that, in addition to the scientists and the people in New Mexico, Chinese Americans and Asian Americans across the country were angry and taking action in support of my case. In many communities, there were demonstrations, protests, informational discussions, and fund-raising events for my legal defense. All year there had been many protests. English-language newspapers had only occasional news about their activities, but in Chinese-language newspapers, the coverage of my case and the community response was almost daily. My wife subscribed to one of the largest Chinese-American newspapers, *The World Journal*, and she kept me updated during her Saturday visits to the jail.

On January 27, 2000, Chinese for Affirmative Action, led by civil rights attorney Diane Chin, organized a rally in San Francisco's Chinatown for me. Alberta flew from North Carolina to be there, and the next day attended a fund-raiser at Ming's Restaurant in Palo Alto arranged by Cecilia Chang for the Wen Ho Lee Defense Fund. In March 2000, Cecilia also organized a demonstration in San Francisco to mark my 100th day of imprisonment. Professor Chang-lin Tien, former chancellor of the University of

California at Berkeley, spoke in support, and member of Congress Nancy Pelosi of California sent a letter saying she had expressed her concerns to Janet Reno and other administration officials. Cecilia's website, *www.Wenholee.org*, was a central site for information about progress in my case and how people could help, though of course I couldn't see her website while I was in jail.

Before this happened to me, I had never paid attention to Asian American people creating organizations and raising their voices. I don't think I even knew of any protest rallies by Chinese or Asians in America. I was quite amazed to discover that there were so many demonstrations about my case and the impact it was having on other people. As time went on, the protests seemed to gather momentum in their increasing number. In New York, on April 9, 2000, Leo Yu-Wan Lee of the Organization of Chinese Americans' New York chapter organized a rally and protest march from Chinatown to the Federal Building. On May 3, the Seattle chapter of the OCA held a march and rally at the federal building seeking my release on bail. The OCA raised money from around the country for a family fund to help us out with our personal needs, in addition to seeking support for the legal defense fund. On May 31, a rally was held in San Jose, in California's Silicon Valley, organized by *Wenholee.org*, the South Bay Labor Council, and the Asian American Public Policy Institute.

There were so many events that I can't list them all. In some months, Alberta was flying to five or six different cities to speak to groups and news reporters about me. Sylvia and I worried about her health and safety with all the traveling. Even Chung, who hated public speaking, was going to different cities to talk, now that his classes were over.

A "National Day of Outrage" was called for June 8, 2000, by several groups in San Francisco from the Asian Law Caucus, Chinese for Affirmative Action, the Organization of Chinese Americans, the Japanese American Citizens League, and others; the effort was led by Phil Ting and Ted Wang. They created a national network called

the Coalition Against Racial and Ethnic Scapegoating—CARES—
that had many organizations joining them. Besides the organizers, it
included the Association of Asian American Studies, the Chinese
American Citizens Alliance, Filipino Civil Rights Advocates, the National Lawyers Guild, the National Baptist Convention, and many
local and regional groups. On that same day, June 8, CARES coordi-
nated protest activities in Albuquerque; Detroit; Dallas; Houston;
Irvine; California; Los Angeles; Miami; New York City; Salt Lake
City; San Francisco; and Seattle. The protests got the attention of
Bill Richardson, who in response issued a press statement that he is
against racial profiling and discrimination of any kind. Member of
Congress David Wu of Oregon wrote a letter in support of the National Day of Outrage, pledging "that I will closely monitor Dr. Wen
Ho Lee's case, and I will work hard to uphold American values of jus-
tice and due process."

At the Republican and Democratic parties' national conven-
tions, which took place in June and July 2000, Asian Americans in
those parties pushed for resolutions seeking fair and equal justice
for my case. At the Democratic National Convention in Los Angeles, Richard Chao of the Joint Chinese University Alumni Association of Southern California organized a protest rally outside the
convention center to let the delegates know that Asian Americans
were very concerned about my case. Members of this association
are alumni of more than 30 universities in Taiwan, including former
classmates of Sylvia's and mine. Throughout my case, they collected
signatures for petitions at shopping centers and raised money for
my legal defense. Sylvia's 87-year-old father, who lives in Los Angeles's Chinatown, took a bus to participate in the demonstration at
the Democratic Convention.

As I've said, I was surprised and touched that Asian Americans
who were not Chinese would get involved in supporting my case.
Commissioners of President Clinton's newly appointed White House
Initiative on Asian Americans and Pacific Islanders expressed their

concern about my case in their nationwide public forums. The Japanese American Citizens League passed a resolution at its national convention, in which they condemned "the racial profiling and discrimination against Dr. Lee, which threatens the civil rights of all Americans," and urged that the government uphold my "rights of American citizenship of equal protection before the law."

Two public interest law groups sent their own legal research, or amicus briefs, to Judge Parker, in support of my legal team's motion for discovery of evidence on my selective prosecution claim that the government had singled me out because of my Chinese ethnicity. The American Civil Liberties Union Foundation, ACLU of New Mexico, and the ACLU Foundation of Northern California together cited numerous legal cases to show Judge Parker that my defense should be allowed to obtain government documents. The other amicus brief, prepared by Victor M. Hwang, the managing director of the Asian Law Caucus, made a similar point on behalf of eight Asian American groups: the Asian American Legal Defense and Education Fund, Chinese for Affirmative Action, the Committee of 100, the Japanese American Citizens League, the National Asian Pacific American Bar Association, the National Asian Pacific American Legal Consortium, the National Lawyers Guild, and the Organization of Chinese Americans. Their legal brief showed how racial stereotyping of Asian Americans as suspicious aliens has been used many times before—and was being used in the investigation and prosecution against me. I never knew of this history before; I guess I never paid enough attention. But this brief gave examples of what had happened to Chinese Americans more than 100 years ago that opened my eyes. Two cases cited in the brief went all the way to the U.S. Supreme Court:

> More than a century ago, when Asian Pacific Americans were still
> barred from citizenship and full participation in American society,
> the Supreme Court took a strong stand in vacating the conviction
> of a Chinese laundryman based upon the principle that:

"[t]hough the law itself be fair on its face and impartial in appearances, yet it is applied and administered by public authority with an evil eye and an unequal hand, so as practically to make unjust and illegal discrimination between persons in similar circumstances, material to their rights, the denial of equal justice is still within the prohibition of the Constitution." *Yick Wo v. Hopkins*, 118 U.S. 356, 373–74 (1886).

Yet, only ten years later, Justice Harlan opined in his memorable dissent in *Plessy v. Ferguson*, 163 U.S. 537, 561 (1896):

"There is a race so different from our own that we do not permit those belonging to it to become citizens of the United States. Persons belonging to it are, with few exceptions, absolutely excluded from our country. I allude to the Chinese race."

One item I received while I was in jail was a full-page ad from the *New York Times* that read: "Wen Ho Lee and the Nuclear Witch Hunt: Charged with Being Ethnic Chinese," with a picture of me and my family. The ad was organized by Ling-chi Wang and Chinese for Affirmative Action of San Francisco, and was paid for by donations from nearly 100 concerned people. The ad read, in part:

Why is American scientist Dr. Wen Ho Lee still languishing in prison? He is not charged with espionage. Early news leaks to the contrary, the FBI cleared Dr. Lee of sharing warhead information with any foreign government. . . .

The chief of Los Alamos counterintelligence says that Dr. Lee was singled out for investigation because of his "ethnicity."

The search warrant for his home was obtained on the U.S. Attorney's affidavit that Dr. Lee is "overseas ethnic Chinese."

Charged with being ethnic Chinese, how can he prove his innocence? And why, of all Americans, should he be forced to?

Caught up in a classic witch hunt built on racist stereotypes and racial profiling, Dr. Lee faces life in prison because of domestic politics, not international intrigue. The 1950s-style nuclear hysteria whipped up in Congress last year made Dr. Lee the scapegoat because he is ethnic Chinese, and for that reason alone.

It should chill us all that our government is still persecuting Dr. Lee and bankrupting his family long after any basis for prosecution has evaporated.

As Chinese Americans—as Americans—we demand justice. Drop all charges. Free Dr. Wen Ho Lee now.

I felt extremely grateful to all of the people who were doing things for me—things that I had never imagined doing myself. Their support helped to motivate me, after so many months in jail, facing all these charges and life sentences. And I hoped that the American people and politicians in Washington, D.C., would pay attention to so many people speaking up about my case. In the courtroom, I could feel the spirit of the many friends I knew in New Mexico, as well as people I had not yet met. In the last week of July, Janet Reno, Norman Bay, the FBI, and the prosecutors finally determined that it would be okay for the jail to remove my leg shackles during my one hour of exercise. Some people said it was because my bail hearing was coming up and the government wanted to give the appearance that they had listened to Judge Parker's request, made so many months ago. It was such a small thing for the government to do, but I know the letters and demands by people across the country during these many months had forced the government to do something. I wondered how I could ever thank all these people.

———

All the public support energized our whole team in the vault-type room as we prepared for several hearings that were scheduled toward the end of July and into August 2000. Chief among them were the hearings on discovery for our claim of selective prosecution and the renewed request to release me on bail. We spent hours in and out of the courtroom, in open session where I could see all of the people who came to give moral support, and in closed sessions, where the two dozen or so attorneys and their teams crammed themselves into a small conference room. At one point in the open hearings, a fire alarm for the building went off and everyone in the courthouse was forced to evacuate. But not me or the other prisoners. During the building evacuation, I was taken down to a jail cell, shackled and chained, and locked up. Had there really been a fire or bomb, I would have been trapped and probably incinerated.

From these three long days of court hearings, two witnesses stood out to me. One was Dr. John Richter, who, like Harold Agnew and Walter Goad, is a preeminent nuclear weapons scientist. John Richter had worked at LANL for many years, as one of the nation's most experienced nuclear weapons designers. He designed more than 40 different nuclear weapons in the U.S. arms stockpile, including the W-88, which I had been accused of stealing for China in the Kindred Spirit investigation. Richter, with the portly air of a senior scientist, took the stand and told Judge Parker that at least 99 percent of the "secrets" I downloaded were unclassified, published in open literature, and not especially helpful to a foreign nation. He also noted that, for all the chest-thumping and finger-pointing that comes out of Washington, D.C., the worst national security violations come from "inside the Beltway," including from Congress, in the form of leaks. And that they go unpunished.

Dr. Richter explained at length that actual test data from the thousands of nuclear tests conducted by the U.S. were not in the codes, the input decks, or the data files I downloaded. He said firmly that they would not change the global strategic balance. If the downloaded files fell into foreign hands, he said, "I don't think it would have any deleterious effect at all. I think keeping him locked up is much more injurious to the reputation of the United States. That's why I'm here."

At one point Judge Parker asked Richter to comment on the testimony that my downloading to tapes was "inconceivable," "unimaginable," and "nefarious." Richter responded, "Well, what comes to my mind, sir, is that there is an old saying, 'Never attribute to malice what can be adequately explained by stupidity.' And I really think it was something pretty dumb to do. . . . There has been a great effort to find a connection, an espionage connection, and that hasn't been found. And so what is left? Stupidity is the best I can come up with." I don't know if what I did was stupid, but, as I sat in the courtroom, I believe he made an impact with his caveat against assuming that there was malice behind my every deed.

The other part of the hearings that really stood out was Mark's cross-examination of FBI agent Robert Messemer. Because of Mark's brief, Messemer was prepared to be questioned with regard to his faulty testimony about the "resume." Messemer squirmed under Mark's respectful but pointed questioning, his ruddy face turning beet red at times. Messemer admitted in open court that he had provided "incorrect" testimony at the December 1999 hearings that sent me to jail all these months. He told U.S. District Court Judge James Parker that he made an "honest mistake" in characterizing my actions as deceptive, and apologized to the court: "Your honor, I regret that error. My credibility in your court is important to me. But I will tell you that at no time did I intend to mislead you or anyone else in this court." I silently laughed at Messemer's words, which Mark described to the court quite accurately as "false testimony." In other words, he lied to the judge.

Messemer asked the court to consider his misstatements in the most charitable light, as simple errors, yet he so singlemindedly concluded that *my* every word was "deceptive."

The lie about the resume wasn't his only admission of wrong testimony against me. He provided inaccurate testimony on several other crucial points.

Messemer testified that I failed to disclose contacts with several

Chinese scientists when I went to China in 1986 with LANL approval. Mark caught him again, by showing Messemer a copy of the trip report that I filed when I returned, in which I listed the names of the scientists. As if that weren't enough, Messemer had told the court that I failed to disclose correspondence with Chinese scientists, beyond receiving a Christmas card—which he had said was an example of my pattern of deceptiveness. The implication was that I had lied to cover up this correspondence. Mark's questioning forced Messemer to agree that I had indeed told FBI agents Carol Covert and John Hudenko back on March 5, 1999, that I had exchanged letters with Chinese scientists in which they discussed mathematical problems.

With Richter and the other nuclear science experts disputing the "crown jewels," and the impeachment of Messemer's testimony citing my "nefarious and deceptive" activities, I believe that Mark, John, and the legal team seriously damaged the prosecution's case. Their arguments swayed several newspapers across the country to issue editorials calling for Judge Parker to release me on bond, including the *Los Angeles Times*, the *Chicago Tribune*—and the *New York Times*.

————

We had to wait for Judge Parker's decision. The waiting was the hardest part, especially Friday through Sunday, when I stayed in my jail cell for twenty-three hours a day. Even at my courthouse office, the days of waiting after the hearings and all the motions were stressful. Fortunately, Judge Parker didn't take long to render his decision.

On Wednesday, August 23, 2000, Judge Parker granted our motion for CIPA, ruling that Files 1–19 were relevant to my defense, for use in trial. These were the "crown jewels" I was charged with downloading. On Thursday, August 24, 2000, Judge Parker ruled that the case "no longer has the requisite clarity and persuasive character" necessary to justify keeping me behind bars until the trial. He ordered the prosecutors to work with my attorneys to come up with the terms of bail so that I could be released on September 1, 2000. Last, on Friday, August 25, 2000, Judge Parker granted our motion for discovery for selective prosecution.

With these three decisions, we won the legal equivalent of the Grand Slam, the World Series and the Super Bowl. I had never watched any of these, but I knew that winning them was a big deal. The judge's rulings pretty much acknowledged that I did not pose the kind of threat to national security that the prosecution had claimed.

Following these rulings, on August 30, 2000, the three most prestigious scientific academies in America publicly criticized the government, saying that I appeared to be "a victim of unjust treatment" that "reflects poorly on the U.S. justice system." The presidents of the National Academy of Sciences, the National Academy of Engineering, and the National Institute of Medicine sent an open letter to U.S. Attorney General Janet Reno—marking the first time that the three congressionally chartered academies ever intervened on behalf of an American scientist. The academies had written hundreds of letters to authoritarian governments—the former Soviet Union, China, Iran, and others—in protest of mistreatment or unjust detention of scientists. In their letter, the academies said that my case raised questions "identical to those that our Committee on Human Rights regularly poses to foreign governments." Congress created these national academies and mandated their 4,800 members to give independent advice on issues of science and technology to the federal government. Their advice to Reno: "We also urge that those responsible for any injustice that he has suffered be held accountable. Even more importantly, perhaps, we urge that safeguards be put in place to ensure that, in future, others do not suffer the same plight."

Judge Parker's decisions sent a devastating political blow to the government, whose entire investigation and prosecution of me depended on the frightening specter they had invented. Now it was clear that court of public opinion was also rejecting the case that they had built, in Bob Vrooman's words, "on thin air."

My team would be able to obtain and use the documents we needed to defend me at trial and to show that the government had singled me out because I am Chinese. Best of all, I would finally get to go home on bail. I began to let my hopes rise, just a little.

CHAPTER 15

Judge Parker issued his order to the lawyers on both sides to agree on the conditions of release that would allow me to get out of jail. The proposed bail conditions were, of course, the most restrictive terms that the government could think of. But they could not come up with anything more draconian than I had already experienced in prison, with their Special Administrative Measures. So whatever they wanted, we accepted.

I would not be able to leave my house or even venture into the front yard. No communications devices could be allowed in my house except for one telephone, which would be monitored at all times, with Mandarin-speaking agents and surveillance officers listening in. Sylvia would also be subjected to stringent conditions, as though she were under house arrest as well. She would have to fax the FBI a notice at least four hours in advance of going shopping or any time she planned to leave the house. Sylvia would be subject to search, as would all packages and mail coming into or leaving the house. My children could only visit me during the daytime, only after making arrangements in advance with law enforcement officials, who would be present during the visits. My neighbors Don and Jean Marshall were designated as "third party custodians" to watch over me, and each day I would have to check in with them. Together, we would contact federal authorities twice each day. I could not leave the premises unless prearranged with the FBI, for visits with my attorneys, or for emergency medical attention, accompanied by Don or Jean. We were required to post $1 million bond, which was secured by my own personal assets and the homes of Don and Jean Marshall and my brother Wenming and his wife. Several other friends and supporters offered to put up their homes as collateral, too, but these were the assets that Judge Parker selected to secure my bail bond.

Legal experts said that these restrictions were virtually unprecedented except perhaps for bosses of organized crime syndicates, but I didn't care. At least I would be home, out of the shackles, out of a small jail cell with no hot water, away from guards who watched me when I used the toilet. I was scheduled for release on bail on September 1, 2000. Before that date, the FBI conducted another search of my house, this time in the presence of Nancy Hollander and K. C. Maxwell. They dismantled the TV and light switches and the electric wiring inside the walls, and they dug up the ground in the yard. They didn't even bother to reconnect the TV hookups—Sylvia had to ask Don Marshall to come and fix things. This time they found nothing except an old beer can buried in my yard.

Despite the restrictions, I was very excited at the prospect of going home. I heard that my neighborhood was planning a welcome home celebration for me. I was all set to go, but then the prosecutors filed an appeal to the Tenth Circuit Court of Appeals, claiming that my release would cause irreparable harm to the country. They said that the restrictions would be too burdensome to the government—even though they were the ones who came up with the restrictions. With their appeal, Judge Parker postponed my release for another week, until the Appeals Court could hear the arguments.

I can't even express how disappointed I was, thinking I was going home, only to have my chains jerked, pulling me back to jail. I tried to keep my head up high; the last thing I wanted to do was to let the government think they were getting to me. So we were back to hearing arguments in court. Even with their appeal to keep me imprisoned, the government had some deadlines coming up to release the many documents that Judge Parker ordered as discovery for my defense.

In September, the judge was to make final determinations on the CIPA issues. And on September 15, 2000, the government had to turn over several items related to selective prosecution. The list drawn up by Judge Parker included all DOE and DOJ statements made by Notra Trulock related to focusing investigations on ethnic Chinese; the suspects in the Kindred Spirit investigation; the full, classified transcripts of any statements involving my case made by Janet Reno, the DOJ, the FBI, and the DOE to any congressional committee; various FBI memos; final reports on all administrative inquiries for improper handling of classified information conducted by the DOE of LANL employees from 1987 to the present; reports by the DOE Task Force Against Racial Profiling; a security video; and other information. My attorneys and many others were looking forward to the release of this information.

———

While these courtroom hearings were taking place, there was another behind-the-scenes legal negotiation to see if a plea bargain could be made. Back in July, Judge Parker had directed the prosecutors and my lawyers to confer with a mediator. Both sides agreed to consult with Judge Edward Leavy, a senior federal judge in the Ninth Circuit Court, based in Portland, Oregon. The first meeting with the mediator took place on August 25, 2000—the same week as Judge Parker's multiple rulings in our favor. Then a second meeting was held on Thursday, September 7. The attorneys and the mediator negotiated all day on Friday, and by late that night, they had agreed to some major points—that I would plead guilty to one count, and that the government would drop the other fifty-eight. I would also submit to five days of FBI questioning, my passport would be held, and I would notify the government of any foreign travel for six months.

I wasn't happy about pleading guilty to the one count. I felt that I had not committed a criminal offense, and no one else who had violated security rules was ever treated this way. I was willing to stay in jail to fight it out. On the other hand, the legal costs were enormous, and my imprisonment was so hard on my family. They were suffering. When the prosecutors offered to make a plea bargain, John Cline and Mark Holscher told me this: "There is a ninety-five percent chance that we will win this case if it goes to trial, but a five percent chance that we could lose. If we lose, you could face life in prison. Are you willing to take that risk?"

I gave my answer: No, it was not worth the risk of spending the rest of my life in prison. I knew I would be pleading guilty to a felony offense, that I would lose some important rights—the right to vote, to bear arms, to run for public office, to serve on a jury. But I didn't want to own a gun or to be a politician. I actually had never voted in the 24 years I had been a citizen. Now, since this happened to me, I understood the importance of voting. But it was less of a sacrifice to lose these rights than to risk a prison sentence, potentially for the rest of my life. So I agreed to the plea bargain.

Over the weekend, the attorneys worked out the language for the plea agreement. The news was already out—someone in Washington leaked to the media that there was a plea bargain in the works and I would be released on Monday, September 11, 2000. I was excited, again, at the prospect of getting out of jail and going home. Alberta and Chung flew into Albuquerque; so did my brother Wen Ming and his wife, and one of my nieces from San Francisco. Many people were once again planning a celebration that afternoon in White Rock.

But then there was a hitch. I met in our courthouse "office" early Monday morning with Mark, John, and Richard Myers, just a few hours before I was to be released. We were going over the state-

ment I was to give, about what I had done with the tapes. As we
went over the details, I told them I had made copies of the tapes
and that they were destroyed, too.

John and Mark got quiet, and Richard closed the door. John became very serious and asked me to say more. I told him, I always
said I destroyed all the tapes. To me, all the tapes were copies and
they were all destroyed. I felt terrible that somehow I had made a
big miscommunication. I thought they knew. John then called
George Stamboulidis to tell him there had been some imprecision
about copies of the tape, and that I had made more than one copy
of some of them.

This news set Stamboulidis off, and after he conferred with
U.S. attorney Norman Bay, and other DOJ people, he said the plea
agreement was off. We walked into the packed courtroom that
Monday morning, where everyone, including the news media, expected me to be released on bond and sent home. Instead, the attorneys said that something had come up. The judge adjourned the
court to go into closed sessions. The stunned gallery was silent, but
then a voice rang out from among the people and shouted, "Hang in
there, Dr. Lee." At that, the people in the gallery began to applaud
in support, as the federal marshals took me out of the courtroom, to
be shackled and chained.

I spent the rest of Monday in my office, the vault-type room,
with Richard Myers, talking about what might happen. Richard was
very kind, and said the problem was due to the language barrier,
since my first language is math, my second language is Chinese, and
my third language is English—and my lawyers didn't speak math or
Chinese.

Mark and Dan Bookin met with the prosecutors, who wanted to
call the deal off, but Judge Parker wouldn't let them. The lawyers
would have to meet again the next day, Tuesday, September 12. The
mediator, Judge Leavy, was going to fly in from Portland. I went
back to my jail cell, not sure what was going to happen. But John
Cline, K. C. Maxwell, and Richard Myers worked all night long,

preparing a brief on why the plea agreement was an enforceable contract. They filed their brief on Tuesday morning. Judge Leavy arrived late in the afternoon. Keeping the prosecutors in one room and my lawyers—Mark and Richard—in another, the judge went back and forth until past 2 A.M. negotiating new terms for a plea bargain. According to the new terms, I agreed to 10 days of questioning with the FBI instead of five; to submit to a polygraph conducted by a tester who is mutually acceptable to the government and my defense team; to be available for further questioning; to give advance notice to the government for the next twelve months of any travel outside the country. Judge Leavy would hold my passport for that period. If I gave false or misleading testimony on the disposition of the tapes, the plea agreement would be voided.

The next morning, Wednesday, September 13, I stood before Judge Parker in the packed Rio Grande courtroom with my very tired attorneys, Mark and John, on either side of me, as the judge spoke.

"Count Fifty-seven charges that on a date in 1994 up through the date of the indictment, within the District of New Mexico, you had unauthorized possession of and control over documents and writings relating to the national defense, which was restricted data that had been gathered onto Tape L and that you willfully retained and failed to deliver Tape L to an officer and an employee of the United States who was entitled to receive it. Do you understand specifically this charge that is made against you?"

I said, "I understand."

"Do you understand, Dr. Lee, that Count Fifty-seven charges you with the commission of a felony crime?"

I said, "I understand."

"If I accept your plea of guilty to Count Fifty-seven, it will be the same as though you have been convicted of that felony charge. Do you understand that, sir?"

I answered, "Yes."

———

I made a written declaration, under penalty of perjury, that first, I never intended to pass, disclose, or cause or allow to be disclosed to any unauthorized person or third person the tapes and never allowed any unauthorized person or third party access to those tapes. Second, that I did not in the past and cannot in the future pass, disclose, or cause or allow to be disclosed the tapes to any unauthorized person or third party. Third, that I never intended to pass, disclose, or cause or allow to be disclosed to any unauthorized person or party the files and I never allowed any unauthorized person or third party access to those files. And fourth, that I do not and did not in the past and cannot in the future disclose or cause or allow to be disclosed the files to any unauthorized person or party. Before the proceeding was final, I also provided the government a written declaration, under penalty of perjury, stating how I disposed of the tapes, as well as how, when, and where copies of the tapes were made and the manner in which they were disposed of.

Judge Parker gave George Stamboulidis an opportunity to state why they were accepting the plea agreement. He said, "The plea and cooperation agreement gives us the best chance to find out with confidence precisely what happened to the classified materials and data that the defendant down-partitioned and downloaded onto unsecured tapes. As it has been clear throughout this prosecution, for national security reasons, the location and fate of the tapes was always our transcending concern. Moreover, this agreement allows us to fully explore with the defendant, through his cooperation as set forth in the agreement that you just reviewed with him, under oath, all national security concerns implicated by his conduct.

"Had this case proceeded to trial and resulted in a conviction on all counts, the defendant might have faced many years in prison, but we might never have learned exactly what happened to those tapes. . . . This guilty plea disposition, under the strict terms of the cooperation agreement, puts us in that optimal position.

"The second component is that this disposition is a serious

felony and in itself carries all that that implies, as a deterrent to others who are entrusted to work on our nuclear weapon design codes and to safeguard them in the process. It's a deterrent that they not violate that sacred oath and trust for any reason, as unfortunately happened here.

"Finally, this disposition avoids the public dissemination of certain nuclear secrets which would have necessarily occurred on the way towards proceeding towards conviction in this case at trial. So for this and other reasons, this disposition is in our nation's best interest."

———

Judge Parker asked me, "How do you plead, sir, to the charge in Count Fifty-seven of the indictment, guilty or not guilty?"

And I responded, "Guilty."

After a few more technical matters, the judge sentenced me to 278 days in jail, the exact number of days I had already served. In a few moments, I would be free to go home and begin the process of putting this nightmare behind me. The judge asked if there were any other concerns from the prosecutors or my attorneys. When all their business was completed, Judge Parker began to read aloud from handwritten notes on a yellow notepad.

Then the judge apologized to me.

———

The Welcome Home party at the Marshalls' house was a big shock to me. I couldn't believe how many people showed up to support me in court, and then to see my entire neighborhood packed with people—it was simply incredible. I had no idea that so many people cared about my case, that so many people across the country were watching. I was overwhelmed. The party was such a joyful celebration. I was very happy to see so many friends and supporters, and I wanted to thank them all. But it also seemed a bit unreal to me. When the criminal justice system is finished with you, you get tossed back into society. Then you have to adjust. My shackles were removed, I was released from my jail cell and solitary confinement, and now I was home.

Alberta and Chung had to leave that night for Albuquerque in order to appear on "Good Morning America," "CBS Morning News," and CNN very early the next morning. So on my first night home, I had only a few minutes to talk with my children. Chung and I had a few moments alone around 11 P.M. Before he left he asked me, "What are you going to do now, Dad?" I said I didn't know. It was awkward. I didn't usually sound so uncertain with my children. Chung says that I seemed tired and pensive that night. I said I thought I would try to rest for a couple weeks, and then I'd see.

I spent the next few weeks taking care of my house, the lawn, the roof. I was back in my kitchen, fixing my favorite dishes for Sylvia and me—making gallons of fresh soybean milk. At lunch I fixed noodles with shrimp, chicken, tomato, ginger, and mushrooms. For dinner I prepared my special marinated chicken, browned in olive oil; omelettes with tomato, mushroom, and shrimp; cauliflower with tofu, or whatever I felt like cooking. If I couldn't find work using my science, I figured I could open up a Chinese restaurant featuring Wen Ho Lee's Top Secret Recipes. I think it could be a hit. I was never so glad to be digging the weeds in my sorely neglected lawn and garden. I tilled the soil with a hoe, then planted some vegetables that would mature in the remaining months before winter. I climbed atop the roof to replace some shingles and soaked in the warm New Mexico sun. My neighbor Mary Norris walked by with her dog, and I waved. It was good to be home.

Stacks of newspapers, magazines, and copies of Internet stories had accumulated in piles while I was in jail. I sat at my desk for a few days, cutting them out and gluing them into a scrapbook. It was especially interesting for me to read the news articles now that I was out of jail. It wouldn't be completely over until a year after my release. Because of the travel restrictions on me until the year is up, I didn't go to Taiwan when my older sister died. That was very sad for me. But I took heart in the fact that each day brought me closer to the end.

I can still make a contribution to my country and do something useful with my science. I'm finishing the mathematics textbook I started writing in jail, about differential equations, for graduate-level students. A few months after I got out of jail, I also sent off a new scientific paper for publication, one of the papers I began before I was fired from LANL, a paper I tried to get out of my office after my access to X Division was removed. My paper was accepted. In it, I apply my knowledge of hydrodynamics and explosives to special techniques in oil-well drilling, using shaped charges. Some of my designs can shoot a small metal projectile through a 6-foot-thick steel wall. I think it could be helpful in producing new oil wells and alleviating the energy shortage. I know a lot about nuclear reactor safety, which should be useful with all the new energy initiatives. Unfortunately, I probably won't get a chance to use my skill. Perhaps one day I will be able to teach.

I tell people that if you want to get a lot of work done, jail is a good place to be. No phone calls, no e-mail, no distractions, no people to talk to. You don't have to worry about when and what to eat, when to bathe—there are very few options in jail. I would rather make a joke about it than dwell on the bad times. My lawyers and Alberta and all the people outside did the really hard work to get me out of jail. I didn't have to do much. So I joke and tell people they can get a lot done when they're in jail. Maybe I feel bad for about five minutes a day.

Sylvia and I are working very hard to put this behind us. Our efforts to move on are made harder when politicians continue to twist my case for their political advantage, when the government continues to spew leaks and lies, and some newspapers still print them without question. After I was released, President Clinton said he was "quite troubled" about my case and told reporters, "I always had reservations about the claims that were being made denying him bail." Attorney General Janet Reno said she didn't know how bad my jail conditions were or that I was in shackles and chains. Some of the very politicians who demanded my head suddenly were saying what a terrible miscarriage of justice had occurred, while others held hearings to find out how the spy got away. It was all more play-acting.

I do not follow the new stories about my case that continue to come out. But it is hard to avoid, and sometimes I find some interesting insight into how this happened to me, such as this story from the *Washington Post* that came out two weeks after I was released from jail. It concerns the meeting at the White House, when important and powerful national officials made the sorry decision to use the power of the federal government to force some kind of "confession" from me:

> The decision to prosecute Lee was made at a meeting in Reno's conference room shortly before Thanksgiving. Despite lingering questions about Lee's motives, according to participants, there was unanimity among the federal prosecutors from New Mexico and their superiors in Washington that the government should bring a massive, 59-count indictment against Lee, using the Atomic Energy Act. Indeed, officials in Washington had decided to charge Lee with intent to injure U.S. national security and (not "or") to aid a foreign adversary.
>
> Crossing a final hurdle, Reno called a meeting of senior national security officials in the White House Situation Room on Dec. 4, 1999, to explain how much classified information prosecutors were prepared to reveal in court. In addition to Reno, Kelly, Freeh and Richardson, those present included national security adviser Samuel R. "Sandy" Berger, CIA Director George J. Tenet and deputy defense secretary John J. Hamre.
>
> Robert D. Walpole, the national intelligence officer for strategic and nuclear programs, began the meeting with a formal assessment that loss of the data downloaded by Lee would be a serious blow to national security.

The meeting ended after Reno offered her assurance that prosecutors were prepared to drop the case immediately if the judge were to grant a motion, sure to come from the defense, that the data downloaded by Lee had to be introduced, in full, in open court.

Six days after the meeting, Lee was indicted and arrested on 39 counts of violating the Atomic Energy Act and 20 counts of unlawfully retaining classified information. The Atomic Energy Act violations, carrying maximum life sentences, enabled Kelly and Gorence to ask for Lee to be held in jail while awaiting trial.

Richardson, as secretary of energy, sent Reno a certification that also enabled the Justice Department to direct jail authorities to keep Lee in solitary confinement, segregated from other inmates through whom he might be able to communicate with the outside world.

Richardson and other senior administration officials contended at the time, and still contend today, that it was necessary to hold Lee without bail because he posed a danger to national security. But some officials also acknowledge that they threw the book at Lee and kept him in solitary confinement to squeeze him into confessing why he had downloaded the data and what he had done with the missing tapes.

"We pushed for solitary confinement to make life as difficult as possible, because if he were sent home, there would not be a lot of incentive for him to come clean," said one senior official, speaking on condition of anonymity.

Then, on December 17, 2000, a year after I was imprisoned and only a few months after I was released, "60 Minutes" aired an interview with Notra Trulock, in which he admitted leaking the government's investigation of me. In a previous account in the *Washington Post,* Trulock said that Bill Richardson told him that Richardson had leaked my name to James Risen of the *New York Times,* which

Richardson denies. But on national television, Trulock told the "60 Minutes" reporter that he himself reached out to the *New York Times,* declaring on camera, "I went to them." Trulock said that he was "delighted by the story" Gerth and Risen wrote—this was the March 6, 1999, story for which the *New York Times* has been strongly criticized by other journalists. On the same "60 Minutes" broadcast, former FBI official and DEO counterintelligence chief Ed Curran said, "Whoever leaked out the information broke the law." With the camera rolling, Trulock stated that he deliberately leaked classified information to the news media—in other words, he mishandled classified information, the federal offense I was charged with. Then Trulock told "60 Minutes" that my legal defense injured *him,* when it was his own actions that backfired against him.

In February 2001, the *New York Times* and the *Washington Post* once again ran stories with information leaked from the government, this time from the ongoing FBI questioning, which we are not permitted to speak about. The papers said that I had received a $5,000 counsulting fee from the Chung Shan Institute in Taiwan, and that I was being investigated for "small family accounts in Taiwanese and Canadian banks." But LANL knew about and approved my consulting work, which was commonly done by lab scientists; the *Washington Post* inaccurately stated that the lab did not know. The Taiwan bank account was set up for my sister, who had since passed away, to help her with treatment of some serious health problems and other family emergencies. It never contained more than $3,000. My wife opened an account with a Canadian bank when she was visiting New York—that account never had more than $10 in it, and the bank finally sent us a letter that they were closing the account because it was such a small amount. The FBI had that letter from the bank, but of course they only leaked the information that made me sound bad.

Meanwhile, the *Washington Post* has published stories stating that some government officials are accusing me of being a potential spy for Taiwan. Does this mean we begin the same farce all over again, this time with Taiwan as the villain instead of the PRC? And here I thought Taiwan was an ally that America has sworn to defend. Mark Holscher has had to tell the newspapers that any suggestion of wrongdoing was false, and pointed out that these "unnamed government officials" who leak to the news risk violating federal criminal law by talking about the investigation.

When I see these news reports, I feel very disgusted, as if I'm watching two gangs of hoodlums—the government and the news—joining forces to keep the FBI employed and to sell newspapers. I feel that it has been irresponsible of the *New York Times* to continue to print these leaks, expecially after they printed two long, self-critical yet self-congratulatory articles which did admit that their tone might have been more balanced and they might have treated me as more human, but then also said they had got most of it "right," and they did nothing wrong. I agree with one point—they should have treated me more like a human being instead of just some Chinese dog or cat whose life and reputation means nothing. In Russia, the government has tortured people by beating them or sending them to Siberia. Here in America, people can be tortured by the media, which involves a highly developed technique. The government gives leaks to reporters, and too often, the newspapers print them. I realize that not all reporters are like this, and that they have a job to do; I also saw many stories that I thought were very balanced and fair. But when a little guy like me gets destroyed in the media by a behemoth like the government, it is impossible to change the minds of all people who wrongly conclude, "Oh, you're Wen Ho Lee, the spy who stole the W-88!" This is how torture-by-media works.

———

With the continued insinuations by the government, in the news, to try to justify all the falsehoods, of course people have questions about me. It is understandable that people would wonder how one day I could be the most dangerous man in America, who might kill 270 million Americans if I am not kept locked in solitary confinement, and the next day be free to walk the streets.

What I did with the tapes, and why, is not mysterious, even though the government tries to cloak everything in secrecy. It is not complicated or nefarious. I have said many times why I made the tapes. I have also said many times that I destroyed them. In the declaration I made as part of the plea bargain, and in the 60 hours of interviews with the government, I said everything there is to say about the tapes. In the news it was reported that I had made 20 tapes. I don't know where that number came from, maybe a false government leak, but that was wrong. Under court order, I cannot discuss the FBI and DOJ questioning; if I acted as the government continues to do, I would be back in jail.

This is what I can say about the tapes:

I made the tapes for the reason I have always maintained, to protect my files, to make a backup copy. More than one backup copy, actually. There were no lab rules against making copies—and most prudent people keep copies of their important documents. These were my most important work products. In John Richter's opinion, that was stupid, but I thought I was doing a smart thing, to keep my codes in the version that could be reconstructed, in case the operating systems changed again. I had lost some important codes before when the operating systems changed and I didn't want that to happen again. When the lab says that nobody lost any work during that period, they're being deceptive. If it were to happen again for any reason, this time I would be prepared, and I would not lose five years' worth of work that would take another five years to recover. I kept my codes safe. By keeping my codes safe and secure in a version that could be restored, by assuring that my country's hydrocodes for nuclear explosions would not get lost, I believed I was doing something good for America. If Richter had known this, he very well might have concluded differently.

Many well-meaning people, including my friends and former colleagues, think that I downloaded the tapes to have my work product in case I needed to find a new job, because I had been given a RIF notice. They say that they could understand why I would do that. But that's not why I made the tapes.

In order to restore my codes in case of a system failure, I needed to save more than just my codes. I needed the equations of state, the input decks and the data files that corresponded to that particular version of my code at that particular point in time. If I saved my code today, and if for some reason the system failed two years from now, the data that would be recovered from that future time would not work with my code, because they wouldn't correspond one to one with my version. The government said I didn't need all these files for my work, but I did—they are all associated with my work product, just as John Deutch's downloaded files were for his work. I wasn't the ony scientist who did this, but I was the one who got caught. Also, I am Chinese.

When I later got my own tape drive in my X Division office, I was able to reorganize the files on the tapes to remove the PARD files from the unclassified files. I reconfigured my tapes and that's how copies came into being. If, back in 1993, I had been able to make tapes of these files from the red, classified system from inside my own X Division office, as I could at the time that I was fired, then there would have been no security infraction at all. Making the tapes and having the tapes were only a problem because the government wanted to make me look like a spy.

After I had my X Division access removed on December 23, 1998, after my DOE polygraph test by Wackenhut, I tried a number of times to get back into my office inside the fence. I had two scientific papers I was working on, and they were in my office. One actually got published in the *International Journal for Numerical Methods in Fluids* while I was in jail: It was titled "The basic character of five two-phase flow model equation sets," by W. H. Lee and R. W. Lyczkowski.

Lyczkowski was a friend and former coworker from Argonne National Laboratory. I thought that if I tried to use the badge swipe card late at night it might work. A few days later, a manager let me into my office to get my papers. One of the times when someone let me in, I decided to take the tapes out.

I kept the tapes in a drawer in my office, which was locked with a key that cannot be duplicated. I protected them very well, and I felt that no one could see them. As I've said, for my files on the open system, I had three passwords, and for all the forensic searches they did on the LANL computer systems, they had to conclude that no unauthorized access occurred to any of those files in the five or six years they sat on the open system.

Back in 1993 and 1994, when I downloaded my files, the X Division wasn't even hooked up to the Internet, so there was little discussion or concern about hackers. But even if a hacker had been able to break into my files, they could only compile the codes by using some utility programs located in the C Division. Without the utility programs, and the users' manuals, the codes can't be compiled. Without compiling, the codes aren't executable. If they aren't executable, they can't be run and the code is worthless. I didn't download the utility programs. These old codes are tied up with utility programs that are only at the lab. In addition, the users' manuals were essential to run these codes. I did not download the users' manuals to the codes. I always kept the manuals locked in my safe. Yet these LANL managers judged me and testified against me even though they were ignorant about these codes—*that* was extremely hard to sit through in court. It was another form of suffering that I had to endure.

After I was transferred from X Division to T Division on December 23, 1998, I realized the tapes and the downloaded files were a problem. I got worried—I didn't want people to know I had the files or the tapes, because I knew they were not proper and would probably be a security infraction.

I took the tapes from my office in order to destroy them. I put them into a trash Dumpster sitting inside the fence, the secured area of the lab, next to the Admin Building where the X Division is located. I couldn't dispose of them in the classified waste containers, which are just for paper, so I threw them into the Dumpster right outside of the X, C, and T Divisions. It was the only Dumpster in the area.

I also began deleting files from my office in the T Division. I didn't need access to the classified partition to delete the files, because they were on the green, open system and I had access to them. But I was now not supposed to have access to them; so, in early 1999, I deleted them. Sometimes I asked the LANL computer help desk for instructions on what to do.

Once I erased the files, I figured they were gone and that was that. I didn't destroy all my tapes because some had only unclassified information, like codes I had written for nuclear reactor safety, back when I worked at Argonne and in my earliest days at LANL, in the Q division. The tapes they found in my T Division office were 100 percent unclassified, but the codes were still useful to me for my research related to the papers I intended to work on while I was in the T Division.

The FBI has heard everything from me, many times over. I would have been happy to tell them much earlier. It wasn't necessary for them to lock me up, to spend enormous amounts of taxpayer dollars on the surveillance, incarceration, and court hearings, to subject all of us to this farce.

The FBI assigned several agents to dig in the city dump to try to find the tapes. They dug for a few weeks, and found some tapes, but they said they weren't mine. They gave up when the weather got cold, but they could have begun digging a lot earlier had they really been willing to talk to me. While the FBI was busy chasing after me, they could have been cleaning their own house, giving their own agents lie detector tests. But then again, Robert Hansen is not Chinese. My case was a huge make-work project for the FBI, the DOJ, and the government. Now that my case is over, they will find some-body else to prey on.

I pled guilty to Count 57, which said I kept Tape L in my posses-sion illegally, and that Tape L contained Secret files. But actually that was wrong—the files on Tape L were PARD files, not Secret. That tape was related to Source Code G, which can be used for the hydro-gen bomb and its hydrodynamics, radiation transport, and neutron transport. I worked on this code for one and a half years, and took some of the Code G and put it into Code A. That's why I wanted to make a backup of this tape. But it didn't really matter that I took a plea with this particular tape. It could have been any of the tapes.

While I was in jail, I wondered, if I hadn't thrown the tapes away, it might have made my life a little easier, because then the government would have the tapes. There was no video of me throw-ing the tapes away—how could I prove it? On the other hand, even if the government had all the tapes to begin with, I think they would have come up with some other story to get me.

I do not regret making the tapes, although I do regret using an unclassified computer outside the fence. I know that was a security violation. But I also know that had it not been for all the hysteria from Washington and the spinelessness of bureaucrats who went along with the wild accusations, my downloaded files would never have turned into a criminal case. Had I not been Chinese, I never would have been accused of espionage and threatened with execu-tion. However, there's nothing I could have done about these factors.

———

In hindsight, there are some things I might have done differently. I might have made different career decisions, maybe going to work in private industry, or teaching at a university, rather than devoting more than twenty years to the national laboratories. This is not be-cause I regret strengthening our country's security, but now I know that political whimsy can destroy the contributions of a life's work, especially if you're an Asian American in a high-security position.

I never thought trouble would fall out of the sky onto my lap like this. But it did, and I learned that we have to stand up and speak up and get involved. Otherwise, we will never get anywhere. To progress even 1 percent, we have to get involved. If you don't get involved, whatever you have can be taken away from you. Like the government took away my liberty. That was the worst.

Something else was taken from me. My American Dream is gone. It died in February 1999 when I realized the FBI was lying to me, trying to trap me. My American dream ruptured then. Before that, when I came in 1964, I thought Americans were good and honest people. I liked that because I was honest, too. Now I've seen the ugly side of people who have lots of power and who are not good and honest. Now I know that any government can turn bad, if we let it. If I could rewind the clock, I would have paid more attention to the issues and the concerns around me and I would have been more involved as an American citizen, using my voice to speak against discrimination and my vote to elect better leaders.

My generation of immigrants came to America thinking that we could work hard, get an education, mind our own business, and take care of our own families. We didn't think it was important to get involved in politics. I came to this country and decided to stay here, raise a family, and make the United States my home.

I have learned a lot in these years. For one, I've learned to be more open-minded. For example, I never knew any lawyers before. I thought they were all a waste of time. But then I met Mark and John and all the attorneys who worked so hard on my case. In the jail, I met so many different kinds of people, and I could see how much of a difference educational opportunity makes in a person's life. If America is going to solve the jail problem and the drug problem, it has to do something about education. I also never knew the power of so many people coming together, even as strangers, to speak up together. These people opened my eyes, my way of thinking. All this is new to me.

These days, when I go out, lots of people recognize me. They come up to me to shake my hand and wish me well. Kids on the street, at shopping malls, shout "Wen Ho Lee!" I don't quite understand what the big deal is. I know some people still think I am a bad guy, the evil spy. At LANL, some people blame me for the new polygraph testing and the tighter security policies. I don't agree. I didn't create the lab culture, and I didn't blow this incident onto the front page of the *New York Times*. But they are entitled to their opinions.

Other people think I'm a martyr. I think that's wrong. I have no interest in being a symbol. But my case did bring many Chinese American people together who are raising their voices to say, "We are not weak. We are not going to let the government screw us up." This case will remind people of what needs to be done, for a long time. I can see that. If it hadn't been for the Chinese American people and all the many other American people who supported me, who got involved to fight the government, I might still be sitting in jail.

I hope Chung and Alberta and their generation will get more involved in politics than my generation did. If one clear message comes out of my persecution, it is this: The Chinese American and Asian American people have to stand up. I've heard that some of the Asian American Members of Congress, like Patsy Mink from Hawaii, David Wu from Oregon, and Robert Underwood from Guam, are seeking answers to the questions that Judge James Parker posed in his apology to me: "What was the government's motive in insisting on your being jailed pretrial under extraordinarily onerous conditions of confinement until today, when the Executive Branch agrees that you may be set free essentially unrestricted? Why were you charged with the many Atomic Energy Act counts for which the penalty is life imprisonment, all of which the Executive Branch has now moved to dismiss and which I just dismissed?"

On April 25, 2001, several months after I got out of jail, the Chinese American group Committee of 100 issued results from a survey they commissioned on how Americans perceive Chinese

Americans and Asian Americans. The findings included these disturbing points:

- 68 percent—two out of three people—feel negatively toward Chinese Americans.
- 32 percent believe Chinese Americans are more loyal to China than to the U.S.
- 34 percent consider Chinese Americans to have too much influence in U.S. high technology.
- 46 percent say that Chinese Americans' passing secrets to China is a problem.

These are exactly the attitudes that tainted everything that happened to me. The survey also found that there was no statistical difference between how people felt toward Chinese Americans or other Asian Americans—all Asian Americans are lumped together, as if we were all the same. I find it interesting that many people spoke out about my case because of the harsh conditions I was subjected to—not because of the underlying suspicion and prejudice toward Chinese Americans that impelled me into those harsh conditions. Of course I am grateful for everyone's support, but as a scientist it is clear to me that unless the fundamentals change, it is highly possible that what happened to me will happen again.

I know that many Americans—including many Asian Americans—have been speaking up long before I learned how important it is to do so. Still, it is not too late for someone, even at my age, to learn the importance of getting involved in the American democracy. This is a country of many races of people—white, black, brown, red, yellow. If the Constitution is right, we should all be treated equally. But we are not, and we all must try to solve this problem. If we do not, the next generation will also face getting locked up the way I was.

My attorneys, at Brian Sun's firm and Sidley and Austin, are working hard on the privacy lawsuit against the federal government for its continual leaks to the media of information about me. In addition, other people continue to fight issues stemming from my case, even though I have no connection to their efforts. For example, several groups, led by the American Civil Liberties Union of North California, the Asian Law Caucus, and Chinese for Affirmative Action, all based in San Francisco, are seeking the discovery documents about racial profiling against Asian Americans that Judge Parker had ordered the prosecutors to produce. Others are independently seeking a presidential pardon for my one felony count, especially since John Deutch was never charged at all, and then was pardoned by President Clinton during his last hours in office.

I do believe that every American ought to be concerned about the abuse of power by the FBI and the government. There is one lesson I learned that everyone should know if the FBI should come to you to ask you questions: No matter how friendly they may seem, no matter what ruse they give you, NEVER speak to them unless you have a lawyer or at least a third party there with you. I was very naïve. Don't let that happen to you.

———

My ordeal is a wound that will be hard to heal. I'm not sure how to recover from it. At my age, I don't want to spend energy feeling hate or bitterness. It will be hard for me to trust people again the way I used to accept people's friendliness and kindness at face value. At the same time, so many Asian, white, black, Hispanic, and Native American people were willing to help me. I wish I could thank every person individually. I also know that if I had been accused of such a thing in China or Russia, I would probably be dead. I would have been shot if this happened in Taiwan under the Kuomintang. The fact that I could be released after being so wrongly accused is evidence of the good in America. I can still say that I am truly glad that I am an American.

My family is doing the best we can, coming out of this nightmare. Chung is well on his way to fulfilling his dream of being a medical doctor. He had a close circle of good friends and classmates who knew that Wen Ho Lee was his father and kept him from being treated differently at school in any way. I'm glad this weight isn't hanging over my children anymore.

Alberta has gone through a metamorphosis, after spending a year of her life going everywhere and anywhere to speak about my case. She wants to devote her life to make society a better place, so that this doesn't happen to someone else's father. She is thinking of changing careers and going back to school to pursue a law degree. I fully support her wish.

Sylvia and I are working hard to stay focused on the positive things in life. For the foreseeable future, we are planning to stay in Los Alamos. For one thing, we think it is the safest place for us. We still worry about being followed, or kidnapped by foreign agents who believe what the FBI, the lab, and the government said about me and the "crown jewels" that I supposedly possess. Even if some Los Alamos people don't like what I did, they won't try to harm us.

The main reason for us to stay here is the warmth of our neighbors, our friends, and the real community we are part of. Sylvia has her places to shop, to hike, to do yoga. I have my work, my garden, my secret fishing holes where I can catch a 27-inch trout, where I can find some peace of mind in the natural beauty that surrounds us. These are the important things that make a place a home.

This is my home, this is my place in America. This is why America is, after all, my country.